W9-BDQ-180

COASTAL CALIFORNIA

A Camping Guide

George Cagala

HUNTER
PUBLISHING

Hunter Publishing, Inc.
300 Raritan Center Parkway
Edison NJ 08818
Tel (908) 225 1900
Fax (908) 417 0482

ISBN 1-55650-695-3

Cover photo: *Carmel, California*
Superstock
All others by author

Although every effort has been made to ensure the correctness of the information in this book, the publisher and author do not assume, and hereby disclaim, any liability for any loss or damage caused by errors, omissions, misleading information or potential travel problem caused by this guide, even if such errors or omission result from negligence, accident or any other cause.

Hawaii: A Camping Guide, by George Cagala, is also available from Hunter Publishing.

Dedication

For Bob, Terry, Brian and Tracy of Hickory Hills, and Dar and Jane of Portland – *rootless* people

Contents

Wri
Wil
P
For
Sti
Sa
C
Mend

Introduction

The late comedian Fred Allen once quipped that "California is a great place to live... if you happen to be an orange."

Well, Fred could just as easily have said that about campers. In fact, California is a superior place to be if you happen to enjoy "living" in the great outdoors. Campers can roam virtually anywhere they want, from deserts to hills, mountains, and along the coast. There are nearly 1,300 campgrounds operated by federal, state and county agencies, hundreds more if you include privately-owned facilities, and most can accommodate you whether you're camping in a pup tent, trailer or motorized mansion.

As a camper in California you have a plethora of options available to you. Stake your tent at the very edge of the continent with the waves of the Pacific Ocean just inches away, or bivouac in a motor home beneath a grove of centuries-old redwoods 200 to 300 feet tall and several yards in diameter. You can rent a teepee on an island a few miles off the mainland, or a cabin on a tiny peninsula of stubborn rock. You may also opt to sleep out in rolling sand dunes, within a secluded cove, or alongside a salmon-swollen river.

Perhaps one of the most amazing aspects of camping in this state is the accessibility of such settings. Certainly, there are many isolated areas requiring vigorous hikes and heavy backpacks but, for families with young children, seniors, or those simply pressed for time and not quite ready for the backcountry experience, California is most convenient and accommodating.

Choosing Your Camp

California is a big place, third largest state in the union (outsized only by Alaska and Texas). It measures 780 miles long and from 150 to 350 miles wide, adding up to 158,297 square miles or more than 100 million acres. Deciding where to camp within this vast expanse can be a massive undertaking. The state park system alone offers close to 18,000 campsites.

California is a land of many climatic and geophysical variations. You can find yourself as low as 280 feet below sea level (Death Valley, the lowest point in the U.S.) or as high as 14,495 feet (the summit of Mt. Whitney, highest point in the contiguous 48 states). You can experience extremes of heat and cold, rain and sun, landscapes as voluptuous with flora as they can be void of it. You'll discover snow-capped mountains, spectacular canyons, vast expanses of flat, fertile valleys, thick, verdant rainforests, barren deserts, as well as balmy seashores. And, remarkably, you'll find a campground in almost every corner.

Each milieu will have its own unique mood and allure, each inarguably worthy of exploration. But, chances are, if you're going to camp in California, you'll be near the state's magnificent coastline. Out of a total of 126 state parks with camping facilities, 44 are located on the coast or within a few miles thereof. However, while they account for a little over a third of the total state campgrounds, they attract 62% of the campers.

The reasons are fairly obvious. Foremost is weather: The coastal climate is far more temperate than the mountains and deserts, where extremes of hot and cold significantly limit camping activities in certain seasons. Coastal campgrounds, on the other hand, are generally hospitable – and in operation – the year round.

Population also helps account for this phenomenon. In terms of population density, California is a rather lopsided creature, with nearly 70% of the state's 29 million people living within the 19 counties edging the coast. The remaining population is sifted thinly throughout California's other 39 counties.

Yet a third reason is the inherent, almost primordial attraction of the coastal environment itself. And California's coast, which pouts, puckers, shrinks and warps for more than 1,200 miles, is among the most celebrated in the world.

"The beaches are the essence of California and provide its most important aesthetic and recreational asset," writes one state ocean-ographer.

With these facts in mind, this guide focuses on campgrounds along the coastal strip, an area defined primarily by the path of the Pacific Coast Highway (Hwy 1), portions of Interstate 5 and 101.

The Myths

For those of you whose image of the California coast has been shaped primarily by Beach Boys tunes and *Baywatch*, it's suggested that you tuck that picture into a small corner of your cranium and make space for additional data. Along a good portion of the coast you may be surprised to learn the water is barely warm enough to wade in – even in the summer. On the shores of La Jolla, for instance, the jewel of Southern California, water temperatures typically peak at just 72°F during the summer, a far cry from the tropical temperatures anticipated by many. The further north you travel along the California coast, the cooler temperatures become, bottoming out at around 58°. Winter averages range from about 59° in the warmest latitudes to a bracing 51° in the coolest.

The coast is not always sunny, sandy and lined with palms, either. Much of it isn't even swimmable. Along parts of it, particularly in the north, the sea seems to be in a perpetual battle with the land, pummeling the shoreline and exploding against the cliffs with unflagging fury. It's wonderfully scenic, but treacherous, too.

Although it really does exist, even the mythical Southern California beach holds some surprises.

"This beach usually features suntanned beauties and hunks posing alluringly with surfboards or exotic cars along vast stretches of sand," writes Dr. Reinhard Flick in his paper, *The Myth and Reality of Southern California Beaches*. "The beauties, hunks, surfboards and cars may be real enough, but the pristine, broad, sandy shoreline, where it does exist, is not a natural condition in most places."

Dr. Flick, a state oceanographer, explains that it has only been through human intervention that the region's widest and sandiest beaches exist. Prior to large-scale human interference, natural conditions sustained only relatively narrow strips of sand in the majority of cases.

"In Southern California, it is precisely the acts of humans that have made many previously narrow beaches wide, or created new ones altogether. The popular opinion, often reflected in the media, is that coastal development has somehow led to the erosion of beaches that were naturally wide and sandy. In contrast, the truth in many places seems to be the exact reverse: coastal development and other human intervention has widened naturally marginal beaches. This is especially true of the two widest beaches in Southern California, Santa Monica Beach and Coronado City Beach."

Weather

California weather may not be what you expect either. It is as varied as the landscape and depends as much on *where you are* as *when you're there.*

For much of the early summer and winter, you'll find fog and low-hanging clouds regularly violate the images of ceaseless sunshine along the entire coast, obliterating the sun for days at a time, burning off into a smoke-like haze by the late afternoon if at all.

The ocean, of course, plays a dominant role, keeping the coast warmer in the winter and cooler in the summer. But it doesn't take very long to lose its moderating effects. On a typical August day in Southern California, for instance, if you drive a straight line from a point on the coast to a point 100 miles or so due east, you would experience temperatures ranging from a high of about 71° at water's edge, to about 90° within 25 miles, and well over 100° at the 100-mile mark.

A similar though less extreme variation occurs as you travel from north to south. For example, on the same August day in Crescent City (on the coast near the northern end of the state), the normal daytime high is about 66°. But, at the opposite end of the coast in San Diego (almost 800 miles to the south), temperatures could easily be 11 to 12° warmer.

In winter, coastal highs average 10 to 15° cooler than during the summer; lows as much as 20° cooler. And the further you get from the coast, the more extreme these highs and lows will become.

Changes in elevation will also result in temperature variations, the higher the elevation, the cooler the temperatures.

Rain

Precipitation rates vary drastically, the result of a complex set of variables consisting of geographical position, topography, prevailing winds, and relatively stable high pressure zones.

According to the National Climatic Data Center, Crescent City's normal annual rainfall totals 83 inches, while San Diego is lucky if it receives a scant 10 inches.

The coastal mountain ranges figure significantly in any discussion of rain along the coast. As moisture-laden winds arrive on shore, these mountains reach up and wring most of the precipitation from the air, leaving little for east-lying regions.

In California, though, rain is a season. It usually hints at its coming in September, becoming bolder throughout November and December, and typically peaking in January and February before beginning its hiatus in March or April. By the time May or June rolls around, rain is nothing but a faint memory throughout most of the state. Even Crescent City, with its high rainfall average, reports less than an inch in either July or August. Dry summers are pretty much a statewide phenomenon.

Snow is virtually impossible along the coast; for that, you'll need to get further inland and higher into the Sierra Nevadas or other inland mountain ranges. So forget about snow tires!

The Lay of the Land

As the climate along the coast changes, so will the landscape. Starting in Southern California, the undeveloped hills and bluffs are typically covered with a drought-tolerant fuzz of chaparral – endemic grasses and low-growing scrub brush – that will change from a deep green during the wet season to a dull, highly flammable blue-gray and burnt umber by summer. It's a veritable desert next to the ocean.

As you proceed north along the coast, the chaparral gradually gives way to rolling grass-covered hills with stands of sturdy evergreen oaks. Again, colors range from a bright green during winter to a wheat gold during the dry months.

The first sizeable showing of real forest – redwoods, pines, eucalyptus and others – occurs around Big Sur, south of San Francisco; it's a sample of what you have to look forward to in the northernmost part of the state.

Availability of Campsites

As with the rest of the U.S., you will find that California's campgrounds receive the biggest crowds and most intense use throughout the summer months, starting with Memorial Day Weekend and continuing all the way up through Labor Day. Competition for space is keen and reservations are vital. But by mid-September, when the school year begins, campground usage begins to diminish. This is, perhaps, the best time to hammer your pegs into the ground. The days are still warm, but the competition for space has noticeably cooled and there may actually be a vacant space next to you.

By late October, campground stores, where they exist, begin closing up shop or curtailing operations to weekends only. Many parks also block off whole sections of campgrounds or shut down completely, even in areas where weather remains mild all year. When that happens, though, there are usually more than adequate facilities nearby to take up the slack.

With the drop in crowds, you'll also enjoy a reduction in fees at many of the state parks, a matter of a couple of dollars per day. At the same time, the maximum length of time you may stay at any one park is often doubled.

Aside from summers, the only other times you can expect a surfeit of campers are spring break and the Christmas Holiday.

Check In/Out

Most campgrounds ask that you to vacate campsites by 11 a.m. or noon and many let you check in whenever sites become available. *Officially*, though, state parks don't have to admit you until 2 p.m.

Types of Campgrounds

Campgrounds are administered by county, state and national agencies. As indicated above, the majority are easily accessible by car and designed to accommodate both RVs and tents. Most don't have hookups for sewer, electricity or water, but virtually every site does have a picnic table and fire ring with grill top. Where wild animals, such as bears and raccoons, can be nuisances, campsites frequently include food storage lockers. Most, but not all, also have modern restrooms with flush toilets and coin-operated hot showers.

Restrictions on how many consecutive days you may stay at a particular campground will vary according to the park, the agency administering it, and the season. National Parks allow stays of from four to 30 consecutive days. Some county parks have no limits at all, while state parks usually range from seven to 15 days. Most also have established yearly limits as well. At state parks, for instance, the annual limit is 30 days total.

In addition to standard family campgrounds as described above, there are some that have been specially designated as *En Route*, *Hike & Bike*, and *Environmental*.

- A growing number of parks are offering **En Route campsites** for RV campers who are passing through and are in need of a short respite for the night. En Route campgrounds are typically located in day-use parking areas; thus, all En Route campers must be in self-contained RVs equipped with running water and toilets. Spaces are first come, first served, and must be vacated by 9 a.m. Maximum stay is usually a single night. No tent campers are permitted. Rates are the same as regular campsites.

- **Hike & Bike campgrounds** are intended exclusively for those who walk or pedal their way into a state park campground. Depending on the park, Hike & Bike areas are more or less segregated from the standard campgrounds and sometimes less convenient to amenities such as showers. However, rates are typically just $3 a night per person. Maximum stays are usually limited to one or two nights.

- **Environmental campsites** are designed for those who want to delve deeper into the wilderness. After driving into a park, you leave your car in a lot, then hike into the backcountry. Such hikes vary from a few hundred feet to several miles. Facilities are generally more rustic, pit toilets typically taking the place of more modern conveniences. Most have tables and fire rings, but not all have potable water and virtually none have showers. Pets are usually not permitted. Fees range from free to the same as those charged for standard campgrounds.

Although not listed in this guide, there are many privately-owned campgrounds which can serve as viable alternatives to the public facilities. Some of these offer pools, laundromats and other luxuries not available in government campgrounds, while others pale in comparison. Most cater to RV campers with full hookups including cable TV, but many will also accommodate tent campers.

Obtaining Permits

When to obtain permits and reservations is as important to know as where to obtain them.

When is largely a matter of season. During June, July, August, spring break and Christmas, reservations should be made as far in advance as possible. How far ahead you can book varies from eight weeks to a year depending on who operates the campground. Of course, even during the peak season, campers can try their luck and simply show up in the hope of obtaining a space. Be forewarned that this is a long shot, fraught with uncertainty and anxiety, that may very well ruin your plans, if indeed you have any. No-hassle camping along the coast during peak season virtually dictates thorough advance planning and firm reservations.

The off-season, however, is an entirely different story; reservations are often not required. Many campgrounds fall back to a first-come, first-served system, but reservations for cabins and group campgrounds are still required.

State Parks

For most state park campgrounds and cabins, reservations can be made a maximum of eight weeks in advance, and as late as 48 hours prior to the date of the reservation. This is done through MISTIX, a private organization under contract to the state.

About MISTIX

MISTIX reservations can be made from anywhere in the country, seven days a week between the hours of 8 a.m. and 5 p.m. Pacific Standard Time. Simply call the toll-free telephone number: 1-800-444-PARK.

Calls are answered by an automatic answering system which will direct you to enter the first four letters of the park name where you want to camp, the number of people in your party, the type of equipment you have and the dates you want to go camping. If you don't feel comfortable with this just ignore the recording and hang on. Within 30 to 45 seconds, you'll be connected to a live operator.

If you prefer, reservations may also be made by mail. In order to do that, you first need to obtain a reservation application form, available from most state park campgrounds or by calling MISTIX . The application *with payment* must then be mailed to MISTIX as early as nine weeks in advance. The address is: HSN MISTIX, P.O. Box 9029, Clearwater, FL 34618.

VISA, MasterCard, Discover or American Express cards are welcome. Checks and money orders are also accepted. Regardless of how you pay for your reservation, however, MISTIX charges a $6.75 *non-refundable* fee per reservation.

If you have to cancel for any reason, try to do it with a minimum of eight days notice and MISTIX will refund the cost of the campground fee minus a $6 cancellation fee. Cancellation of reservations less than eight days in advance will result in a partial refund.

National Parks

Of the three National Park facilities that accommodate campers along the coast, permits are obtained by calling the parks directly. Reservations can be made from two to three months in advance of the first night of camping. (Phone numbers and addresses are provided with the park descriptions.)

National Forests

There's only one area designated as a National Forest that offers coastal camping, and these are first come, first served throughout the year, except for group camping arrangements. (See section on Los Padres National Forest.)

County Parks

Permits needed to camp in County parks vary with each county. Refer to the park listing for details.

Cost

Saving money is not the sole benefit of camping, but it's certainly an important one. Public campground fees range from no charge up to $25 a night and are typically around $15. Generally, the better equipped campgrounds cost more than the more primitive ones, the difference usually marked by the availability of potable water, hot showers and flush toilets. For RV campsites with sewer, water and electrical hookups, expect to pay a few dollars more. Specific cost information is provided with each campground listing on the following pages.

Discounts

Senior citizens, disabled veterans and others with disabilities may be eligible for waived or discounted fees within the state park system.

If you're 62 or older, you will receive a $2/day campsite fee discount, but you have to request it when making the reservation, then have proof of age when registering at the park.

Disabled persons can receive a 50% discount from state park fees (excluding Hearst Castle tours and $6.75 MISTIX reservation fee) once they obtain a *Disabled Discount Pass.*

If you're a veteran who was held as a prisoner of war or have a 70% or more service-connected disability, you may be exempt from paying most state park fees (excluding the $6.75 MISTIX reservation fee) with a *Disabled Veterans/Prisoner of War Pass.*

Both of the above passes have a one-time fee of $3.50. For additional information, write to:

> Department of Parks and Recreation
> P.O. Box 942896
> Sacramento, CA 94296-0001

Other Considerations

Pets

"A state park is not necessarily a safe place for your pets. Dogs get bitten by wild animals (which can put them in danger of contracting rabies); they get lost; they get hit by cars; they suffer painful, sometimes fatal falls. And the park's strange sights, sounds and smells may make the most friendly dog nervous and nippy."

So begins a notice distributed in many of the state parks. It's hardly an encouragement to bring along your four-footed friends, and yet you'll find they are permitted at the majority of campgrounds. In all cases, however, you'll be required to keep them on a leash (maximum six feet) at all times. Failure to do so can result in a $42 citation. At night, most campgrounds insist they be kept inside a tent or vehicle due to nocturnal visits by local wildlife. What's more, pets are never to be left alone. That can put a serious crimp in one's activities, especially when you realize that many park areas are off-limits to pets, including most hiking trails and beaches.

"Pets are one of the park system's biggest law enforcement issues," admitted one state park ranger. "Many pet owners feel that they should be able to take their animals anywhere. But dogs can be very damaging to plant and wildlife," he said. And they often lead to confrontations, "dog versus dog and even people versus people. It's a very emotional issue."

Most campgrounds charge an extra dollar per night per pet. Always carry the animal's rabies certificate in the event of a mishap.

Gas or Liquid Fuels

If you're flying into the state, remember that the airlines prohibit carrying on or checking in any kind of fuel normally used for camping stoves and lanterns. This includes Coleman fuel, propane and Gaz (popular in Europe). And while charcoal briquets are okay, lighter fluid is not. You'll find such fuels readily available in any of the larger population centers along the coast. Check the local Yellow Pages for stores such as K-Mart, Target, Walmart, Sears, Longs Drugs and camping specialty stores.

Camping Gear

Before you start packing, remember that the airlines *officially* limit each passenger to a maximum of three bags, packages or boxes weighing no more than 70 pounds each. (Anything over this limit will result in an additional charge of $45 per extra bag each way!)

Unofficially, each passenger can also count on carrying up to two additional bags on board as long as they are small enough to fit under the seat or in one of the overhead storage bins. Purses, camera bags and briefcases typically fall into this category.

Now that you know your limitations, you can better analyze your requirements. At first, it may seem an impossible task. But have faith. It can be done. Naturally, what you pack depends a lot on *how long* you're going to be camping, *where* you will be camping, and *how comfortable* you really want to be. A suggested check list follows:

> Tent with rainfly (stakes)
> Ground tarp
> Backpack (for campgrounds requiring hike-ins)
> Sleeping bag (especially for upper elevations)

Air mattress or other sleeping pad
Small pillow
Pillow case
Lantern and/or flashlight
Plastic garbage bags
Camp stove
Portable grill (*grills are not always available or in good operating condition*)
Camping cookware
Coffee pot
Eating utensils
Swiss Army knife
Waterproof matches
Dish towel
Scouring pads
Small bottle of dishwasing liquid
Ice chest (*may be loaded with supplies and checked in with the airlines as baggage*)

Buying or Renting Equipment

Of course, virtually anything you require is easily obtainable in California, either to rent or buy. Familiar stores like Sears, K-Mart, Walmart and Target stock complete lines of tents, sleeping bags, stoves, lanterns and all other manner of gear. Prices are comparable to any other region.

You'll also be able to rent equipment by the day or week from camping supply stores in the larger towns and cities. Condition of the equipment will vary from good to good-and-used.

How to Dress

Regardless of the season, you'll do well to plan your wardrobe in layers, something you can peel or add to as conditions change. Although summer days are normally warm and sunny, ideal for sandals, shorts and sleeveless shirts, they can start off and end up brisk enough for a sweatshirt. After a sizzling day, it's not unusual for a blanket of fog to move in quickly and cool everything off.

Regardless of how warm it is, however, always remember to protect yourself from the sun. Sunscreen is mandatory, but light, loose-fitting, longsleeved shirts and a wide-brimmed hat are even better protection. This is important even on grey, overcast days, when ultraviolet rays continue to cook.

Winter days are similar except that temperatures are 10 to 20° cooler day and night. The sun is further south and less likely to burn. As winter is the rainy season, you'll find a plastic poncho very handy.

The nature of your activities will also help determine your wardrobe. Casual hikers can usually get along with a good pair of sneakers, but for extended hikes, you may want to consider hiking boots. When venturing through heavily forested regions, consider wearing long pants and long-sleeved tops to protect yourself against irritating plants and insects such as poison oak and ticks (see *Coastal Critters*, page 15).

Following is a suggested list of basics. And don't forget, California merchants are well equipped to fulfill any requirement that may arise along the path of your adventure.

> Lightweight athletic shoes
> Thongs or sandals
> Cap or wide-brimmed hat
> 4-5 pairs of socks
> 4-5 pairs of underwear
> Swim suit or trunks
> 2-3 pairs of shorts
> 1-2 pairs of long pants
> 3-4 short-sleeved shirts or tops
> Plastic poncho or other rain gear (winter months)

Transportation

Automobiles

You can bike, hike, hitch rides, or board a train or bus to get from one point to another, but the most flexible means of moving up and down the coast is by way of an ordinary car. It'll take you where you want to go, when you want to go. Except on rare occasions, you won't even need four-wheel-drive. A dozen rental car companies will be happy to loan you virtually any kind of automobile, from compact to van, from the latest models to so-called rent-a-wrecks. Offices are located in every major city and airport. Save money by making arrangements in advance and by renting by the week rather than by the day.

Recreational Vehicles

Renting an RV equipped with kitchen, TV, beds, on-board privy and many other comforts of home is a very viable option. It's not an inexpensive one, however. For example, an 18- or 20-foot van conversion that sleeps up to four adults will cost you about $100/day or $665/week during the summer months ($90/day or $595/week through the winter). After a limited number of free miles (about 500 free miles per weekly rental), it will cost an additional 22¢ a mile, plus gasoline, cleaning fees (about $55), and taxes. You'll also have to provide full insurance coverage, including collision, comprehensive and applicable deductibles. Of course, expenses increase as the size of the vehicle gets larger.

Such arrangements must be made in advance, especially during the summer months. Dealers are located in most of the major population centers. See the Directory at the back of this guide.

Bicycles

Thousands of bicyclists each year choose to pedal their way along the highways and through California's numerous parks. Although bikes are often prohibited on hiking trails, many parks allow them on fire roads which provide a wonderful workout as well as a great way to explore backcountry areas. Most cyclists rely on heavy duty, multi-geared mountain bikes with thick tires that can climb dusty dirt roads up steep slopes. Rental concessions are sometimes available in or near parks.

Coastal Critters

With and Without Legs

Robert Frost wrote a poem called *New Hampshire,* and in it there's a whimsical little stanza about California. It goes like this:

> I met a Californian who would talk California
> – a state so blessed,
> He said, in climate, none had ever died there
> A natural death, and Vigilance Committees
> Had to organize to stock the
> graveyards
> And vindicate the state's humanity

Well, ummm... life in California may be good, but it's not quite that good. Although the climate is blessed and the scenery spectacular, you'll find the people here as vulnerable to life's tribulations as they are all over the world. Vigilante committees aren't really needed "to stock the graveyards."

There certainly may be concerns *different* from those to which you are accustomed – mountain lions, earthquakes, poison mushrooms, rip tides, rattlesnakes and sleeper waves to name a few. To be sure, there's no cause for alarm. Your chances of succumbing to any such concerns are slim and extremely unlikely to impact your camping adventure. Millions visit and camp the golden state every year... and they live to tell about it!

It's helpful, however, to know what's "out there." And one of the simplest yet most overlooked ways to do this is to read the bulletin boards that often greet you as you enter a park. They cover a wide variety of subjects ranging from crime alerts, animal advisories and fire warnings to campground program schedules, blurbs on natural history, details regarding fees, rules, regulations and registration procedures. A few minutes spent perusing these boards can make your experience immeasurably safer and infinitely more informative. And while the chance of running into, say, a mountain lion, may be slight, wouldn't you like to know what to do, if you did?

Following are some of the tidbits you'll find on the bulletin boards, along with some you won't.

Animals

Whales

One of the animals you absolutely must watch out for, not because they pose any danger, but because they put on one of the best wildlife shows anywhere in the world, is the gray whale. Every year, beginning in early October, these 40-ton sea-going mammals leave their home in the cold Arctic waters for a two-month sojourn in the warm coastal lagoons of Baja California. It is here that the pregnant cows give birth and nurture their calves from about January through February. By March, they're ready to head back along the coast towards the rich feeding grounds in the Bering Sea and adjacent waters.

The best time to view the whales off the coast of California is during the southward migration. From November through December, these mammoths swim constantly, averaging four to six miles an hour, never stopping to eat or sleep. The best views are from promontories that project well beyond the rest of the shoreline and where the whales often come within a few hundred yards.

Mountain Lions

Dangerous confrontations between mountain lions and humans are on the increase in California. Two people were mauled to death in 1994, the first such happenings in more than 80 years. There were also several injuries and a number of near incidents. And experts predict there will be more. "The mountain lion population is very healthy," says the Department of Fish and Game.

Indeed, the current population has been estimated at between 4,000 and 6,000, indicating the mountain lion has come back and come back strong after being nearly eradicated following decades of unrestricted hunting. By 1920, the population had been whittled to about 600 cats. Part of the increase may be attributed to the *special protected mammal* status that the mountain lion received in 1990 after California voters passed a proposition protecting the cats from sport hunting. With the recent encounters, however, there's already talk of rescinding that status.

The mountain lion, alternately called a puma, panther or cougar, is nothing new to California. It's indigenous to about half the state and can be found from deserts to coastal forests, from sea level to well up into the mountains. Yet, because they usually hunt alone and under the cover of darkness, they normally maintain a low profile. It's quite easy to live in mountain lion country without ever seeing one.

As the mountain lion population increases and humans increasingly encroach on mountain lion habitat, however, confrontations are inevitable. The California Department of Fish and Game offers the following suggestions on how to avoid encounters with a mountain lion and what to do if it happens:

- Don't hike alone. Go in groups.

- Keep children close. Mountain lions seem particularly attracted to young children.

- Don't approach a lion. Most will try to avoid a confrontation. Let them have a way to escape.

- Don't run from a lion. It may stimulate the animal's instinct to chase. Instead, stand and face the animal.

- Do all you can to appear larger. Raise your arms. Open your jacket. Wave your arms slowly and speak firmly in a loud voice. Try to convince the lion you may be dangerous and are not suitable prey.

- Stay standing. Don't crouch or bend over. Experts suggest that a person squatting or bending looks like a four-legged prey.

- Fight back. When attacked, people have successfully defended themselves with sticks, caps, jackets, garden tools and their bare hands. It's crucial to remain standing, if possible, since a mountain lion usually tries to bite the head or neck.

Bears

The only species of bear left in California is *Ursus Americanus*, better known as the black bear even though it comes in a variety of colors, including brown, blonde and cinnamon. It thrives in the evergreen forests and oak woodlands of the Redwood National and State Parks in Northern California where copious quantities of plant and animal foods like grass, berries, ants and termites keep it fat and quite happy. Adult males weigh in at close to 300 pounds, while females are about half that.

Amazingly athletic creatures despite their gawkish appearance, they swim, they climb trees, and they sprint at speeds of up to 25 mph. They're incredibly strong, too, and can easily tear open car doors, windows and coolers to search for food.

Fortunately, bears have a natural fear of people. If they see you first, they run. It's when they learn not to be afraid of people that trouble begins. And that only happens if people get careless. By not storing food securely, by not disposing of garbage properly, bears quickly come to associate people with sources of food. And once they learn to get human food in campgrounds, picnic areas or from garbage cans, they are sure to return again and again. Bears have very good memories, according to the experts. In the process of seeking out human foods, bears sometimes lose their fear of people and become aggressive and dangerous. That can lead to increased likelihood of personal injury or property damage for people, and almost certain death for bears.

To prevent such calamity, campers must take certain precautions when camping in bear country. These include the following:

- Use bear-proof garbage cans and food storage lockers when available, or store food and scented personal care items in the trunk of your car.

- If bear-proof storage facilities are not available, hang food and garbage in a tree well out of reach of bears – at least 10 feet away from the trunk and 12 feet from the ground.

- Cook and store food at least 100 feet away from where you sleep. Wash dishes immediately after use.

- When you leave the site, pack all garbage out with you.

- If a bear approaches, stand up and wave your arms while shouting and making loud noises. Throwing small rocks in the bear's direction will usually send it running. Act boldly, but use good judgment. If you feel threatened, walk away, don't run.

Rattlesnakes

There is only one venomous snake in California – the rattlesnake. With the exception of agricultural and urbanized areas, they can be found in virtually every corner of the state from the coast to the deserts, and on the mountains up to an elevation of 11,000 feet.

Although they have a sinister reputation, they are valuable members of the environment. Without them, rodents, gophers and other potentially harmful critters would breed beyond control. "Please do not kill a rattlesnake if you see one," writes a park ranger from Orange County. "If you find a rattlesnake in your camping area, contact a ranger or maintenance worker and we will be glad to remove the snake and relocate it to an unpopulated part of the park."

Their usefulness aside, about 300 people are bitten by rattlesnakes each year, two-thirds of the bites occuring in Southern California. That's actually a surprisingly low number considering the population of California and the ubiquity of the snake. But it could be even lower if people would do three simple things:

- Learn to recognize a rattlesnake. If the tail rattles, it's certainly a rattlesnake. However, rattlesnakes can lose their rattlers. Their distinctive arrow-shaped heads, on the other hand, easily distinguish them from all other California snakes, whose heads are merely extensions of the rest of the body.

- Don't pick one up. At Torrey Pines State Reserve, which draws a quarter-of-a-million people to its hiking trails each year, only one person has been bitten in more than 33 years. And that wouldn't have happened if the young lad had not tried to touch it. As a park brochure says: "If you are lucky enough to see a snake, please leave it alone. As with all wild animals: if you don't bother it, it won't bother you."

- Watch where you step. Self-explanatory.

In the event someone does sustain a bite, try to keep the victim calm and lying down to slow the spread of poison through the body; lower the bitten area to below the level of the heart, then call 911. It might be helpful to remember, too, that only about 3% of snake bites result in death according to the experts. That's safer than driving.

Raccoons

Raccoons have become a major nuisance at many campgrounds. They've simply gotten accustomed to people who encourage them into a camp with scraps of food. Now they expect it. Stories abound of raccoons boldly walking into camp, ripping through tents and breaking into coolers even as people shout to scare them away.

"If they had a few more IQ points, they could steal a car," quipped one park ranger.

Campers are cautioned to store all food in vehicles and never offer to feed the animals, however cute you may find them. It creates bad habits that are impossible to break. And, besides, raccoons will bite and claw if you get too close.

Sea Monsters

Sure, there are millions of creatures out there in the vast depths of the Pacific, but most will disappear as soon as they know you're around. Some, however, like sea urchins and the Portuguese Man of War, can't move very fast. In cases like that, it's your job to avoid them.

The Man of War is a purplish-blue bubble floating on the surface of the water. But there's more to this man than meets the eye. Below the water, it has tentacles several feet long. Touch them and you'll receive an extremely painful sting. It can happen even if you find the creature beached on the sand.

Sea urchins are like pin cushions attached to submerged rocks and coral. Brush up against one and the pins break off and penetrate the skin.

Then there's coral, which doesn't move at all. It's sharp and quick to cut and scrape anyone who gets too close.

Fortunately, wounds from any of the above are normally not serious, except for the pain and discomfort. Cleaning the wound and applying antiseptic is normally adequate treatment. If unusually severe symptoms develop, see a physician.

Among other animals you may encounter in the water is the stingray, a flat, oval-shaped creature with a long whip-like tail. On uncrowded beaches in Southern California, they like to settle down into the sand close to shore. To avoid stepping on one and getting stung by the venomous barb located on the base of the tail, waders are advised to shuffle their feet as they walk into the water. Once they know you're around, they are more than happy to leave.

Sharks are present, too, but your chances of seeing one, let alone being attacked by one, are slimmer than winning the California State lottery. It happens maybe once or twice a year along the California coast, a minuscule number of times considering the throngs that take to the ocean every year. Far more worrisome is the risk of drowning, which is more than 1,000 times greater than that of dying from a shark attack.

To reduce the risk of an attack, experts recommend that you stay out of the water at dawn, dusk and night when some sharks move inshore to feed. Always swim, surf or dive with other people, preferably at beaches where lifeguards are on duty. And don't enter the water if you have open wounds or are bleeding in any way. Sharks are drawn to blood and other body fluids, even in very small concentrations. Also, avoid wearing high-contrast clothing and shiny jewelry which seem to attract sharks.

In the unlikely event you do encounter one, get out of the water with as little noise and splashing as possible.

Plants

Deadly Harvest

Some of the world's most poisonous mushrooms grow along parts of the California coast, including Mt. Tamalpais State Park. Every year, people die or become violently ill from eating Death Caps or Destroying Angels. "Do not gather!" says a bulletin board warning. "The mushrooms resemble harmless varieties and even experts can be fooled."

More than 90% of all mushroom poisonings are from this group. Vomiting and diarrhea begin 10 to 20 hours after eating, followed by damage to the heart, liver, kidneys and skeletal muscles. About 50% of the victims die in two to five days. Take heed!

Stinging Nettle

Stinging nettle is a plant, not an insect. If you touch it, though, the result is the same. Ouch! Its sting will burn, itch and cause red welts the same as a bee, wasp or spider. It's not serious, fortunately, and should quickly clear up with nothing more than soap and water. The principal ingredient of the irritant is formic acid. It flows through tiny hollow bristles that look like fuzz on the stalks, leaf-stems and underside of leaves. Brush up against a Stinging Nettle and you're sure to get the point, thousands of them.

Poison Oak

Perhaps the most irritating of all California's plant life is poison oak. It grows almost everywhere, from sea level to altitudes almost a mile high. It can take the form of a spindly plant, bush, or climbing vine, but its distinctive leaves, which grow in patterns of three, offer the best indication of its presence. The leaves are shiny with prominent veins. Their color usually changes with the seasons, starting off bright green in spring, turning yellow-green with pink or reddish tones in the summer, ultimately becoming bright red or russet in fall. Leaves typically fall off in winter, leaving stick or whip-like stems or climbing vines.

Brushing up against any part of the plant, including stems, roots, berries and leaves, normally produces itching and blisters. However, the irritant can also be spread by tools, animals, clothes and even your own hands if they've made contact with the plant. Treatment usually calls for a thorough cleansing and an application of calamine lotion. Severe cases should be treated by a physician.

The best treatment is prevention. Learn to recognize poison oak and stay away from it. When hiking, wear long pants and sleeves. Wash contaminated clothing.

Insects

Lyme Disease

Lyme Disease has nothing to do with California's citrus production. But it could have something to do with you if you plan on hiking off established trails for any distance. The disease is caused by a spiral-shaped bacteria that's transmitted by the bite of a tick.

First noted in 1975 at Old Lyme, Connecticut, it is now recognized as a serious concern throughout the Northeast, parts of the Midwest and Southeast, as well as Oregon, Nevada and many European countries. It was discovered in California in 1978.

The good news is that out of 49 species of ticks occurring in California, only one, the western black-legged tick, is known to transmit the disease. The bad news is the tick has been found in 50 of California's 58 counties, most commonly in the humid coastal areas and on the western slope of the Sierra Nevada range. More good news. Ticks don't fly, jump or drop from trees, but they are in the grass and brush lying in wait for a host – animal or human – to brush up against them. Ranging in color from brownish-black to red-brown, they measure about 1/8th of an inch long and are hard to spot unless you're wearing light-colored clothing, which is one of the precautions suggested when venturing through suspect areas. Ticks work by imbedding their mouth parts into the skin of a host and dining on its blood, infecting the host with the disease-causing spirochete in the process.

Early symptoms of the infection usually occur three to 30 days after the bite and include rash and flu-like symptoms such as fever and aches. Long-term complications may show up weeks, months and years later and include disorders of the heart, nervous system and chronic arthritis.

Preventive measures include wearing light-colored clothing, application of insect repellants, avoidance of brushy, grassy areas where ticks may be thriving, and frequent checks of clothing.

If you are bitten, remove the tick as soon as possible. Prompt removal may prevent transmission. Try not to crush or squeeze the insect because exposure to body fluids may transmit Lyme or other disease agents. Using tweezers if possible, grasp the tick's mouthparts as close to the skin as possible and gently pull the tick straight out, avoiding twisting or jerking motions. Wash with soap and water and apply antiseptic. If mouthparts break off and remain under your skin, see a physician.

Killer Bees

Since escaping from an experimental station in Brazil in 1957, Africanized honey bees – so-called *killer bees* – have been moving north steadliy. They established themselves in Texas in 1990 and were expected to arrive in San Diego County sometime in 1995.

Although its killer reputation has been greatly exaggerated, the presence of the new bee will certainly increase the numbers of people and pets that are stung. Killer bees are identical in appearance to the more familiar European honey bee, but they react far more aggresively when they sense danger, attacking in greater numbers and over a greater distance. They will pursue their victim for up to a half-mile, much farther than the 100 yards or so expected from their European cousins. Africanized bees can only sting once.

A couple of simple precautions may help you, your children and your pets from being stung.

- Explore your immediate surroundings before letting you children and pets loose. These bees will often nest underground, in empty cans, buckets and old tires, within piles of lumber, as well as in trees, sheds, low decks and spaces under buildings. If you detect a nest or hear a tell-tale hum of a swarm, alert the nearest park ranger or camp host as quickly as possible.

- Don't disturb bee swarms and hives. Even loud noises can be enough to incite the volatile killer bee.

If you are attacked, follow these tips:

- Don't swat the bees – it only angers them further. Run to the nearest building or vehicle and shut the doors.

- Avoid running into thick brush. It won't stop the bees and will serve only to slow you down.

- Stay out of the water. The bees will only follow you and wait until you come up for air.

- Protect you face and head especially. They are usually exposed and are prime targets for the bees.

- Use a dull knife or credit card to scrape stingers from your skin. Avoid using tweezers or fingers which can squeeze venom sacks attached to the stingers and inject additional poison.

- Call 911 for emergency assistance once you are safe from further attack.

The Ocean

A bulletin board at Wright's Beach in Sonoma County posted the following rather sobering warning:

"Since 1950, at least 81 people have been swept away from Sonoma Coast State Beaches. They didn't know how to protect themselves from the dangerous conditions that exist here."

This and similar warnings are to be expected at beach parks up and down the length of the state. And while inherent dangers will vary from one location to another, a common truth runs through them all: The ocean can be dangerous. Never turn your back on it.

Rip Currents

Images of terrified swimmers flailing the water with their arms in vain efforts to prevent themselves from being sucked underwater and pulled far out to sea are often associated with the words "rip current." Although not without some basis in truth, rip currents don't necessarily portend such tragedy.

A rip current is perhaps less frightening and easier to understand if you think of it simply as a river in the sea. Like water flowing on land, a rip current is nothing more than a stream of water, only instead of running off the land, it's flowing through the waves and swells of the ocean. Such "rivers" are usually no wider than about 50 feet and normally don't go any further out than the surf line. Although not as obvious as a land river, you can usually identify a rip current by its contrast with the rest of the ocean. Look for a strip of ocean with a choppy surface, foam or turbid water.

If you happen to "fall" into this type of river, don't try swimming against the flow, say the experts. It's not any easier swimming against the flow of a rip current than it is swimming against the flow of an earthbound river. And don't panic either. A rip current won't pull you under. You can escape its grip by either floating with the current until it dissipates, normally not far past the point where waves begin to break, and then swim away from it and towards shore. Or, you can swim out of the river by swimming to either side of the rip current (along a line parallel to shore).

Sleeper Waves, Backwash and Drop Offs

Storms and strong winds at sea often create huge waves that break with sudden and tremendous force along portions of the coast with steep beaches. These are called sleeper waves because they appear with little warning and frequently catch swimmers by surprise. Sleeper waves can easily knock adults off balance and against the sand or rock, a dangerous condition by itself. Compounding the danger is the backwash, the powerful flow of water back into the ocean. Once in the grip of the backwash, it's extremely difficult to escape as it pulls you farther and farther into the sea and subjects you to another onslaught of waves.

Swimmers also need to be aware of drop offs, underwater trenches or holes that are created as wave after wave breaks against a beach. Some of the holes may be 100 feet or more across with a rip current flowing out of them. Such depressions are normally dangerous only for inexperienced swimmers, who may panic when they suddenly find they are in water over their heads.

Two-Legged Critters

Caution! Lock your car! Keep valuables with you!

Warnings like this are a familiar sight at campgrounds. You'll see them as free-standing signs and as notices on bulletin boards. Some parks even print out advisories and hand them to campers as they check in.

"Theft is common here!!!," says one such effort. "Normal precautions may not be enough. Items have been stolen in broad daylight. Tents and bicycle cables have been cut. Store your property in your vehicle. Report suspicious persons."

Few places are immune to crime and that, obviously, includes campgrounds. Recently, even the FBI got involved in a crime spree affecting campgrounds in California, Oregon and Washington state. Working with park rangers from each state, the FBI set up a sting operation and eventually nabbed the thief. It turned out to be the same fellow who was arrested several years earlier for the same type of crime.

"We're going to send him to prison forever this time," says Donald Murphy, Director of the California Department of Parks and Recreation.

Murphy credits park rangers for helping solve the recent wave of thefts. "Our rangers are the ones who primarily coordinated this activity and I have to say that we put a tremendous amount of resources in training our rangers, making sure they are competent peace officers," he said in an interview with the *RV Journal* (October-December 1994).

"Some (crime) rings who do campgrounds are professionals and they are very difficult to catch unless you start throwing all of your resources into crime prevention. I think that the resources we have are doing a fairly good job now at policing these areas and doing regular patrols."

Of course, not all campground crime is an organized effort. Sometimes it's local vandals or, perhaps, another camper in a weak moment. Whatever the case, it's the park ranger who's often the first line of defense. It comes as a surprise to many that state park rangers are full-fledged peace officers; they can pack pistols, make arrests and issue costly citations to those breaking park rules and regulations. They have jurisdiction throughout the state with power to intervene even in off-park situations.

In addition to the prominent presence of rangers, many parks – national, county as well as state – also have resident camp hosts. In exchange for free camp space, sometimes including hookups, volunteer hosts help facilitate park operations, assisting state park personnel in registering campers, disseminating information and other such activities. Most valuable, perhaps, is their accessibility. Simply being there to watch over things and offering help when someone needs it is of great comfort to many. Camp hosts, a number of whom are retired or semi-retired couples, are on call 24 hours a day to assist in campground emergencies.

Even with park rangers and camp hosts on duty, however, campers can further reduce their chances of problems by taking a few simple, common-sense precautions:

- Meet with your neighbors and agree to watch each other's campsite and personal belongings.

- Secure your camping gear at night and when you leave your campsite during the day.

- Zip up your tent or lock your camper, trailer or motor home whenever you leave it.

- Make sure you don't leave axes, hatchets and knives out in the open where they can be used as tools to break into your camping vehicle.

- Report suspicious persons or activities to the rangers, noting descriptions, vehicles, license numbers and direction of travel.

- Mark your property with your state driver's license number or other information so that it can be easily identified if lost or stolen.

- Park your vehicle within view of your campsite or in an area patrolled regularly by park personnel.

- Lock your vehicle.

- If you leave the campsite, take your valuables whenever possible. When it's not feasible to do so, secure them in the trunk of your vehicle or at least keep them out of sight.

- Lock bicycles with a case-hardened steel lock and chain.

Earthquakes

Each year, California is subject to about 100,000 earthquakes, but don't be alarmed. Only about 1,000 of them are strong enough to be noticeable. And of those, just five to 10 will measure 5 or more on the Richter scale and result in any significant damage. Thus, odds are excellent that nothing catastrophic will befall you. Driving that vehicle of yours is far riskier!

In the unlikely event that a big one does strike, remember that the primary danger is falling debris and collapsing structures. As a camper, you may find comfort in knowing there's far less danger of that in the undeveloped countryside. Even in the wilderness, though, a good jolt can cause landslides and falling rock. (Rain can cause these as well.) Perhaps the only precaution is to stand back from unstable cliffs and rocky slopes. You'll find most parks are well marked with signs identifying potential hazards. Most of all, try not to panic. Earthquakes are shortlived, usually subsiding after less than a minute, often in a few seconds.

Southern California

California

San Diego, Orange and Los Angeles Counties

Myth & Reality

In the minds of many, the beaches of San Diego, Orange and Los Angeles counties come closest to defining the popular notion of *Southern California*, a mythical paradise of endless summers, surf, sand, youth and beauty. It ignores the fact that the region extends for hundreds of miles east over vast, desolate expanses of parched desert where temperatures reach 120° and water is often just a mirage. Nobody sings about that part of the state and nobody sings about the smog either. Los Angeles County records well over 100 days per year of unhealthful air (Orange and San Diego counties have less at only 40 to 50 days per year). They occur most often in the summer, but you can usually escape such conditions by staying near the coast, where the wind blows the soot and smoke inland.

The myth of Southern California, surreal as it is, is not entirely groundless, however. It does enjoy the mildest weather and the sunniest skies anywhere along the California coast. Daytime summer temperatures average in the high 70s and 80s; winters are in the 60s and 70s. The ocean air makes sure it never gets too hot or cold, although it can dip into the 40s at night and moisture-laden winds can make it feel even cooler. Water temperatures reach a pleasant 70-72° in the summers and about 10-12° cooler in the winter.

Of course, you've all heard the expression, "it never rains in Southern California." Believe it or not, that's also based on fact. You can count on more than 280 days of sunshine per year; summers are essentially rainless. If rain is going to fall, it will undoubtedly be sometime between November and April, from nine to 14 inches of it (depending on where you're taking the measurements). That's just enough to turn the normally brown hills a lively green.

Another part of the myth includes images of lean, muscular bodies baked to perfection by the sun. That's not without its basis in fact

either, but more evident are the millions of other not-so-lean bodies, nearly 14 million to be exact. More people live within these
three counties than any other part of the state – over 46% of
California's total population. In fact, Los Angeles and Orange
counties pack more people per square mile than any other county
in the state, except for San Francisco.

That doesn't mean Southern California is a wall-to-wall Manhattan, however. It's really quite remarkable how airy all but the most
urbanized centers can seem. Almost every inch of the coast is
public property and open to recreation. You'll find most coastal
communities quite pleasant, if not absolutely delightful.

What the large population does mean is keen competition for
facilities, including campsites. It virtually guarantees crowds in the
summers and most holidays, threatens traffic snarls, and all but
assures difficulty in finding parking space. You can avoid it all,
however, just by timing your visit before Memorial Day and after
Labor Day. A trip here in the weeks just after Labor Day will avail
you of the sought-after spaces in the best campgrounds with some
of the clearest, cleanest and most comfortable weather of the year.

Getting There

Getting to the coast of Southern California is an easy matter. The
area's four major airports are right on the coast or within a short
drive of it. They include: Los Angeles International Airport, Long
Beach Municipal Airport, John Wayne/Orange County Airport (in
Santa Ana), and the San Diego International Airport.

You'll probably find the least expensive airfares by flying into Los
Angeles because it's serviced by so many airlines and, even if your
ultimate destination lies to the north or south, you may find it
worth your while to arrive here. In just two hours, you can drive to
either San Diego or Santa Barbara.

Amtrak also provides convenient train service along the coast. For
stations, schedules and fares, contact Amtrak at: 1-800-USA RAIL.

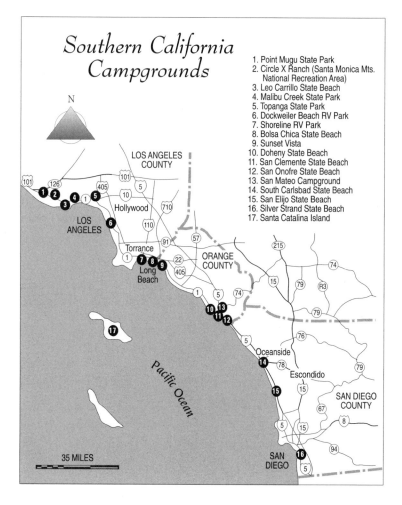

Southern California
Campgrounds

N

1. Point Mugu State Park
2. Circle X Ranch (Santa Monica Mts. National Recreation Area)
3. Leo Carrillo State Beach
4. Malibu Creek State Park
5. Topanga State Park
6. Dockweiler Beach RV Park
7. Shoreline RV Park
8. Bolsa Chica State Beach
9. Sunset Vista
10. Doheny State Beach
11. San Clemente State Beach
12. San Onofre State Beach
13. San Mateo Campground
14. South Carlsbad State Beach
15. San Elijo State Beach
16. Silver Strand State Beach
17. Santa Catalina Island

LOS ANGELES COUNTY

Hollywood

LOS ANGELES

Torrance

Long Beach

ORANGE COUNTY

Oceanside

Escondido

SAN DIEGO COUNTY

SAN DIEGO

Pacific Ocean

35 MILES

Attractions

From the U.S.-Mexico border south of San Diego to the Hollywood film studios of Los Angeles, Southern California offers countless places to enjoy. Venture from your campground for a few hours and explore such attractions as Sea World, Disneyland (the original), the San Diego Zoo and Wild Animal Park, Universal Studios (another original), and the exclusive, world-famous communities of Malibu and Beverly Hills. During the winter, you can even ski in the mountains of Los Angeles. There need never be a dull or empty moment in Southern California.

San Diego County

SILVER STRAND STATE BEACH

500 Highway 75 (between Coronado and Imperial Beach)
Coronado CA 92118. (619) 435-5184

* On-the-beach RV camping; no tents

Relaxing on the beautiful white beach at Silver Strand

This is an absolutely beautiful beach featuring a long, broad stretch of blonde sand. And, if you're lucky enough to have use of a self-contained camping vehicle (minimum requirements include a built-in sink with enclosed drain system and portable toilet), you can camp here up to seven days with nothing but the sand between you and the sea. Anything other than a self-contained vehicle means you're out of luck, although day use is open to anyone paying the $4 entrance fee. The beach's four large parking lots can accommodate nearly 1,000 cars. Lifeguards are on duty all summer long and most holiday weekends.

It's located on a narrow strip of sand known as the Silver Strand or Coronado Peninsula. Five miles to the north of the park's entrance is the city of Coronado and the landmark Hotel Del Coronado. You'll find numerous restaurants and gift shops here, as well as grocery stores, a movie theater and whatever else you can expect to find in a community of nearly 30,000 people.

About three miles to the south of Silver Strand State Beach is Imperial Beach, another full-service community of nearly 30,000.

Within the park, there's a daytime snackbar in operation throughout the summer months. Free interpretive programs for children are scheduled throughout the summer, too. And don't forget the ocean. It's hospitable most of the time and protected by lifeguards throughout the year.

CAMPGROUND: There are 124 RV spaces, including two reserved for the handicapped. Essentially, the campground is nothing more than a paved parking lot that's set aside for recreational vehicles. There are no tables or grills, and the area is absolutely void of trees, shrubs or anything else but ice plants and a few other low-growing plants that help keep the sand in place. The preferred spaces front the beach. When those are gone, you start the next row behind.

RESTROOMS: Modern flush toilets, changing rooms and a single outdoor cold water rinse-off shower.

RESERVATIONS: None; first-come, first-served basis.

CHECK IN/OUT: You may check in anytime the gates are open (8 a.m. to 7, 8 or 9 p.m., depending on season); noon check out.

FEES: $14/day in peak season (March-November); $12/day remainder of the year.

DOGS: $1/day. No access to beach; must be kept in parking lot only.

MAX. STAY: Seven days, although addtional days can be approved by the park staff up to the 14th day, depending on the occupancy rate.

SECURITY: Park rangers and resident camp host. Also, the gated entrance is opened every day at 8 a.m. and closed at 7, 8 or 9 p.m. (depending on the season). Note that this not only prevents anyone from entering the park after hours, but it also prevents anyone from leaving.

HOW TO GET THERE: From downtown San Diego, drive south on I-5; exit onto the San Diego-Coronado Bay Bridge (75); stay on 75 as you pass through Coronado. Watch for entrance to the Silver Strand State Beach Park about five miles south of the Hotel Del Coronado.

Grunion

One of Southern California's most interesting phenomena is the grunion run in Spring and Summer. And Silver Strand is one of many beaches where you can see it happen.

The diminutive silver-colored fish arrive on shore with the highest tides following the fall or new moon. On the beach, females bury themselves tail first in the sand and deposit their eggs. Males then release milt to fertilize them. The reproduction process thus completed, the fish are swept back out to sea by outgoing waves, leaving eggs to develop in the warm, moist sand.

In 10 days, the next series of high tides erodes the beach and washes the eggs into the ocean. Within minutes, new grunion hatch. Spawning takes place from March through September, and you're allowed to catch the grunion every month during that period except April and May, when fish are permitted to reproduce undisturbed. There's no limit to how many you can catch, but only the bare hands may be used; nets, scoops, crates or other traps are illegal. Those 16 and over must have a California fishing license, available at any sporting goods store.

SAN ELIJO STATE BEACH
Highway 101, Cardiff-by-the-Sea, CA 92007
(619) 753-5091

• Oceanfront tent and RV camping

Belly up to the waist-high barrier lining the bluff that rises 30-40 feet above the beach here and you can see some of San Diego County's most beautiful coastline curving and bending into the distance. Or look due west for an unimpeded view of the vast Pacific Ocean, its offshore sheen undisturbed except by an occasional yacht or, if you're here during the winter months, a breaching whale.

With any luck, the edge of this bluff will also be the edge of your campsite; with roughly half of the park's 171 sites built along the ledge, you've got a 50-50 chance.

San Elijo is surrounded by the communities of Solana Beach, Cardiff-by-the-Sea and Encinitas, composed mostly of mid-and up-scale single family homes, condominiums and apartments. A little more than a half-mile south on Pacific Coast Highway is Cardiff's restaurant row, where locals and tourists alike are drawn to a choice of eateries, some right on the sand. Less than a half-mile to the east, across the highway, are several smaller restaurants and a donut shop.

You can also rent bodyboards, soft surfboards, kayaks, snorkeling gear, chairs and umbrellas during the summer months from Hansen Surfboards, located at 1105 First Street in Encinitas, about two miles north on 101.

CAMPGROUND: San Elijo's 171 campsites may be used for either tents or RVs up to 35 feet. There are no hookups, although there is a sanitary disposal station. Each space is little more than hard packed sand and dirt separated from the other spaces by evergreen shrubs. There are few tall trees and, thus, shade is at a premium.

The campground is arranged in basically three tiers. There is a row of spaces at the edge of the bluff (most desirable); a row at the edge of busy Pacific Highway railroad (least desirable), and islands of spaces in between the two rows.

At the south end of the campground a few sites are at the beach level. However, most of the access to the usually broad, sandy beach below the bluff is by way of six long stairways that zig-zag down the 35-foot descent. Fishing, swimming and surfing are good here. Lifeguards are on duty throughout the summer and most weekends.

RESTROOMS: Flush toilets, sinks, mirrors and coin-operated showers (25¢ for 2½ minutes).

RESERVATIONS: Up to eight weeks in advance through MISTIX: 1-800-444-PARK. **Note:** Although this park has historically stayed open all year long, it has been closed for the winter months the last couple of years.

CHECK IN/OUT: 2 p.m in; noon out.

FEES: $21/day for beachfront; $16/day for interior in peak season (Mar. 1-Nov. 30); $19/day for beachfront and $14/day for interior in off-peak.

DOGS: $1/day. Permitted on the beach *only* south of the main lifeguard tower.

MAX. STAY: Seven days (June-September); 15 days remainder of the year.

SECURITY: Rangers are on duty throughout the day; on-site camp hosts are on call for emergencies around the clock.

HOW TO GET THERE: From San Diego International Airport, drive north on Interstate 5 about 26 miles; exit at Lomas Santa Fe and turn left; stay on Lomas Santa Fe until you reach Pacific Coast Highway (101); turn right at 101 and drive 2.2 miles north. San Elijo State Park is on the left side of the highway. If coming from the north, exit I-5 at Encinitas Boulevard and drive west (right) to 101; turn left onto 101 for 2.5 miles to the park entrance.

SOUTH CARLSBAD STATE BEACH
2680 Carlsbad Boulevard (Pacific Coast Highway)
Carlsbad, CA 92008. (619) 438-3143

• Oceanfront tent and RV camping

Like San Elijo State Park a few miles to the south, South Carlsbad State Beach is located on a bluff about 50 feet above the beach with panoramic views of the coastline. Ramps or stairs lead to the long beach, which is frequently denuded of sand and covered with smooth, worn rocks and pebbles. (The sand is to be restored as part of a complete park renovation project in the near future.)

The east end of the park parallels the Pacific Coast Highway, which bears the name "Carlsbad Boulevard" as it passes through this area. The AMTRAK railway also runs alongside the park and rumbles past the campground day and night.

A camp store, from which you can rent body boards and buy food items, beverages, fishing bait, etc., is open through the summers (closed after Thanksgiving through March). But with a city the size of Carlsbad, which has 65,000 residents, you won't have any problem finding anything you need. In fact, there's a large shopping center with a major grocery store, cleaners, coffee shop, restaurants and fast food just minutes away (east of the park on Poinsettia

Lane). Carlsbad is also site of a soon-to-be-built theme park by the makers of Lego toy building blocks.

A wooden stairway leads the way to the rocky beach and blue sea

CAMPGROUND: Two rows of sites line campground. They're on hard packed dirt and can be used for either tents or RV. The first and most desirable locations are those on the edge of the bluff, which is lined with a waist-high chain-link fence. These sites are said to be as much as 10°F cooler than those in the second row, which are located just across the narrow access road.

That's because of the wind, explains one of the park's year-round camp hosts. The bluff deflects the sea breeze upwards, cooling the first row of spaces, but passing over the second row of spaces just 20 to 25 feet away. In addition to being slightly warmer, the second row is less desirable because it's closer to the highway and train tracks.

There are no hookups, although a sanitary disposal station is on site. The spaces are generous, measuring about 25 x 35 feet, with fire pits, picnic tables and some grills. Hedges of acacia, bottlebrush and other shrubs divide one space from another for reasonable privacy.

RESTROOMS: Flush toilets, sinks, mirrors and coin-operated-showers (25¢ for 2½ minutes).

RESERVATIONS: Up to eight weeks in advance through MISTIX: 1-800-444-PARK. Drive-ups okay if space is available.

CHECK IN/OUT: 2 p.m. in; noon out.

FEES: Peak season (March 1-Nov. 30); $21/day beachfront; $16/day interior. Off-peak: $19/day beachfront; $14/day interior.

DOGS: $1/day; not permitted on beach.

MAX. STAY: Seven days (June-Sept.); 15 days rest of the year.

SECURITY: Rangers are on duty throughout the day; on-site camp hosts are on call for emergencies around the clock. This is normally a safe campground, although thefts of bikes (using bolt cutters to cut locks and chains), radios, surfboards and other unsecured valubles have been stolen recently.

HOW TO GET THERE: From San Diego International Airport, drive north on I-5 about 30 miles; exit at Poinsettia and turn left; the park entrance is at the end of Poinsettia where it intersects with the Pacific Coast Highway (101), but you'll have to make a right turn onto 101, so that you can make a left turn (within a half-block) to cross the highway and reach the park entrance.

SAN ONOFRE STATE BEACH
3030 Avenida Del Presidente, San Clemente CA 92672
(714) 492-4872

- Oceanview tent and RV camping
- Walk-in camping
- Hike & Bike camping
- Group camping
- En Route camping

If you don't mind sleeping next to a nuclear power plant, and experts maintain that you shouldn't, you might consider camping at 3,000-acre San Onofre State Beach.

San Onofre is squeezed between the Pacific Ocean and busy Interstate 5 about three blocks from where nuclear reactors churn out millions of kilowatts of power for thousands of customers throughout Southern California. But you won't hear a sound, nor smell any odor; in fact, from your campsite, it's unlikely you will know it's there.

A sandy trail takes you to the white sandy beach

The park is essentially a broad, sun-baked bluff 3½ miles long and 400 to 600 yards wide, covered with a grey-green fuzz of indigenous grasses and shrubs. There are few trees offering shade.

The campsites are located along a narrow asphalt road that parallels I-5 just a few feet away. This section of I-5 is also the location of a U.S. Border Patrol Inspection Station where motorists must stop for a usually cursory vehicle check.

In addition to the main campsite, which accommodates both RVs and tents, the park also has a primitive campground, a section for organized groups of up to 50, space for En Route campers, and a Hike & Bike camp.

CAMPGROUNDS: The main campground consists of 221 asphalt-covered spaces that can accommodate either RVs (max. 30-ft.) or tents. Tents are restricted to the dirt area immediately behind the asphalt. The rest of the bluff is closed to camping (with the exception of Echo Arch; see below). Each space features a picnic table and fire pit, but there are no hookups for electricity, water or sewer.

Six dirt trails gradually descend from the campground to the beach; the shortest trail is about 100 yards, the longest 300 to 400 yards. They drop approximately 150 feet in elevation, making the hike back up something to consider for the very young, very old and very lazy.

Tenters desiring a location just a few yards from the beach may opt to camp at Echo Arch, a quarter-mile hike from the park entrance. But this is considered a primitive site with minimal conveniences. Because it is in an environmentally sensitive area, radios and dogs are prohibited. This area has 26 sites, each of which can accommodate up to eight persons and includes a fire pit and table. **Note:** Echo Arch is open only from June 1 to the first big rain, usually around October or November.

RESTROOMS: The main campground features private flush toilets with sinks on the outside of the building. Cold water showers are also outside. Echo Arch has four chemical toilets and one outdoor cold water shower.

RESERVATIONS: Reservations for the main campground and the group site may be made up to eight weeks in advance through MISTIX: 1-800-444-PARK. Reservations for Echo Arch are accepted from June 1-Sept. 15.

CHECK IN/OUT: 2 p.m. in; noon out.

FEES: *Main campground* and *En Route* - $16/day in peak season (Mar. 1-Nov. 30), $14/day off-peak. *Hike & Bike* -$3/day per person. *Echo Arch* - $16/day.

DOGS: $1/day; not permitted on beach or at Echo Arch.

MAX. STAY: 15 days (June-Sept.); 30 days remainder of the year. En Route and Hike & Bike limited to one day.

SECURITY: Park rangers. The U.S. Border Patrol also routinely checks the campground.

HOW TO GET THERE: San Onofre State Beach is 21 miles north of Oceanside. From Oceanside, take I-5 north; exit at Basilone Road; turn left and follow the road three miles to the park entrance.

Orange County

SAN MATEO CAMPGROUND
3030 Avenida Del Presidente, San Clemente CA 92672
(714) 361-2531

- Ocean-vicinity tent and RV camping

Open only since 1992, the San Mateo Campground is one of the newest in the state. Officially, it's part of San Onofre State Beach about six miles to the south. Physically, though, it's much closer to San Clemente State Beach, just 2.3 miles drive to the north and west.

Although just 1½ miles from the amenities of San Clemente, site of the "West Coast White House" under the late President Nixon, the campground itself is quite by itself. Situated on one side of a wide, vacant valley of stubby coastal scrub and woody riparian growth, you'll see little development on the hills flanking either side of the valley, quite unusual in this part of Southern California.

You may very well hear the distant "rat-ta-tat" of a machine gun or an occasional "boom" of artillery. That's coming from Camp Pendleton, where Marines by the thousands hone their combat skills. You may also encounter a variety of native wildlife out here, including mountain lions, bobcats, quail, rabbits, squirrels, road-runners and, yes, rattlesnakes. Shortly after opening, there were so many rattlers that they had to be rounded up and moved offsite. Although the park is without incident to date, parents are routinely cautioned to watch small children closely.

Trestles Beach, a famous surfing spot, is a 1½-mile walk from the campground along an easy dirt pathway.

CAMPGROUND: There are 162 spaces, including two reserved for the handicapped; 69 of them have hookups for electricity and water. Both tenters and RVs up to 36 feet are welcome. Each camp space is comprised of an asphalt parking pad and a generous section of earth covered with wood shavings and/or other plant material. Chances are you'll be separated from your neighbor by leafy shrubs 6-12 feet tall. A wooden picnic table and fire pit with grill top are also provided for your convenience. There are also water spigots and a dump station.

RESTROOMS: First class restrooms featuring private flush toilets, electrical outlets, sinks and mirrors; private showers cost 25¢ for 2½ minutes; accessible to the handicapped.

RESERVATIONS: Up to eight weeks in advance through MISTIX: 1-800-444-PARK.

CHECK IN/OUT: 2 p.m. in; noon out.

FEES: *With hookups* - $20/day in peak season (Mar. 1-Nov. 30); $18/day off-peak. *Without hookups* - $16/day in peak season; $14/day off-peak.

DOGS: $1/day; not permitted on trails.

MAXIMUM STAY: 15 days (June-September); 30 days remainder of the year.

SECURITY: Park rangers and resident camp host.

HOW TO GET THERE: From Oceanside, drive north on I-5 and exit on Cristianitos; follow Cristianitos to the right for one mile to the park entrance.

SAN CLEMENTE STATE BEACH
3030 Avenida Del Presidente, San Clemente, CA 92672
(714) 492-0802 or (714) 492-3156

- Oceanfront tent and RV camping
- Hike & Bike camping
- Group camping

This park is located on a breezy bluff about 100 feet above a broad, golden sand beach popular with surfers, swimmers and divers alike.

Topside, the bluff is a woodsier place than you might expect for Southern California, particularly after visiting San Mateo, San Onofre and the other state parks further south. Stands of tall, leafy eucalyptus create cool islands of shade here and there, while shrubs and grass help give the area added depth and color.

A waist-high fence of chain-link meanders along the rim of the bluff, undoubtedly having prevented hundreds, perhaps thousands, from falling to certain injury or death down the sheer, wrinkled cliffside. Looking down on the beach below, the umbrellas, towels, blankets and the people using them resemble dollhouse miniatures.

Sandy shores at San Clemente

To join them, it's a relatively short and easy descent along either of two asphalt pathways that wind and bend along the face of the cliff. Count on a three- to five-minute walk going down, perhaps double on the way back up.

The park is situated on the south end of San Clemente, a bedroom community of nice homes built on a hillside overlooking the Pacific. There's no need for a camp store because you're just a minute or two from the San Clemente business district, where restaurants, fast food, gas stations, liquor stores and convenience marts are abundant.

CAMPGROUNDS: Unlike most other state parks along the coast, the tent campers and RV campers have their own separate campgrounds.

The RV section has 72 spaces with hookups for water, electricity and sewer and can accommodate vehicles up to 30 feet long. Mature eucalyptus cast shade over select spaces. Asphalt pads are variously separated from one another by trees, shrubs or, in some cases, nothing at all. Each space also has a fire pit and picnic table.

The tent campground is dotted with bushy acacias, scrubby pines as well as an occasional eucalyptus tree, although it's generally less woodsy than the RV section. Shade is nevertheless assured beneath covered mini-pavilions sheltering picnic tables at each of the 85 campsites. These spaces also feature grills and fire pits. Campers park right next to their plot on an asphalt pad. The ground area is typically dirt covered with a thin, short, dry stubble of grass.

There's a section for bicyclists and hikers who enter under their own power (no motor vehicles) and a bluff-top group campground for up to 50 people and 20 vehicles that overlooks the ocean.

RESTROOMS: Each campground has restroom facilities, including flush toilets in tiled stalls, coin-operated showers and laundry tubs.

RESERVATIONS: Up to eight weeks in advance through MISTIX: (800) 444-PARK.

CHECK IN/OUT: Noon.

FEES: *With hookups* - $20/day in peak season (Mar. 1-Nov. 30); $18/day off-peak. *Without hookups* (tentsites) -$16/day in peak season; $14/day off-peak. *Group rate* -$75/day for up to 50 persons. *Bicyclists/hikers rate* -$3/day.

DOGS: $1/day; not permitted on beach.

MAX. STAY: Seven days (June-Sept.); 15 days remainder of the year.

SECURITY: Park rangers and resident camp host.

HOW TO GET THERE: From San Diego, drive north on I-5 for 53 miles; exit at Cristianitos and turn left; follow Cristianitos until it turns to Avenida Del Presidente for about a mile to Calafia; turn left at Calafia for about 1/5th of a mile to the park entrance. (San Mateo State Campground is just 2.3 miles away).

If driving south on I-5, exit at Calafia and follow that just 500 feet to the park entrance.

DOHENY STATE BEACH
25300 Harbor Drive, Dana Point, CA 92629
(714) 496-6172

- Oceanfront tent and RV camping
- Hike & Bike camping

There's no towering bluff and no steep trails or stairs to get between you and the beach at Doheny. Here, spaces for both RVers and tenters are right on the edge of a big, broad curve of golden sand.

The beach runs about a mile in length and is fun for swimming and body surfing. Lifeguards are on duty throughout the busy season and weekends. Its rocky north end is best for fishing and those interested in tide pools. A free Visitor Center has a limited selection of souvenirs and features an indoor tide pool as well as several aquariums with local sea creatures.

The 62-acre park is surrounded by the very pleasant community of Dana Point, named after Richard Henry Dana, Jr., author of *Two Years Before the Mast.* He probably wouldn't recognize the town today, which has boomed in recent years and undergone a major remodel. It maintains its original nautical nature, although the ships in its two marinas now harbor thousands of yachts and fishing boats instead of whaling ships.

On-beach camping at Doheny

CAMPGROUND:
There are 120 tent and RV spaces at Doheny, and these are divided into three distinct categories: (1) tentsite; (2) RV site; and (3) beachfront, which may accommodate either tents or RVs. None have hookups, but there is a dump station and freshwater fill-point next to the large parking lot at the north end of the beach. Spaces also include tables and fire rings.

When making reservations, campers must specify the type of space required. RVs are limited to 35 feet maximum length.

RESTROOMS: Flush toilets and individual hot showers (25¢ for 2½ minutes).

RESERVATIONS: Up to eight weeks in advance through MISTIX (1-800-444-PARK). Drive-ups okay if space is available. Park rangers indicate this is a very popular park all summer long, even on weekdays.

Note: During the peak season, the rangers at Doheny assign spaces by lottery. Visitors who arrive before 11:45 a.m. will pick a number out of a box. This is a random number and places campers in numerical order for registration according to the number they've drawn. At 10 a.m., a list of available campsites will be posted for campers to choose from. Campers entering after 11:45 a.m. will be placed at the bottom of the lottery list and registered as their name comes up. The lottery begins at noon. Campers may choose campsites only from within their reservation type (beachfront, tentsite or RV site).

CHECK IN/OUT: Noon.

FEES: *Beachfront* - $21/day peak season (Mar. 1 through Nov. 30); $19/day off-peak. *Interior* - $16/day peak season; $14/day off-peak. *Bike & Hike camping* - $3/day.

DOGS: $1/day; not permitted on the beach.

MAX. STAY: Seven days (June-September); 15 days remainder of the year. Hike & Bike maximum: one day.

SECURITY: Park rangers and resident camp host.

HOW TO GET THERE: From San Diego, drive north on I-5; turn off at the Beach Cities exit and follow that 1.2 miles to the Pacific Coast Highway (1); turn left onto Del Obispo for a short distance to the park entrance.

If driving from the north, exit at Camino Las Ramblas and follow that to Pacific Coast Highway (1) south to Del Obispo and turn right.

SUNSET VISTA

103 Pacific Coast Highway, Huntington Beach, CA 92648
(714) 969-5621 (information) or (714) 536-5280 (campground gate)

* Beachfront RV camping
* En Route camping

Sunset Vista is 38 miles southeast of Los Angeles on the western edge of Huntington Beach, a sparkly, upscale city that works extremely hard at being the "Coastal Playground" of choice for shoppers, surfers, sailors and others interested in year-round action. It's the 13th largest city in California with an estimated 200,000 residents. Due to its low crime rate, the FBI designated it the safest large city in the state in 1993, and the 12th safest in the nation. Unofficially, Huntington Beach is also known as "the surf capital of the world" and boasts "the most reliable surf in the continental U.S." At the heart of the city is its new $10.8 million pier, which juts out more than 1,800 feet off shore, affording visitors a fascinating walk above the sea and a fantastic view of the city and the mountains behind it.

The wide, sandy beach extends for 8½ miles and is served by lifeguards throughout the year.

CAMPGROUND: If you have a self-contained recreational vehicle, you can camp at the edge of this beach across from the Pacific Coast Highway and the myriad of shops, restaurants, hotels and malls that line it. The campground is essentially a parking lot with space for 120 vehicles up to 40 feet long. There are no hookups, but there is a dump station and drinking water.

RESTROOMS: There are two modern restroom facilities with flush toilets and sinks. Showers are outside and cold water only.

RESERVATIONS: The campground is open September 15 to May 31 each year. Reservations during this period may be made at the park (camper facility booth) or through the mail no earlier than one calendar month prior to occupancy. No reservations are accepted over the phone. Reservation fees are nonrefundable and nontransferable.

Sunset Vista becomes an En Route camp exclusively from June 1 to Sept. 14 and is available on a first-come, first-served basis after 6 p.m. En Route campers are limited to a single day's stay and must leave by 8 a.m.

CHECK IN/OUT: Except for En Route campers, check-in time is from 2-10 p.m.; check out by 2 p.m. Campground entrance is open from 7 a.m. to 10 p.m. daily.

FEES: $15/day.

DOGS: Prohibited.

MAX. STAY: 15 days per month (five days must elapse before reentering). *En Route camping* - one day.

SECURITY: Patrolled by city police and lifeguards. Very little trouble noted.

HOW TO GET THERE: From Los Angeles, take the 405 south; exit west on Route 39; turn right on Pacific Coast Highway (1) to 1st Street; turn left into park entrance.

BOLSA CHICA STATE BEACH
18331 Enterprise Lane, Huntington Beach, CA 92648
(714) 846-3460

• Beachfront RV camping

Three miles west of Huntington Beach, well out of the din and dither of the city, is Bolsa Chica State Beach, 100 acres of unsurpassed Southern California sand and surf that draws almost 1½ million visitors each year. While Sunset Vista (see previous page) abuts one of the most commercial sections of the city, Bolsa Chica neighbors an ecological reserve considered to be one of the best spots for birdwatching in the country. Thousands of human visitors *flock* to the reserve each year to stroll and observe as many as 320 species and tens of thousands of birds throughout the seasons.

The beach is among the friendliest in the state and very popular. A bike trail runs along its entire three-mile length and connects with Huntington Beach. Other activities include surfing, fishing and volleyball. A snack bar operates throughout the summer.

CAMPGROUND: More than 22,000 RV campers visit here annually and camp on an asphalt parking lot at the edge of the beach. There are no hookups and the nearest dump station is about four miles south at Huntington State Beach (Magnolia Street entrance).

RESTROOMS: Modern flush toilets with sinks and mirrors. Cold rinse-off showers on the beach.

RESERVATIONS: Up to eight weeks in advance through MISTIX, 1-800-444-PARK.

CHECK IN/OUT: Noon.

FEES: $14/day throughout the year.

DOGS: $1/day; allowed on paved areas only.

MAX. STAY: Seven days (June-September); 15 days remainder of the year.

SECURITY: Park rangers and resident camp host during summer months.

HOW TO GET THERE: From Huntington Beach, drive north on Highway 1 for three miles (if you reach Warner Avenue, you've gone too far).

Los Angeles County

SHORELINE RV PARK
200 W. Shoreline Drive, Long Beach, CA 90802
(310) 435-4960

• Waterfront RV camping

This is another in a series of parking lot-type RV camps run by the city or state that you encounter along the densely-populated coastline in and near Los Angeles. Here, as at the others, you're surrounded by city life, which isn't necessarily bad. The nice thing about Shoreline is its proximity to big city attractions like the *Queen Mary*, major shopping centers, the harbor where you can hop a ferry to Santa Catalina Island 22 miles offshore (see section on

Santa Catalina, page 56), and the Long Beach Convention and Entertainment Center where major trade shows and popular entertainers are often scheduled. It's an easy walk to Shoreline Village where you'll find a variety of good restaurants, an antique carousel and numerous specialty shops.

Shoreline RV Park is attractive and well-maintained. It's set on the edge of an alcove of water that opens out onto the Pacific Ocean, but you wouldn't want to swim here; it's much too close to the Port of Long Beach. A far better beach is located just a mile or so away.

The adjacent park looks across the bay to where the *Queen Mary* is permanently docked and open to touring, shopping, eating and even staying overnight. Very picturesque. You can fish from the edge of the bay or just sit and picnic at one of the barbecue stations spaced about the palm-graced grounds.

CAMPGROUND: There are two sections to the campground. Area I is closer to the water and much preferable to Area II, which is located back beneath a section of elevated freeway. Essentially, however, both campground locations are the same, consisting of a pad of asphalt with a few palm trees. All 70 spaces, regardless of what area they're in, include full hookups, picnic tables and barbecue grills, and can accommodate RVs up to 40 feet long. Laundry and vending machines are near the campground entrance next to the security office.

RESTROOMS: Modern facilities including flush toilets, sinks and showers.

RESERVATIONS: Reservations must be made at least five days prior to arrival. Call: (213) 435-4960. There is a non-refundable service charge of $3.50 for all reservations.

CHECK IN/OUT: Noon. $10 fee for late check out.

FEES: *Area I* - $23/day; *Area II* - $20/day.

DOGS: $1/day; maximum two dogs.

MAX. STAY: 30 days per year.

SECURITY: Both areas are fenced, gated and patrolled 24-hours a day. Campers receive a key for entrance to Area I, a card key for Area II.

HOW TO GET THERE: From Los Angeles, get on the Long Beach Freeway (710) south; take the Downtown Shoreline Drive exit; turn right at Shoreline Park entrance. Follow signs to the Shoreline RV Park office.

DOCKWEILER RV PARK
12001 Vista Del Mar, Playa del Rey, CA 90293
(310) 322-4951

- Beachfront RV camping

Although a state beach, this facility is operated by the Los Angeles County Department of Beaches & Harbors, probably because it's right next to Los Angeles International Airport. The airport is something you'll notice right away because every minute or so a plane takes off, the line of flight passing almost directly over the RV park. *Varoom!*

People don't seem to mind the noise, however, which does diminish with the number of flights after 10 or 11 p.m. You'll find the park is frequently filled throughout the summer months.

No doubt Dockweiler's long, wide and sandy beach helps compensate for the unfortunate proximity of the airport. The nearby public golf course doesn't hurt either, nor Marina del Rey, the world's largest man-made small craft harbor which is just a few miles to the north. Besides the more than 6,000 boats that make their home in the marina, there's a public boat launch ramp, guest docks, and numerous specialty shops, harbor tours and restaurants. A bike trail also parallels the beach from the marina as far south as Manhattan Beach.

CAMPGROUND: This is another parking lot for RVs of virtually any size. Washer/dryer facilities are on site as is a dump station. There are 117 sites, 80 of which have full hookups.

RESTROOMS: Modern flush toilets, sinks, mirrors and hot showers (no charge).

RESERVATIONS: Up to eight weeks in advance through MISTIX, 1-800-950-PARK.

CHECK IN/OUT: Noon.

FEES: *Beachfront w/full hookup* - $25/day peak season (May 27-Sept. 17); $22/day off-peak. *Middle row w/full hookup* - $17/day peak season; $15/day off-peak. *Back row w/no hookup* - $15/day peak season; $12/day off-peak.

DOGS: $1/day; not permitted on beach.

MAX. STAY: 30 days in summer (Friday before Memorial Day to Labor Day); 90-day maximum in winter.

SECURITY: Security service all night.

HOW TO GET THERE: In Los Angeles, take the San Diego Freeway (405) to Imperial Highway; follow Imperial Highway west to the end at Vista Del Mar. *Varoom!*

SANTA CATALINA ISLAND

There's a well-known song (an oldie but goodie from what must be the 50s) that romanticizes a 76-square-mile island just 20 miles off the coast of Los Angeles. Once you hear the song, you'll find it almost as hard to forget as the place itself, Santa Catalina, the island of romance.

Measuring 21 miles in length by eight miles at its widest, Catalina, as it is commonly referred to, looks like a chunk of mountain range that got separated from mainland California. Thousands of years ago, in fact, Native Americans referred to it as the "mountain ranges that are in the sea."

Today, reaching those sea-blocked mountains is a routine matter. Large 700-passenger boats as well as speedier yacht-style ships make the easy one- to two-hour crossing several times a day, every day of the week (except in extremely rough weather).

Despite its proximity to Los Angeles, however, Santa Catalina is surprisingly untouched by development. There are only two centers of population: Avalon, a charming Mediterranean-style resort town built along the rim of the island's busiest harbor, and Two Harbors, built on the slender isthmus 11 miles to the northwest.

Avalon is the heart of the island, home to 2,400 year-round residents, most of the shops and all but one of the island's more than 40 hotels and inns. It's a compact town, one square mile that's easy to explore by shuttle bus, cab, bicycle, golf cart or walking. That's fortunate because, except for golf carts, there isn't a car, moped, motorcycle or any other motor vehicle to be rented here or anywhere else on the island. What's more, outside of Avalon's narrow thoroughfares there are only 10 miles of paved road.

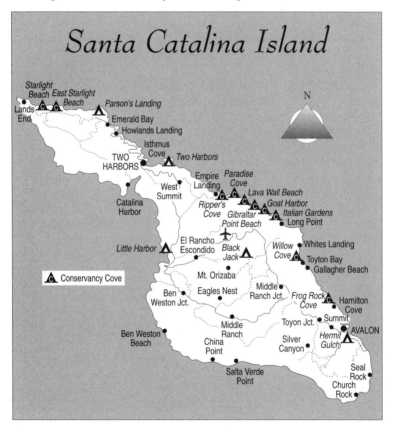

Two Harbors is a village of about 65 people. The island is a scant half-mile wide at this point and you can walk from one side of the island to the other in just five minutes. There's a harbor on both sides of the isthmus, thus the name *Two Harbors*, which caters to the yachts moored to either side. Although small, Two Harbors is completely self-contained with its own general store, restaurant, lodge, dive center and visitor services office.

The rest of Santa Catalina is a dry, sparsely vegetated fusion of uninhabited valleys, 2,000-foot peaks, isolated coves, beaches and sheer oceanfront cliffs. More than 42,000 acres – 86% of the island – is a natural preserve administered by the Catalina Island Conservancy. The island is home to more than 100 species of birds and nearly 400 species of native plant life. It's also the only one of the eight channel islands that hosts rattlesnakes.

Its climate is actually milder than that of nearby Los Angeles. Temperatures rarely exceed 75° in the summer or dip below 50° during the winter. Rainfall averages 11 inches annually. May, June, July, September and October are practically rain-free.

The summer months also happen to be the peak of the tourist season. The island's hotels are frequently without a vacancy. You can expect much the same of the island's several campgrounds, particularly on holiday weekends. During the off-season, though, you'll find camping along pristeen beaches or near the top of the island's tallest peaks among California's most delightful experiences.

Most visitors arrive by boat at either Avalon or Two Harbors. However, helicopter service is also available. Roundtrip fares range from $21 to $110 per person, depending on point of embarkation and vehicle type. For current schedules, contact the companies below:

From Long Beach:

Catalina Express, featuring jet-powered ships with airline-style seating. Departs from Catalina Express Port, 1046 Queensway, Long Beach at the *Queen Mary*. Call (800) 464-4228 or (310) 519-1212. Roundtrip fares - Adults $35; children (2-11) $26; under 2, $2. Estimated travel time: 1 hour.

Catalina Cruises, featuring large 700 passenger vessels, departs from 320 Golden Shore Blvd., Long Beach. (800) CATALINA.

Ferry arriving at Avalon

Roundtrip fares - Adults $21; children (2-11) $19; under 2, $2. Estimated travel time: 1 hour, 50 minutes.

From Newport Beach:

Catalina Flyer, featuring the largest passenger-carrying catamaran in the United States. Departs from Balboa Pavilion, 400 Main Street, Balboa. Call (714) 673-5245. Roundtrip fares - Adults $32.50; children (2-12) $16.50; under 2, $2. Estimated travel time: 75 minutes.

From San Pedro:

Catalina Express featuring jet-powered ships with airline-style seating. Departs from Catalina Terminal, Berth 95, San Pedro. (800) 464-4228 or (310) 519-1212. Roundtrip fares - Adults $35; children (2-11) $26; under 2, $2. Estimated travel time: 1 hour.

Helicopter Service:

Island Express, offers daily flights from Long Beach at the *Queen Mary* and San Pedro at the Catalina Terminal. Lands at Pebbly Beach on Catalina, three-quarters of a mile from Avalon. Call (310) 510-2525. Roundtrip fares: $110. Estimated travel time: 15 minutes.

Campers Note: Luggage is restricted on the above services. Some can accommodate bicycles and scuba tanks; others can't. Camp stoves, lanterns, fuel, firewood, charcoal, and other flammable or combustible materials are prohibited on all of them. For specific information, contact the carrier of your choice.

Hiking/Biking Permits

Most of the island is a natural preserve; hiking and biking are rigidly controlled. Permits are required when venturing beyond the immediate vicinity of both Avalon and Two Harbors. Hiking permits are free; biking permits are $50 per person or $75 per family for one year (valid from May 1 through April 30). The permit includes coverage for accident, liability and life insurance while bicycling on Catalina and may be obtained from any of the following locations:

Avalon – Catalina Conservancy Office, 125 Claressa, from 8:30 a.m. to 4 p.m. daily, (310) 510-1421; and Brown's Bikes, 120 yards from the boat dock, (310) 510-0986.

Two Harbors – Visitors Services, at the end of the pier, (310) 510-2800.

Airport-in-the-Sky – 8 a.m. to 5 p.m. (7 p.m. from April 15 to Oct. 15), (310) 510-0143.

Hermit Gulch Campground
Box 737, Avalon, CA 90704
(310) 510-TENT

• Inland tentsites, teepees, and tent cabins

This is the only campground in or near Avalon. It's located 1½ miles from Avalon Harbor, a mile uphill of the town's stores and beaches and only a five-minute walk from the Wrigley Memorial and Botanical Garden.

Surrounded by chaparral-covered hills, Hermit Gulch rolls gently with a sprinkling of young Torrey pines and leafy sycamores. During the summer, the sycamores offer oases of shade throughout the campground, but by winter the leaves have left. The grass is sparse and pretty well stomped.

The road leading past the campground to the Wrigley Memorial can be heavy with shuttle busses, walkers, golf carts and bicyclists.

CAMPGROUND: There are approximately 50 tentsites, eight teepees and three canvas cabins which can, combined, accommodate more than 200 persons. Three of the teepees are 18 feet in diameter and sleep up to six people; the other five are 16 feet in diameter and house four to five persons. Of the cabins, two can take up to four persons, the third cabin up to six. Neither teepees nor cabins con-

Colorful teepees offer fun for the family

tain bedding or any other equipment. Thus, campers need to bring their own gear or rent what they need from the campground. Tents, sleeping bags, ground pads, cots, lanterns and propane stoves are available. Picnic tables and grills are located at most of the tentsites.

A small campground store, open from 8 a.m. to 5 p.m. daily, sells ice, charcoal, propane, mantles and white gas and snack foods. There are also vending machines for soft drinks, juice and snacks, a microwave, a change machine and storage lockers.

RESTROOMS: Private individual restrooms with flush toilets, sinks and mirrors. Also, coin-operated showers, fountains and utility tubs.

RESERVATIONS: Always recommended; required in July in August. Call the campground at (310) 510-TENT.

CHECK IN/OUT: 11 a.m.

FEES: *Tent* spaces - $7.50/day per person. *Small teepees* (16 feet) - $20/day plus $7.50/day per person; *large teepees* - $25/day plus $7.50/day per person. The *four-person tent cabins* - $20/day plus $7.50/per person; the *six-person cabin* - $25/day plus $7.50/day per person. Campers opting to rent the teepees or tent cabins can save money by purchasing package rentals, which includes sleeping bags, pads and lanterns. Contact the campground for details and current prices.

There is no charge for children six and under.

DISCOUNTS: For groups of 20 or more, the per person rate drops to $6/day Friday and Saturday, and $5/day Sunday through Thursday.

DOGS: Not allowed.

SECURITY: Ranger lives on site. Few problems reported.

HOW TO GET THERE: From the Avalon boat landing, it's about one mile up a slight incline. Count on 20 to 25 minutes. Walk towards town along Crescent, the main street fronting the harbor; turn left at Catalina; right on Tremont; then left again at Avalon Canyon Road. Taxis are also available (current rate is $6 for up to four persons). If you prefer, catch the Safari Shuttle Bus from the Island Plaza bus depot, corner of Catalina and Beacon. The cost is

$1 each way ($2 with baggage). **Note:** shuttle service may not be offered during the non-peak season.

Two Harbors Campground
Two Harbors Visitor Services, P.O. Box 5044
Two Harbors, CA 90704-5044
(310) 510-2800

• Oceanfront tentsites, teepees, and tent cabins

It would be hard to improve the location of Two Harbors Campground. It sits on a gently sloping hillside that overlooks and eventually slides into the cyan-tinctured bay of Two Harbors.

Like most of the island, the hillside is essentially naked with the exception of some cactus and an annual grass that browns out during the arid summers. But the growth of anything more substantial would serve only to block the picture-perfect vista that spreads out before you.

Although secluded, Two Harbors Campground is less than a quarter-mile walk along a dirt trail from the village, where you'll find a well-stocked general store, restaurant, bar and laundromat. So, while you have your wilderness, civilization is never very far away.

A perfect spot to relax and watch the sailboats drift by

CAMPGROUND: There are approximately 30 tentsites, several of which are on a cliff just above the beach; in addition, there are five teepees and 10 tent cabins. The teepees have a canvas floor and their entrances can be tied together (more or less) for privacy at night; cabins have single beds with foam mattresses. Bring your own sleeping bags. A stove and lantern is furnished with both teepees and cabins.

You'll find fresh water conveniently located near each site. Some sites also have patio covers as well as picnic tables, fire rings and grills.

The tentsites can accommodate four to six persons depending on their placement and size; the teepees hold up to eight adults (or 10 children) each, and tent cabins from five to eight persons (depending on size).

RESTROOMS: Rather primitive: Chemical toilets and cold, outdoor rinse-off showers. However, private coin-operated hot showers are available in the village.

RESERVATIONS: Always recommended; required in July and August. Call (310) 510-2800 as far in advance as possible. Penalties for cancellations. Camping permits can be picked up in Avalon at 211 Catalina Avenue, directly inland from the green Pleasure Pier, or in Two Harbors at the Visitors Services Office.

CHECK IN/OUT: 2 p.m. in;11 a.m. out.

FEES: *Tents* - Most are $7.50/day per person, two-night minimum on weekends from Memorial Day to mid-September. A few of the sites will cost $8.50/day per person based on location and size. **Note:** During the busy season, you may be required to pay the "site minimum," i.e., if a site can accommodate four persons, but your party has only two, you may be charged for four persons unless you're prepared to share the site with another couple. *Teepees* - $60/day for up to 6 persons, $10 for each additional person, with two-night minimum on weekends during the summer. Off-peak rates drop to $50/day plus $8 per additional person. Available April-October. *Tent cabins* - Small cabins (max. 5 persons): $48/day for four persons, $10 per additional person. Off-season: $40/day and $8 per additional person. Larger cabins (max. 8 persons): $72/day for up to 6 persons, $10 per additional person. Off-season: $60/day and $8 per additional person. Available April-October.

DISCOUNTS: Groups of 20 or more receive a 25% discount off tent cabin and teepee rates Sunday through Thursday all year long (excluding three-day holiday weekends).

DOGS: Not allowed.

MAXIMUM STAY: None.

SECURITY: On-site ranger day and night.

HOW TO GET THERE: You can reach Two Harbors directly from the mainland as well as from Avalon.

From Avalon you have two options: (1) By shuttle bus, a 23-mile ride that takes about an hour and 30 minutes and costs $14.50 each way, or (2) by Catalina Express Coastal Shuttle, a 14-mile trip that takes about 45 minutes and costs $12.50

Catch the shuttle bus in Avalon from the Island Plaza Bus Depot, corner of Catalina and Beacon Streets; board the Coastal Shuttle at Avalon Harbor. Both offer regular service during the peak summer season. However, service during the off-peak season is extremely limited, if available at all. For current schedules, call Two Harbors Visitor Services at (310) 510-2800.

From the mainland, you may cruise directly to Two Harbors via either of two cruiselines: Catalina Cruises and Catalina Express.

Catalina Express offers speedy 60-minute crossings via compact, yacht-style boats with airline-type seating. Ships leave from the Port of San Pedro and cost $35 roundtrip. Call (800) 995-4386 or (310) 519-1212 for schedules and directions to the port.

Catalina Cruises offers the comfort of roomy 700-passenger boats at significantly less cost: $21 roundtrip. However, the crossing takes about twice as long as the express boats and embarks from the Port of Long Beach. Call (800) 228-2546 for schedules and directions to the port.

Little Harbor Campground

Two Harbor Visitors Center, P.O. Box 5044
Two Harbors, CA 90704-5044
(310) 510-2800

• Oceanfront campsites

If Hollywood wanted to remake the movie of *Robinson Crusoe*, they could do it very convincingly right here. The broad crescent of vacant beach, the empty teal-blue cove, the golden desert hills all around – looking today exactly as they must have looked hundreds of years ago – practically scream "isolation" at Little Harbor Campground.

The only inconsistencies Hollywood would have to contend with are a few porta-potties, a couple of outdoor showers, some picnic tables, patio covers and a gravel road that runs right through the middle of the campground. Oh, and maybe a small herd of bison that graze their way through the area now and then.

The craggy coastline at Little Harbor

The columns of Canary Island palms, standing out in bright green contrast to the surrounding cactus and toasted ground cover, lend a very tropical feel to the scene and complete the illusion of Crusoe's desert island. It would be best, of course, if Hollywood would do the filming during the low season, when the campground is often empty and shuttle busses are few and far between. Even during the peak season, however, Little Harbor limits occupancy to about 150 persons, substantially less congested than the larger, less isolated campgrounds at either Hermit Gulch or Two Harbors.

Little Harbor does have a telephone and firewood. Charcoal and propane are available from the ranger when he is on site. If you require anything more, you'll have to go to Two Harbors, about seven miles away.

CAMPGROUND: 17 tentsites, some of which may also accommodate a trailer or moderate-sized RV (should you be a resident of the island and have access to such vehicles). There are no hookups, however.

The sites are well spaced and furnished with fresh water, patio covers, picnic tables, fire pits and grills.

RESTROOMS: Chemical toilets and outdoor rinse-off showers.

RESERVATIONS: Always recommended, especially during the peak season. Call (310) 510-2800 as far in advance as possible. Penalty for cancellations. Camping permits can be picked up in Avalon at the Catalina Camping Office (shuttle bus depot), 211 Catalina, or in Two Harbors at the Visitors Services Office.

CHECK IN/OUT: 2 p.m. in; 11 a.m. out.

FEES: $7.50/day per person. No weekend minimum.

DISCOUNTS: Rates drop to $5/day per person for groups of 20 or more.

DOGS: Not permitted.

MAX. STAY: None.

SECURITY: Ranger patrols the site during the day.

HOW TO GET THERE: The easiest way to get to Little Harbor is to take one of the ferry boats from the mainland directly to Two Harbors. From there, a shuttle bus can take you to Little Harbor, 6.8 miles further east. Cost is $7.25 one way. If you're coming from Avalon, the 16-mile ride will cost you $11.75. It's important to note, however, that regularly scheduled shuttle service is offered during the peak season (generally from the end of May through October). At other times, you may have to charter a shuttle or hike in. Call Two Harbor Visitor Services for current schedules (310) 510-2800.

Parson's Landing Campground
Two Harbor Visitors Center, P.O. Box 5044
Two Harbors, CA 90704-5044
(310) 510-2800

• Primitive oceanfront campsites

If isolation is what you're after, you can't do much better than Parson's Landing, about seven miles from Two Harbors on Catalina's northwest shore. This is a remote campground limited to a maximum of 50 people and designed for backpackers. Everything that you will need, with the exception of firewood and water, has to be carried in. And when you leave, you're responsible for packing out your own trash as well.

Parson's Landing serves as a trailhead for day hikers wishing to explore the rugged, sharply eroded hills surrounding it. Fishing, swimming and diving along the small, sheltered curve in the shoreline are favorite pastimes, too.

CAMPGROUND: There are only six campsites, all situated right on a brownish-grey sand beach. Each site can accommodate up to eight people and includes a picnic table, fire ring and grill. A ranger also comes by once a day to deliver firewood and water. You'll find the provisions stored in a locker on a bluff above the beach. The locker key will be given to you when you check in at the Two Harbors Visitors Center to obtain your camping permit. (Those caught camping without a permit may be fined $50.)

RESTROOMS: Chemical toilets; no showers.

RESERVATIONS: Always recommended, especially during the peak season. Call (310) 510-2800 as far in advance as possible. Penalty for cancellations. Camping permits can be picked up in Avalon at the Catalina Camping Office (shuttle bus depot), 211 Catalina, or in Two Harbors at the Visitors Services Office.

CHECK IN/OUT: 2 p.m. in; 11 a.m. out. All campers must check in at the Visitors Center in Two Harbors.

FEES: $15/day for the first person and $5/day for each additional. No weekend minimum.

DISCOUNTS: None.

DOGS: Not permitted.

MAX. STAY: None.

SECURITY: Camp ranger patrols daily.

HOW TO GET THERE: The first trick is getting to Two Harbors (see Two Harbors Campground). Once there, you have two ways of reaching Parson's Landing: Hike approximately seven miles, or take a shoreboat to Emerald Bay. From there you have to hike an additional 1½ miles to the campground. Be advised that the shoreboat operates on a regular schedule only during the peak season and reservations are required. Cost is $9 roundtrip. For current schedules, call (310) 510-2800.

Blackjack Campground
Two Harbor Visitors Center, P.O. Box 5044
Two Harbors, CA 90704-5044
(310) 510-2800

• High country tent camping

Blackjack is no beachfront campground. This one's nestled 1,600 feet above sea level near the center of the island and beneath a grove of pine and eucalyptus trees. To either side of the campground are Catalina's two tallest peaks, Mt. Black Jack (2,006 feet), and Mt. Orizaba (2,069 feet).

Blackjack affords you great panoramic vistas of the island's coastline and undulating interior. On an exceptionally clear day, you may even have a view of the mainland and the other channel islands.

A huge barbecue, a remnant of times when the area was part of a large cattle ranch, serves as a kind of centerpiece for the campground and is frequently used by camping groups.

CAMPGROUND: There are 11 sites spaced generously beneath the shade of the evergreen grove, each including a picnic table, fire pit and grill. There's also a telephone and water. You can purchase firewood, charcoal, propane and butane from the camp ranger. Maximum occupancy is 75 persons.

RESTROOMS: Chemical toilets; outdoor rinse-off showers

RESERVATIONS: Although Blackjack is less likely to fill up than the other campgrounds, reservations are still recommended, particularly on holidays and summer weekends. Call (310) 510-2800 as far in advance as possible. Camping permits can be picked up in Avalon at the Catalina Camping Office (shuttle bus depot), 211 Catalina, or in Two Harbors at the Visitors Services Office. Penalties for cancellations.

CHECK IN/OUT: 2 p.m. in; 11 a.m. out.

FEES: $6.50/day per person. No weekend minimum.

DISCOUNTS: Rates drop to $5/day per person for groups of 20 or more.

DOGS: Not permitted.

MAX. STAY: None.

SECURITY: A camp ranger patrols in the late afternoon.

HOW TO GET THERE: The campground is nine miles west of Avalon and 5½ miles east of Little Harbor. You can hike there or take the Safari Shuttle Bus from Avalon (depot at Beacon and Catalina) or Two Harbors (look around for the busses). The shuttle stops at Black Jack Junction, near the Airport-in-the-Sky and from there you must hike about 1½ miles further. The bus operates on a regular schedule through the peak season only. Call (310) 510-2800 for current fares and schedule.

Catalina Conservancy Coves
Two Harbors Visitors Center, P.O. Box 5044
Two Harbors, CA 90704-5044
(310) 510-2800

• Primitive oceanfront camping

Ten secluded coves along Catalina's leeward shore offer a unique opportunity for real wilderness camping. There are no phones, no tables, no fire pits, no grills, and no restrooms or showers. To reach these coves, however, you'll need your own boat (no drop-off service is available) and you'll have to bring all camping gear, including porta-potties.

CAMPGROUNDS INCLUDE: Frog Rock Cove, Willow Cove, Italian Gardens, Goat Harbor, Gibraltar Point Beach, Lava Wall Beach, Paradise Cove, Rippers Cove, Starlight Beach and East Starlight Beach. All can accommodate a maximum of 12 campers, with the exception of Willow and Paradise Coves, which are limited to six.

The coves are inaccessible by land, all protected by sharply eroded canyon walls speckled with cactus and scrub brush. Palm trees grace some of the beaches, which are usually sandy, although that's subject to change, depending on the time of the year and tidal ebb and flow patterns. The beaches at Rippers Cove and Paradise can so narrow, in fact, they literally disappear.

Until recently, campers also had the option of camping in one of two yurts which are built on redwood platforms above the beach at Goat Harbor. Modeled after the circular tents used by Mongols and Turkic peoples of central Asia, these yurts were closed in 1994 due to the fire code, and there is uncertainty as to whether or not they will ever be allowed to reopen.

In the event they do, you should know that the main yurt is a luxury-appointed, insulated tent with indoor gas fireplace, TV, stereo, a complete kitchen, gas barbecue, carpet, hot shower and queen size bed. It can accommodate six people.

The smaller yurt is a little further up and contains egg crate mattresses and a small vanity with portable lanterns. It can house an additional two or three people. Daily rental rates before closure last year were $50/day per person, double occupancy.

RESERVATIONS: May be made up to a year in advance, although two weeks is usually sufficient except during summer weekends. Call (310) 510-2800.

FEES: $4/day per person; $3/day per child under 12; no charge for children under six.

MAX. STAY: No restrictions.

TOPANGA STATE PARK
Topanga Sector Headquarters
1501 Will Rogers State Park Road, Pacific Palisades CA 90272
(310) 455-2465 or (818) 880-0350

• Primitive walk-in tent & horse camping

Although Topanga State Park is situated entirely within the boundaries of the city of Los Angeles, its 11,000 wild, brush-covered acres bear little evidence of it. A rugged, rolling terrain with forests of oak and peaks up to 2,100 feet, hikers, mountain bikers and equestrians find its 36 miles of trails and fire roads offer a quick and easy escape from the bustling city below. High points offer good views of the coast and surrounding mountains and valleys.

The park's thick, flammable coat of chaparral makes it a tinder box, particularly in the hot, dry months of summer when daytime highs soar well into the 90s. This necessitates the prohibition of fires throughout the park. During the winter months, nighttime lows in the mid-30s are common.

Three or four miles from the park entrance is mile-long Topanga State Beach, popular among swimmers and surfers. Neighboring Malibu offers the nearest services.

CAMPGROUND: Topanga's sole campground is about 1,500 feet above sea level in a level clearing surrounded by hills of coastal scrub brush and oak.

There are eight primitive, little-used tentsites with tables, but no fire rings. Hitching rails and troughs are provided for horse campers. Running water is available in the restrooms. From the parking lot at the park entrance, the campground is accessible by way of an easy, mile-long hike up the Musch Trail.

RESTROOMS: Modern facilities with flush toilets, sinks and mirrors; no AC outlets or showers.

FEES: $3/day.

DOGS: Not permitted.

MAX. STAY: Seven days (June-Sept.); 15 days remainder of the year.

RESERVATIONS: First-come, first-served basis.

CHECK IN/OUT: Noon out.

SECURITY: Park rangers on patrol.

HOW TO GET THERE: From Santa Monica, drive north on Highway 1; turn right at Topanga Canyon.

MALIBU CREEK STATE PARK
28754 Mulholland Highway, Agoura, CA 91301
(818) 706-8809 or (818) 880-4089

- High country tent and RV camping
- Group camping

The next time you watch an episode of the MASH television series, pay special attention to the opening sequence. It was filmed in Malibu Creek State Park.

Although the series has long since ended, those scrubby, chaparral-covered slopes are still here, still wild and still offering escape from the megalopolos of Los Angeles just a 30- to 45-minute drive south.

Situated in the Santa Monica Mountains six miles inland of the coast, Malibu Creek is comprised of 10,000 acres of rugged valleys and towering peaks, some of which rise to over 2,000 feet.

It's a dry, sunny region popular among hikers (there are 30 miles of trails), and great for mountain biking, horseback riding and fishing (12 creeks host bass, bluegill and sunfish).

It should be noted that this area lays claim to both the hottest and coldest temperatures in the Santa Monica range, with winter extremes ranging from lows of 10 or 12°F and highs up to 115° when the dry, desert-driven Santa Ana winds begin to blow.

CAMPGROUNDS: The park includes a family campground and group camp, both situated about 500 feet above sea level in a grassy clearing. Oak and drought-tolerant shrubs grow all around and up the hillsides surrounding the park. Gophers and ground squirrels have done an amazing job of burrowing through the area. Tunnel openings are everywhere and the ground is subject to collapse beneath an unwary footstep. Campers need to watch where they walk.

Other things to be mindful of include food-bandit raccoons and, to a lesser degree, rattlesnakes, mountain lions, fox, coyotes, mule deer and badgers, all of which keep a very low profile.

The family campground includes 62 sites; three are large enough to accommodate RVs up to 35 feet, the others are suited to tents or trailers and RVs up to 24 feet in length. Each site includes a gravel-covered parking pad, picnic table and fireplace with grill. Water spigots are nearby.

Groups of 10 (minimum) to 60 persons can be accommodated in the hike-in campground, located a few hundred yards from the family section. This is a tent-only facility requiring an easy hike of about 100 yards from the parking lot. Fireplaces, tables and water are provided.

RESTROOMS: Modern restrooms are located in each campground and feature flush toilets, mirrors, sinks and coin-operated, solar-heated showers.

FEES: *Family campsites* - $14/day peak season (March 1-November 30); $12 non-peak. *Group campground* -$90/day.

RESERVATIONS: Family campsites are available on a first-come, first-served basis throughout the year. No reservations are accepted. Expect keen competition for sites during the summer months, especially weekends.

The group camp may be reserved up to eight weeks in advance through MISTIX, 1-800-444-PARK.

CHECK IN/OUT: Noon.

DOGS: $1/day. Must be leashed at all times and are restricted to the campground and day-use areas. Dogs are not permitted on trails.

MAX. STAY: Seven days (June-Sept.); 15 days remainder of the year.

SECURITY: Park rangers and live-in camp host.

HOW TO GET THERE: From Los Angeles, take 101 north; exit at Las Virgenes Road and head south (to your left) about four miles.

From Santa Monica, take 1 north; turn right on Malibu Canyon Road and follow for about six miles.

LEO CARRILLO STATE BEACH

c/o Angeles District Headquarters
1925 Las Virgenes Road, Calabas CA 91302
(818) 706-1310

- On-beach vehicle camping
- Near-beach tent and RV camping
- Hike & Bike camping
- Group camping

Like Malibu Creek State Park to the southeast, Leo Carrillo State Beach is no stranger to Hollywood film makers. Its scenic 1¼-mile shoreline often serves as a setting for commercials, films and TV shows, including David Hasselhoff and *Baywatch*. In fact, the park is named after an actor, perhaps best known for his portrayal of Pancho, the comical sidekick in the *Cisco Kid* television show. Beyond the beach, however, there lie 2,000 acres of hills and valleys that help form the Santa Monica Mountain range.

Hikers of virtually any age can explore this wilderness along Yellow Hill Trail, from the top of which you can see Anacapa and Santa Cruz, two of the eight Channel Islands, on a clear day. More experienced hikers may want to venture along the Nicholas Flat Trail, which meanders up and down the steep canyons.

Offshore, extensive kelp beds provide for one of Southern California's best scuba diving spots. There are also several good fishing areas that hold the promise of catching thresher shark, corbina, white sea bass, surf perch and halibut. On the beach, tidepooling and whale-watching in February and March are popular pastimes.

CAMPGROUNDS: There are three.

North Beach Campground: This is actually just a parking lot located on the extreme northern end of the beach. It's intended for vehicles only; no tents. Officially, vehicles are supposed to be self-contained, meaning they should have their own toilets; but that's not closely administered. Cars, campers and trucks also frequently park here. The only real restriction is vehicle height; they can't be any higher than eight feet in order to pass through the Pacific Coast Highway underpass leading to the campground.

There are 32 spaces, each equipped with a table and fire ring.

Chemical toilets and outdoor rinse-off showers are on the beach. However, campers may use the more complete facilities, including flush toilets and coin-operated showers, across the road in the canyon campgrounds.

Canyon Campground: The canyon across Highway 1 provides camping for families, groups and hikers & bikers. It's a well shaded area loaded with mature sycamores and occasional oaks. The ground is hard packed dirt. There's a dump station and camp store, which is open from 8 a.m. to 8 p.m. during the peak season and holidays.

Family sites offer tables and fire rings, and can accommodate either tents or RVs up to 31 feet. Parking spurs are positioned alongside each site.

The group campground can accommodate up to 50 people. This is a tent-only area. Campers must park their vehicles in a parking lot, then hike about 500 feet to the campsite. Two barbecue pits are provided as well as tables, restrooms and coin-operated showers.

The *Hike & Bike Campground,* near the park entrance, normally accommodates four to six campers. There's a fire pit and chemical toilets.

RESERVATIONS: May be made up to eight weeks in advance through MISTIX, 1-800-444-PARK.

CHECK IN/OUT: Noon.

FEES: *Family campsites* - $16/day peak season (March 1-November 30); $14/day non-peak. *Group campground* -$75/day. *Hike & Bike* - $3/day per person.

DOGS: $1/day; permitted in campgrounds only. Trails and beaches are off-limits.

MAX. STAY: Seven days (June-September); 15 days remainder of year.

SECURITY: Park rangers and resident camp host.

HOW TO GET THERE: From Santa Monica, drive north on Highway 1 about 25 miles.

CIRCLE X RANCH
c/o National Park Service
Santa Monica Mountains National Recreation Area
30401 Agoura Road, Ste. 100, Agoura Hills, CA 91301
Visitor Center: (818) 597-9192/Ranger Station: (310) 457-6408

- Mountain tent camping
- Group camping
- Backcountry camping

Circle X Ranch is comprised of 1,700 acres six miles east of the coast within the folds of the Santa Monica Mountains.

Sandstone Peak, the highest point in the Santa Monica Mountains at over 3,100 feet, is more or less the center of the park. Hike to the top of it on a clear day and you may see the Channel Islands as you look to the northwest. A myriad of trails will lead you there and to numerous other points within this rugged backcountry. Bike it or ride horseback if you don't want to hike.

CAMPGROUND: Circle X Ranch features three campgrounds. All sites are for tenters only:

Happy Hollow Campground is tucked in the bottom of a steep canyon graced with the shade of mature oaks and pines. There are 23 sites, each furnished with a table and fire pit. However, wood fires are prohibited here; you'll have to rely solely on charcoal grills and/or camp stoves. Water is nearby. Access to the campground is by way of a 1½-mile dirt road that's quick to get muddy and slippery and certain to close at the first sign of wet weather. Trailers are prohibited. The road leads to a parking lot, from which campers must walk 10 to 100 yards to reach their site.

The *Group Campground* is located up the canyon from Happy Hollow right next to the ranger station. It's accessible by vehicles and can handle a maximum of 75 persons. The area has a few oaks, but is mostly cleared ground surrounded by chaparral; thus, there's limited shade. Water and tables are provided. Parking is in a lot adjacent to the campsites.

A Backcountry Camp was scheduled to reopen sometime during 1995. However, the exact date and location is still undetermined. The previous camp was accessible only by foot, bike or horse along a three-mile uphill trail. It was closed following a fire and subsequent erosion damage.

RESTROOMS: Pit toilets.

FEES: $6/day at *Happy Hollow* (max. six persons, two tents and two vehicles per site); $2/day per person at the *group camp;* no fee at the *backcountry camp.*

RESERVATIONS: First come, first served for Happy Hollow and the backcountry camp. The group camp must be reserved by calling (310) 457-6408 up to three months in advance.

CHECK IN/OUT: Noon.

DOGS: No additional fee; must be leashed at all times. Permitted on trails. **Note:** Dogs are *not permitted* in the backcountry camp.

MAX. STAY: 14 consecutive days.

SECURITY: Park ranger resides on site.

HOW TO GET THERE: From Santa Monica, drive north on Highway 1 to Yerba Buena Road; turn right on Yerba Buena and follow approximately five miles to Circle X Ranch entrance.

POINT MUGU STATE BEACH

c/o Angeles District Headquarters
1925 Las Virgenes Road, Calabas CA 91302
(818) 880-0350

- Beachfront tent and RV camping
- Canyon (near-beach) tent and RV camping
- Group camping
- Hike & Bike camping

Pt. Mugu is much like Leo Carrillo State Beach just four miles to the south, only it's almost eight times as large, with 15,000 acres of jagged pinnacles, open meadows, canyons filled with oaks and sycamores and five miles of oceanfront. Meandering through it all are more than 70 miles of trails and fire roads for hikers, bikers and horseback riders.

Campers can enjoy Pt. Mugu's four campgrounds. More than 78,000 do so every year.

Sycamore Canyon

This is a family campground located directly across Highway 1 from Sycamore Cove, a well groomed area of swimmable sandy beach, picnic tables and barbecue grills. The canyon is a flat, shady area of sycamores and oaks surrounded by chaparral-covered hills, a down-sized version of Leo Carrillo's main campground.

Monarch butterflies frequently nest here in the fall. It has 55 spaces capable of accommodating either tents or RVs up to 31 feet in length. Each space includes a parking pad, table and fire ring. Water spigots are near each site, but there are neither hookups nor dump station. There is a Hike & Bike campground in the canyon as well.

RESTROOMS: Modern restrooms with sinks, mirrors, AC outlets and private coin-operated showers (50¢ for 5 minutes).

RESERVATIONS: Up to eight weeks in advance through MISTIX, 1-800-444-PARK.

CHECK IN/OUT: Noon.

FEES: $16/day peak season (March 1-November 30); $14/day off-peak. *Hike & Bike* - $3/day per person.

DOGS: $1/day. Must be leashed at all times. Permitted on fire roads and beach, but not on trails.

MAX. STAY: Seven days (June-September); 15 days remainder of the year. Hikers & Bikers maximum two days.

SECURITY: Park rangers and round-the-clock camp host.

HOW TO GET THERE: From Santa Monica, drive on Highway 1 for 31 miles to the site.

Thornhill Broome Beach Campground

This campground offers an opportunity to tent or RV on or beside a broad stretch of beach paralleling Highway 1 and a ridge of sunburned hills. It's a good place for surf fishing, clamming and beachcombing, but entering the water is not recommended. There's a steep drop-off which usually results in treacherous wave action, and the water is often colder than elsewhere along the coast due to cold upwellings caused by a deep underwater rift.

Thornhill Broome Beach, Point Mugu

There are spaces for 75 tents or RVs up to 31 feet. Each is furnished with a table and fire pit.

RESTROOMS: Chemical toilets. No showers.

RESERVATIONS: Up to eight weeks in advance through MISTIX, 1-800-444-PARK.

CHECK IN/OUT: Noon.

FEES: $9/day peak season (March 1-Nov. 30); $7 non-peak.

DOGS: $1/day. Must be leashed at all times; permitted on beach.

MAX. STAY: Seven days (June-September); 15 days remainder of year.

SECURITY: Park rangers on patrol.

HOW TO GET THERE: From Santa Monica, take Highway 1 north about 1½ miles past Sycamore Canyon and Cove.

Central

California

Ventura, Santa Barbara, San Luis Obispo,
Monterey, Santa Cruz, San Mateo and
San Francisco Counties

The Best of the North & South

If you're limited by the amount of time and travel you can afford, consider Central California. Along its 350 miles of coastline, you can sample some of the best that the state has to offer.

Within a couple hours, you can drive from the jagged cliffs and heavy redwood forests of Big Sur to the near-naked dunes of Pismo Beach. And 1½ hours further south, you're in Ventura – essentially Southern California without the congestion or frantic pace.

As you proceed from north to south, the sea and air subtly warm, skies brighten, shores broaden and turn friendlier, trees thin and mountains yield and soften. The mood changes, too. The hard, rocky, brooding drama of the north eases into a lighter, less-formal *mellow-drama* if you will, a feeling closer to the spirit of television and movies than the legitimate theater and serious film. Note the change in people, too. Nothing is more evident than their clothes, the long-sleeved plaid and windbreakers of the north inevitably being shed for shorts and halter tops.

The overwhelming impression along Central California's coast is fresh and open. Communities don't ramble on and on and melt into one another as they can in the southern part of the state. There are definite cities and towns that actually end and give way to long, vacant, rolling stretches. Along some portions, you even risk running out of gas if you're not careful.

Regardless of the time of year, temperatures along the Central coast are mild, ranging from the mid-70s in summer to the mid-60s in winter. Once you leave the coast, of course, temperatures climb quickly. Summertime highs of 90 to 100° are common in the inland valleys. Annual rainfall averages 14 inches in Ventura and almost 20 inches in San Francisco. Midway between the two, however, Big

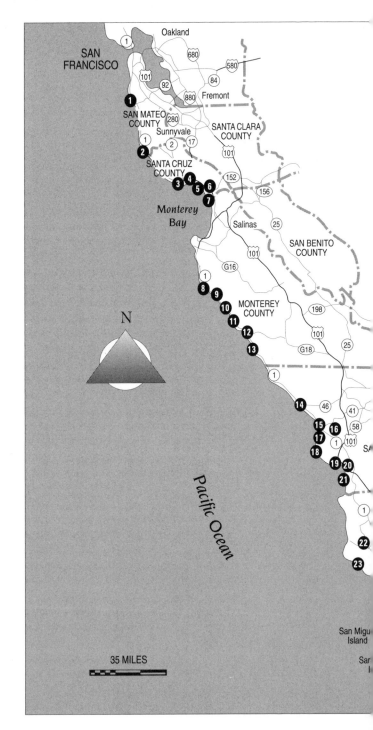

Central California Campgrounds

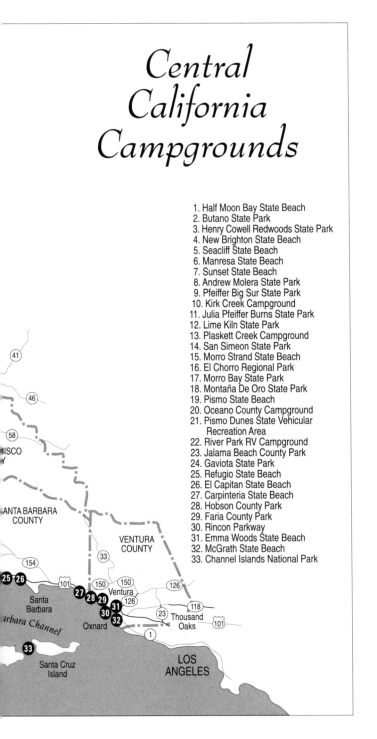

1. Half Moon Bay State Beach
2. Butano State Park
3. Henry Cowell Redwoods State Park
4. New Brighton State Beach
5. Seacliff State Beach
6. Manresa State Beach
7. Sunset State Beach
8. Andrew Molera State Park
9. Pfeiffer Big Sur State Park
10. Kirk Creek Campground
11. Julia Pfeiffer Burns State Park
12. Lime Kiln State Park
13. Plaskett Creek Campground
14. San Simeon State Park
15. Morro Strand State Beach
16. El Chorro Regional Park
17. Morro Bay State Park
18. Montaña De Oro State Park
19. Pismo State Beach
20. Oceano County Campground
21. Pismo Dunes State Vehicular
    Recreation Area
22. River Park RV Campground
23. Jalama Beach County Park
24. Gaviota State Park
25. Refugio State Beach
26. El Capitan State Beach
27. Carpinteria State Beach
28. Hobson County Park
29. Faria County Park
30. Rincon Parkway
31. Emma Woods State Beach
32. McGrath State Beach
33. Channel Islands National Park

Sur reports more than 40 inches, its higher elevation precipitating the increase.

Although the population is relatively light along most of the Central Coast in comparison to Southern California, competition for the most desirable campgrounds is keen, especially during the summer and long weekends. The area is within easy reach of those living in the major population centers north and south. Good planning and reservations are essential throughout the summer months.

Getting There

If you're flying, you'll find the most economical commercial flights will be to San Francisco or Los Angeles International Airports. You do have other options, of course, but you'll undoubtedly pay a premium to land in Santa Barbara, Santa Maria, Monterey, San Luis Obispo or Ventura. What's more, these airports are serviced by far fewer airlines and, therefore, flights.

Amtrak rail service, on the other hand, has convenient service all along the coast. For stations, fares and current schedules, contact Amtrak at: 1-800-USA RAIL.

Attractions

You will find a number of unique attractions, including Pismo Beach, the only beach in the state where you can drive your car or RV up to the water's edge; Hearst Castle, one of the most magnificent estates ever built; and the world-acclaimed Monterey Bay Aquarium, featuring more than 6,500 sea creatures. There are also quaint fishing villages and a growing number of wineries of increasing renown.

However, it is this coast's natural gifts for which it is most famous. Its jagged cliffs and the small, isolated beaches of sand hidden among them; the unspoiled hills and mountains that parallel the sea; and the spectacular pockets of redwood forests that can only hint at the grandeur of those growing further north are all major attractions. It is arguably one of the most scenic locations on earth and, fortunately, most of it is easily accessed via the sinuous Pacific Coast Highway (1), along which there are more than 30 parks with camping.

Ventura County

CHANNEL ISLANDS NATIONAL PARK
1901 Spinnaker Drive, Ventura, CA 93001
(805) 658-5730

• Primitive tent camping

As you're driving along the California coast near Ventura or Santa Barbara, look out over the ocean. If the weather's clear, you'll see the outline of an island or two, the closest of which is just 11 miles offshore. These islands are part of the eight-member chain called the Channel Islands. Five of the islands – Anacapa, Santa Cruz, Santa Rosa, San Miguel and Santa Barbara – form the Channel Island National Park. Four of them are open to camping and offer a unique and wild outdoor adventure.

Although people have resided on, hunted, fished and ranched the islands for hundreds of years, the five islands forming the national park have been in "protective custody" for many years. Anacapa and Santa Barbara Islands became a national monument by presidential proclamation in 1938. San Miguel, much of Santa Cruz and, finally, Santa Rosa subsequently came under the same protective custody. In 1980 legislation was signed establishing Channel Islands National Park as the nation's 40th such park. In the time since, the islands have been restoring themselves, re-establishing the environments that were drastically altered through ranching, farming, bombing practice and other equally devastating activities during the past 100 years.

Camping in the islands is not for the faint of heart. Starting with the cross-channel cruise, which varies from 1½ to five hours depending on which island you're bound for, you can anticipate a more strenuous routine than usual. Even your landing can be a rough, if not wet, experience. In fact, weather and sea conditions may very well prevent passengers from ever leaving the boat. Landings are not guaranteed.

Once on the islands, the weather will continue to be of significant concern. The wind can blow for days at a time up to 40 mph on the outer islands. Spring and winter rains are likely to turn camp-grounds into mudflats, and extended periods of fog may chill and dampen your mornings and nights to uncomfortable extremes even during the summer. When the sun is out, you'll also have to protect yourself with a hat and ample quantities of sunscreen. The islands are nearly barren of trees and shade is as precious as gold.

Because the weather can change so quickly, visitors should dress in layers so they can *peel* or pad their wardrobe as circumstances dictate.

In addition to clothing, you'll have to bring all other necessities, including drinking water – about a gallon a day per person. Abso-

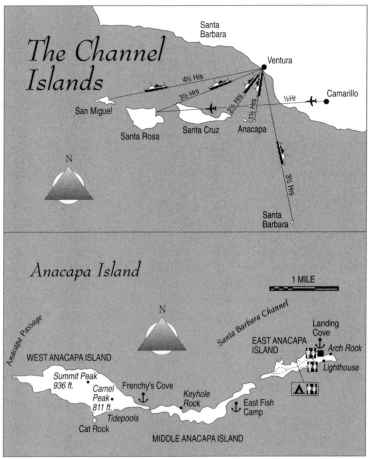

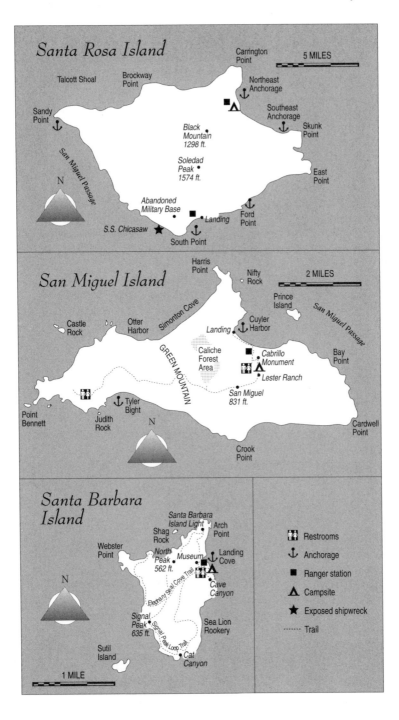

Santa Rosa Island

5 MILES

Talcott Shoal
Brockway
Point
Carrington
Point
Northeast
Anchorage
Sandy
Point
Southeast
Anchorage
Skunk
Point
Black
Mountain
1298 ft.
Soledad
Peak
1574 ft.
East
Point
San Miguel Passage
N
Abandoned
Military Base
Landing
Ford
Point
S.S. Chicasaw
South Point

San Miguel Island

Harris
Point
Nifty
Rock
2 MILES
Prince
Island
Castle
Rock
Otter
Harbor
Simonton Cove
Cuyler
Harbor
San Miguel Passage
Landing
Caliche
Forest
Area
Cabrillo
Monument
Bay
Point
GREEN MOUNTAIN
Lester Ranch
Tyler
Bight
San Miguel
831 ft.
Point
Bennett
Judith
Rock
N
Cardwell
Point
Crook
Point

**Santa Barbara
Island**

Santa Barbara
Island Light
Arch
Point
Shag
Rock
Webster
Point
North
Peak
562 ft.
Museum
Landing
Cove
N
Elephant Seal Cove Trail
Cave
Canyon
Signal
Peak
635 ft.
Signal Peak Loop Trail
Sea Lion
Rookery
Sutil
Island
Cat
Canyon
1 MILE

Restrooms
Anchorage
Ranger station
Campsite
Exposed shipwreck
------- Trail

lutely nothing is available for rent or sale on the islands. Tables, pit toilets and, in some cases, windscreens are the only amenities provided by the park service. A camp stove or grill is an especially important piece of equipment to bring since fires are prohibited. Having said that, you'll be responsible for lugging your own gear to the site after it's brought ashore, and it's important not to bring too much. When you depart, you're the one who will pack everything out, including trash, so backpacks, duffle bags and containers with handles are recommended.

If you're willing and able to deal with such challenges, the pay-off is a rare chance to explore one of the world's most unusual natural resources. The Channel Islands offer miles of trails, tidepools, rusting shipwrecks, huge colonies of sea lions and seals and underwater reserves for snorkelers and scuba divers.

CAMPGROUNDS: Camping facilities can be found on the islands of Anacapa, Santa Barbara, San Miguel, and Santa Rosa. The campgrounds are open all year, although boat service to all but Anacapa is scheduled only from April or May through November. Private boats require a free permit to dock at Santa Rosa. Pets are prohibited on all the islands. Fishing is allowed on Santa Barbara and Santa Rosa (license required); however, it is prohibited on Anacapa and San Miguel because of California State Ecological Reserve regulations.

RESERVATIONS: Call Channel Islands National Park Visitor Center at (805) 658-5730 no more than 90 days in advance (30 days in advance for San Miguel Island) to reserve a permit. A maximum of 30 people per day are allowed at each island. **Note:** It is suggested that campers secure transportation before requesting permits (see *How to Get There,* below).

FEES: Camping permits are free. Transportation fees are given below.

SECURITY: Resident park rangers on all islands.

HOW TO GET THERE:

By Boat - Except for Santa Rosa, which has an airstrip, the only way to reach the Channel Islands is by boat. Unless you have your own, you'll need to contact Island Packers, the only concessionaire authorized to ferry visitors to and from the islands. Call or write for information: Island Packers, 1867 Spinnaker Drive, Ventura, CA

93001 (805) 642-1393. Reservations may be made seven days a week between 9 a.m. and 5 p.m. Pacific time. Current roundtrip camper fares are as follows: *Anacapa* - $48/adult; $30/12 years and under. *Santa Barbara* - $75/adult; $65/12 years and under. *Santa Rosa* - $80/adult; $70/12 years and under. *San Miguel* -$90/adult; $80/12 years and under.

Landing permits and information for those piloting their own vessels are free and may be obtained up to 30 days in advance of a visit from Channel Islands National Park headquarters, (805) 658-5700, or the Visitor Center, (805) 658-5730.

By Air - For those wishing to fly into Santa Rosa, contact Channel Islands Aviation, 305 Durley Avenue, Camarillo, CA 93010, (805) 987-1301. It's open seven days a week from 7:30 a.m. to 6 p.m. Pacific time. Current roundtrip camper fares are $150 for adults, $100 for children 2-12 years old. Maximum 80 pounds of gear per person, two-passenger minimum.

Anacapa

At 1.1 square miles, Anacapa is the second smallest but most visited of the islands, being the closest to the mainland – just 11 miles away. It's actually three separate volcanic islets (designated east, middle and west islands) connected by shallow, normally submerged reefs. Together, they span a slender five-mile length, no point being wider than a half-mile. The shoreline is rugged and rocky and the island's beaches generally inaccessible.

On calm summer days, however, you can swim from either Landing Cove or Frenchy's Cove. There are several scuba and skin diving areas as well, including the wreck of the *Winfield Scott*, which grounded and sank off Middle Anacapa in 1853.

A 1½-mile self-guiding nature trail lets you explore East Anacapa at your leisure. Because West Anacapa is the primary nesting site for the California brown pelican, it has been designated a Research Natural Area, closed to the public with the exception of the beach at Frenchy's Cove. Middle Anacapa can be explored with a park ranger guide.

The boat ride to Anacapa usually takes no more than 1½ hours. Upon arriving, campers must haul their equipment and supplies up a steel rung ladder to the loading dock. From there, a 154-step climb to the top of the island, followed by a half-mile hike will bring them to the campground. Although limited to 30 campers, Anacapa's sites are very close together and when filled to capacity, which may happen on summer weekends, it will feel quite cramped. Visiting during the mid-week and off-summer months is suggested as a way of beating the crowds.

Anacapa is the only island with boat service throughout the year. Maximum stay is 14 days per year.

Santa Barbara

For so small a speck of an island – it's less than one square mile – Santa Barbara has been a busy place in recent history, serving as sheep ranch, potato farm, and military installation before being turned over to the National Park Service in 1938. The island lies 46 miles west of the mainland and 24 miles from Santa Catalina. Only 635 feet at the highest point, its beaches are rocky and difficult to reach, most of the shoreline being sheer rock cliffs. Plant life ranges from cactus to grass and coastal scrub; animal life includes the endangered California brown pelican and night lizard, as well as sea lions, harbor seals and elephant seals.

Although tiny and remote, the island is not without its merit. "To visit Santa Barbara Island is to encapsulate the Channel Islands experience," according to *Channel Islands National Park*, an excellent overview published by the Friends of Channel Islands National Park. "Santa Barbara provides a sampler of the resources, scenic beauty, and remote island experience in a compact and powerful summary – the essences, as it were, of the Channel Islands."

Campers may explore the island along its 5½ miles of hiking trails, as well as snorkel and dive from Landing Cove.

The camping area is adjacent to the ranger station. Following a three-hour boat ride, campers must climb a steel rung ladder to the loading dock, then climb another 275 yards up two steep switchbacks to the campground. Nine sites with tables overlook the anchorage from an elevation of about 100 feet. The campground is flat and grassy.

Boat service is available from April through November. Maximum stay is 14 days per year.

San Miguel

Eight miles long and four miles wide, San Miguel is the third largest island in the Channel Islands National Park, covering a total of 14 square miles. It's 26 miles from the mainland, but 53 nautical miles from Ventura; thus, it takes longer to reach San Miguel than any of the other islands. Count on a crossing time of four to five hours.

Among sailors, San Miguel is best known for its cool, frequently foggy weather, submerged rocks and shallow shoreline, which make boating hazardous. In fact, the island is often referred to as the "Graveyard of the Pacific" because there have been so many shipwrecks here.

Naturalists visit San Miguel for its extraordinary populations of seals and sea lions, which loll by the thousands along the island's isolated coves and beaches.

A windswept plateau with gentler, less rugged features than the other islands, San Miguel features more miles of sandy beaches than any other island in the park. The near-constant wind has created large sections of dunes and bluffs covered with scrub brush. One of San Miguel's most remarkable features is the caliche – sandcastings of large prehistoric trees and other plants – which show the island was once covered by an ancient forest. Although caliche are evident on other islands, the best examples are here.

Because of the island's size, San Miguel's trails are considerably longer, varying from two to 16 miles roundtrip. Hikers normally require a park ranger escort for any hiking beyond the immediate vicinity of the campground.

San Miguel is undoubtedly the toughest campground to reach of any on the islands. The ride is long and can be rough. Once ashore, campers have to make what is described as an "extremely physical" ¾-mile hike up a steep canyon trail to the campground, which sits 700 feet above sea level. Because the island is subject to frequent wind, four of the six campsites have wind breaks, and the two that don't, should. Winds of 30 mph are not uncommon.

Boat service is scheduled from May through November. **Note:** Maximum stay is two days per year.

Santa Rosa

Those cowboys on horseback you may see galloping off on the horizon aren't illusions. They work for the Vail and Vickers Company, which has been cattle ranching on Santa Rosa since 1902. Although the company sold the island to the National Park Service in 1986, the Vail and Vickers Co. retained the right to continue ranching up to the year 2011.

As the second largest island in the park, Santa Rosa's 84 square miles of gently rolling, grass-covered hillsides and ample supply of fresh water make it well-suited to cattle grazing. More than 6,000 head are on the island at any one time.

That cattle operation, as well as a commercial hunting enterprise for introduced elk and deer, is why most of the island is off-limits to visitors unless accompanied by a park ranger. Only Water Canyon, location of the island's sole campground, is unrestricted. Fortunately, the canyon provides numerous opportunities for exploration, including beaches, oak groves, caves and overlooks.

Visitors should count on a 3½-hour cruise to reach the island. From the pier, you must hike a relatively flat and easy 1½-mile trail to the campground, 80 feet above sea level. Frequently, the park service will truck visitors' gear to the site. The campground, enclosed by a fence to keep cattle out, is very grassy with few bushes. Sites are spaced generously and include tables and pit toilets.

Windy conditions prevail and the campground's 15 sites include windbreaks to protect against gales up to 40 mph. Tents have to be sturdy.

Even though the island has an abundant water supply, none is currently available at the campground and campers are required to bring their own. In fact, because weather is so variable here, it's recommended that campers bring an extra day's supply of food and water in the event the boat can't dock when scheduled. Generally, you'll find Santa Rosa's summers are dry and foggy, its winters cool and rainy (about 15 inches a year).

Boat service to Santa Rosa is scheduled from April through November. **Note:** Maximum stay is two days per year.

MCGRATH STATE BEACH

c/o Channel Coast District Headquarters
1933 Cliff Drive, Suite 27, Santa Barbara CA 93109
(805) 654-4744

- Tent and RV camping near sand dunes
- Hike & Bike camping

A massive white sand beach and dune area is McGrath State Park's most distinctive feature. Tufts of reedy grass give a soft, fuzzy look to the rolling mounds of sand that ultimately melt into the impeccably smooth wave-washed shoreline. Beyond, the Pacific Ocean extends to infinity as the coastline curves lazily away. In the distance, homes, condominiums and apartments look like toy building blocks set against the green-tinted mountains to the northwest. To the left, you can see the silhouette of an Edison plant.

Although the beach is extraordinary, the surf is known to be hostile at times, prone to sleeper waves that can arise unexpectedly, knocking down children and adults alike and dragging them into deep water. Rip currents are also common and extreme caution is required. However, lifeguards are on duty throughout the summer and on holiday weekends when the number of visitors require them. Those desiring less powerful currents and calmer waters can find them just 10 or 15 minutes away.

CAMPGROUND: There are 174 developed campsites that can accommodate either tents or RVs up to 34 feet long. Each site has its own parking pad, table and fire ring. Water spigots are nearby, but there are no hookups. The campground is arranged in 18 circular clusters, each cluster having eight to 10 campsites. Some of the spaces are built at the edge of the dunes, about 300 to 400 yards from the beach; those further inland assume more park-like features, including grassy ground and even medium-sized trees. All through the campground, however, large bushes add both greenery and privacy to the sites. More than 100,000 people camp here each year. The Hike & Bike campground is situated near the park entrance.

RESTROOMS: Modern facilities with private flush toilets, sinks, mirrors, AC outlets and individual coin-operated showers (25¢ for 2 minutes).

RESERVATIONS: Up to eight weeks in advance through MISTIX, 1-800-444-PARK.

CHECK IN/OUT: Noon.

FEES: $16/day in peak season (June 1-Sept. 30); $14 off-peak. *Hike & Bike* - $3/day per person.

DOGS: $1/day; not permitted on beach or nature trails.

MAX. STAY: Seven days (June-September); 15 days remainder of the year.

SECURITY: Park rangers and resident camp host.

HOW TO GET THERE: From Oxnard, drive north on Highway 101; exit at Harbor Blvd. and turn left; stay on Harbor for about three miles. Park entrance will be on the right hand side.

EMMA WOODS STATE BEACH

c/o Channel Coast District Headquarters
1933 Cliff Drive, Suite 27, Santa Barbara CA 93109
(805) 654-4611

- On-the-beach tent and RV camping
- Hike & Bike camping
- Group camping

There are two parts to this park: The north section, called North Beach, is pressed between Highway 101 and the ocean on an unused section of the old Pacific Coast Highway. This is where the family campground is located. The other part is a quarter-mile inland of the coast in the usually dry Ventura river bed, between the railroad and Highway 101. This is the location of the group and Hike & Bike camps.

Neither section is what anyone would describe as an ideal campground. Some might be reluctant to give North Beach that title at all. And yet, more than 22,000 campers make use of this area annually, according to statistics.

CAMPGROUNDS:

North Beach: This part is interesting if you like climbing over surf-scrubbed boulders, which take the place of sand on most of the beach. You'll find absolutely no plant life of any aesthetic significance here and, with the highway and railroad to your back, it leaves much to be desired. However, the park is well suited to fishing and surfing. As for swimming, there are far more benevolent shorelines to be found.

There are 61 campsites here. Both tents and RVs up to 40 feet are welcome, although tenters are at a distinct disadvantage – there's simply very little ground available on which to stake

Only hardcore campers can find a place on the rocky beach

a tent. Take your pick between the road and the rocky beach. Don't forget, this is nothing more than an abandoned stretch of highway.

Each of the sites includes a rudimentary fireplace fashioned from piles of beach rock, but there are no tables or hookups. Just pick a spot and park.

RESTROOMS: Chemical toilets; no showers. RESERVATIONS: First-come, first-served basis. CHECK IN/OUT: Noon. FEES: $16/day in peak season (April 1-Sept. 30); $14/day off-peak. DOGS: $1/day. Not permitted on beach. MAX. STAY: 10 days. SECURITY: Park rangers on patrol. HOW TO GET THERE: From Ventura, drive about three miles north on Highway 101; exit at Highway 1 and follow it down a short decline; at the bottom of the decline, make an immediate left U-turn into the park's entrance.

Ventura River: This section includes five group campgrounds and a Hike & Bike camp. Four of the group campgrounds are exclusively for tenters and require a walk of about 20 yards from the central parking lot. Each accommodates up to 30 campers and five vehicles. A fifth campground is for RV groups; it has room for 50 campers and 20 vehicles up to 35 feet long. There are no hookups.

This is a grassy area with some shrubs but little in the way of trees or shade. A narrow rocky beach is about 100 yards away and accessible by way of a trail that crosses the railroad tracks.

RESTROOMS: Flush toilets, sinks, mirrors and AC outlets; no showers. RESERVATIONS: Reservations for group camps are accepted up to six months in advance by calling the park directly at (805) 654-4610. CHECK IN/OUT: Noon. FEES: *Tent group camps* - $45/day; *RV group facility* - $75/day; *Hike & Bike* - $3/day per person. DOGS: $1/day (not permitted on beach). MAX. STAY: 10 days. SECURITY: Park rangers. HOW TO GET THERE: From Los Angeles, take 101 north; exit at Main Street in Ventura and head north until you see the park entrance.

FARIA COUNTY PARK
County of Ventura
General Services Agency Recreation Services
800 South Victoria Avenue, Ventura CA 93009
(805) 654-3951

- Beachfront tent and RV camping
- Group camping

Faria is essentially a flat gravel parking pad on a shelf of land about 10 or 12 feet above Faria Beach. A wall of large boulders separates it from the sand, which is most easily accessed via a concrete stairway at the north end. Its surf appears friendly and easy going, although there are no lifeguards.

Highway 1 runs right along the opposite side of the park on a rise about 20 feet above. Tucked into a small corner of the park is a day-use area with grills, tables and horseshoe pit.

A campstore serves fast-food breakfasts, lunches and dinners from 8 a.m. to 5 p.m. seven days a week all summer long, as well as on weekends and holidays during the rest of the year. It also carries a limited selection of grocery and camping items.

CAMPGROUND: There are 42 sites capable of accommodating both tents and RVs up to 40 feet long. The sites are not much more than oversized parking spaces furnished with tables and fire rings with grill tops. None have hookups and there is no dump station, but water spigots are nearby. A solitary row of palm trees parades down its center.

RESTROOMS: Modern, well-appointed restrooms include flush toilets, sinks, mirrors, AC outlets, and even hand soap. Private, coin-operated showers cost 25¢ for 2½ minutes.

RESERVATIONS: Sites 6 through 39 may be reserved from three weeks to six months in advance by calling Ventura County Parks Monday through Thursday between 8 a.m. and 5 p.m. at (805) 654-3951; there is a two-day minimum.

Remaining sites are first come, first served. Groups may reserve sites only from September 15 through May 15. Fee is per campsite as indicated above, with a five-campsite minimum.

CHECK IN/OUT: 2 p.m. in; 11 a.m. out.

FEES: $16/day, maximum six persons per site, in peak season (April 1-Oct 31); $13/day off-peak.

DOGS: $1/day, maximum two dogs. Must be leashed at all times. Permitted on beach.

MAX. STAY: 14 days.

SECURITY: Resident camp host.

HOW TO GET THERE: From Ventura, drive north on Highway 101; exit at Highway 1 off-ramp and stay on Highway 1 for seven miles. Before you reach Faria County Park, you may notice a sign identifying a section of the coast as Faria Beach. This is private. The county park is a little ways beyond.

RINCON PARKWAY

County of Ventura
General Services Agency Recreation Services
800 South Victoria Avenue, Ventura CA 93009
(805) 654-3951

- Next-to-the-beach RV camping; no tents

If parking alongside the Pacific Coast Highway (1) sounds like a good idea, you may want to consider Rincon Parkway. To one side of the park you'll find a long stretch of sandy beach suitable for fishing and swimming. On the other side, however, are a couple of lanes of traffic. *Zoom!*

There's not much more to Rincon than that. You won't find tables, hookups, fire rings or even water. In fact, you'll need a commercially-built stove if you plan to do any cooking. Campfires are not permitted.

Open to RVs of any size.

RESTROOMS: Chemical toilets only; no showers.

RESERVATIONS: First-come, first-served basis.

CHECK IN/OUT: 11 a.m.

FEES: $11/day in peak season (April 1-Oct. 31); $8/day off-peak.

DOGS: $1/day. Must be leashed at all times. Permitted on beach.

MAX. STAY: Five days (April 1-Oct. 31); 10 days remainder of year.

SECURITY: Periodic checks by park rangers.

HOW TO GET THERE: From Ventura, drive north on Highway 101; exit at Highway 1 and proceed north again for about six miles. Rincon Parkway will be the left shoulder of the highway. Watch for the signs and the row of RVs.

HOBSON COUNTY PARK

County of Ventura
General Services Agency Recreation Services
800 South Victoria Avenue, Ventura CA 93009
(805) 654-3951

- Beachfront tent and RV camping
- Group camp

With the exception of its location, a few miles north of Faria County Park, Hobson is a virtual replica in terms of layout, appearance, facilities, rules, regulations, even the camp store, which happens to be operated by the same concessionaire.

Palm trees tower over Hobson Park

Hobson County Park is located on a gravelly shelf of land just above a reef-protected beach that is reportedly safe for swimming and popular for scuba diving and fishing (perch, cabazon, lingcod and croaker are the most common catches).

As at Faria County Park, large boulders separate the entire outside edge of the park from the beach, which is best reached by way of a short stairway. A tall row of palms is the most notable sign of plant life.

CAMPGROUND: Hobson is a bit smaller than Faria Park. There are just 31 sites capable of accommodating both tents and RVs; a few sites can fit RVs as big as 40 feet. They're not much more than oversized parking spaces furnished with tables and fire rings with grill tops. Water spigots are nearby.

RESTROOMS: Modern, well-appointed restrooms include flush toilets, sinks, mirrors, AC outlets, and hand soap. Private, coin-operated showers cost 25¢ for 2½ minutes.

RESERVATIONS: Beachfront sites 15 through 28 may be reserved from three weeks to six months in advance by calling Ventura County Parks Monday through Thursday between 8 a.m. and 5 p.m. at (805) 654-3951; there is a two-day minimum. Remaining sites are first come, first served. Groups may reserve sites only from September 15 through May 15. Fee is per campsite as indicated above, with a five-campsite minimum.

CHECK IN/OUT: 2 p.m. in; 11 a.m. out.

FEES: $16/day, maximum six persons per site, in peak season (April 1-Oct 31). $13/day off-peak.

DOGS: $1/day. Maximum two dogs. Must be leashed at all times. Permitted on beach.

MAX. STAY: 14 days.

SECURITY: Resident camp host.

HOW TO GET THERE: From Ventura, drive north on Highway 101; exit at Highway 1 off-ramp and stay on that road for nine miles.

Santa Barbara County

CARPINTERIA STATE BEACH
5361 Sixth Street, Carpinteria, CA 93013
(805) 684-2811

- On or near-beach tent and RV camping
- Hike & Bike camping
- En Route camping

Carpinteria State Beach is hardly a wilderness experience. With the exception of its 4,100-foot shoreline, the park is completely surrounded by the city of Carpinteria, a comfortable community of about 13,750 people. Within an easy walk of the park, supermarkets, restaurants, fast foods, banks, laundromats, sporting goods stores and numerous other businesses and services abound, fulfilling the needs of visitors and residents alike.

But, once you are wrapped within the park's 43 acres, it's not hard to forget your proximity to civilization. The periodic freight and passenger trains along the railroad paralleling the park's eastern boundary will, however, remind you of your location several times throughout the day and night.

More than 700,000 visitors flock to this park each year, nearly half of them to camp. Located alongside Carpinteria City Beach, "The safest beach in the world" according to city officials, Carpinteria State Beach shares many, if not all, of the same qualities. It's sandy, shallow and sheltered from rough seas and rip currents by the Channel Islands, the nearest of which are less than 20 miles away.

Extending back from the beach is a moderate stretch of dunes, its mounds of sand and ice plants occasionally highlighted by wind-swept cypress, eucalyptus and small shrubs.

CAMPGROUNDS: Beyond the dunes are four clusters of camp-grounds.

Anacapa (sites 1-39) is a grassy area with shrubs and some shady pine trees where either tents or RVs (maximum 35 ft.) can set camp. The beach is a little distance, perhaps 200 yards, across a large asphalt parking lot for day users and En Route campers. Each space has its own parking pad, table and fire ring. Water spigots are nearby. There are no hookups. The Hike & Bike campground is also located here.

Santa Cruz (sites 40-101) is also grassy, with lots of eucalyptus trees, pines and leafy shrubs. Open to tents and RVs up to 35 feet, the sites feature their own parking pads, tables and fire rings. There are no hookups, but water spigots are intermittently spaced.

Santa Rosa (sites 102-187) is unlike the Anacapa and Santa Cruz sections, looking more like a parking lot designed for RVs. The asphalt is interrupted only by narrow islands of dirt from which spring towering eucalyptus trees and shrubs. There is space enough only for small tents. The largest spaces can accommodate RVs up to 30 feet in length. All spaces have hookups for water, sewer and electricity, as well as tables and fire rings.

San Miguel (sites 188-262) is a lot like Santa Rosa, only less shady. About half of the spaces have no hookups, however, and those that do (spaces 210-243) provide only water and electricity, no sewer. All have the standard table and fire ring. The largest spaces can accommodate RVs up to 30 feet. Some sites also have room for a small tent.

RESTROOMS: Modern facilities include flush toilets, sinks, AC outlets and coin-operated showers.

RESERVATIONS: Up to eight weeks in advance through MISTIX, 1-800-444-PARK.

CHECK IN/OUT: Noon.

FEES: Fees vary according to the type of site and location you prefer. *Hike & Bike* - $3/per person per day, maximum 2 days. *Anacapa* and *Santa Cruz* - $16/day in peak season (April 1-Sept. 30); $14/day off-peak. *En Route* campers pay the same. *Santa Rosa* - $20-$25/day in peak season (for beachfront); $18-$23/day off-peak. *San Miguel* - $16-$21/day in peak season (beachfront); $14-$19/day off-peak.

DOGS: $1/day. Not permitted on beach.

MAX. STAY: Seven days (June-September); 15 days remainder of year.

SECURITY: Park rangers and round-the-clock camp hosts residing within each campground. Note that this is a safe campground, although there have been recent thefts. Tents and bicycle cables have been cut and visitors are warned to store property within their vehicles.

HOW TO GET THERE: From Santa Barbara (just 12 miles to the north), drive south on 101; exit at Route 224 and turn right, following the signs to the park about one mile from the freeway.

EL CAPITAN STATE BEACH
#10 Refugio Beach, Goleta, CA 93117
(805) 968-1033

- Above-beach tent & RV camping
- Hike & Bike camping
- Group camping
- En Route camping

Twenty miles north of Santa Barbara, El Capitan is the first of three state parks strung like beads along a 10-mile section of hilly, undeveloped coast. (The others, Refugio and Gaviota, are described on the following pages.) It's situated along three miles of golden sand beach on 133 acres of gently billowing oak, sycamore and acacia. Although the smallest of the three parks, El Capitan is the most popular, each year drawing more than 262,000 visitors, almost half of whom are campers.

The never-ending beach at El Capitan

The bulletin boards warn that this is mountain lion country, but the only incidents to date have been harmless sitings. More than likely if you encounter a problem with wildlife, it will be with a raccoon or rodent. They're unlikely to hurt you, but they may very well get into your food supply if proper precautions aren't taken. You'll also stand a good chance of viewing sea lions frolicking offshore.

Stairways or ramps, several of which have been closed due to erosion, normally provide easy access to the beach, which is popular for fishing, swimming and surfing. Lifeguards are on duty throughout the peak season. There's also a short nature trail and a 2½-mile bike trail that connects with Refugio State Beach to the west.

A camp store sells groceries, microwavable food items and limited camping supplies throughout the summer from 9 a.m. to 6 p.m. daily. If that's not open, there's another store in a private campground just across the road. It's open the year round.

CAMPGROUND: El Capitan is the largest of the three park campgrounds, with 140 sites which can accommodate either tents or RVs up to 30 feet. Each site features its own parking pad, table and fire ring with grill top. There is a dump station but no hookups. Water is nearby.

The grounds are grassy and mottled with shade from tall sycamores and broad oaks. A variety of shrubs help maintain reasonable privacy between plots. Railroad tracks parallel a portion of the park; you'll be reminded of their proximity numerous times during the day and night.

Three walk-in group camps for tenters are located above the family area. Ortega campground can take up to 50 tent campers with parking for 10 vehicles; Cabrillo accommodates a maximum of 75 people and 15 vehicles; Drake campground can handle 125 people and 25 vehicles.

Hike & Bike and En Route camping is also permitted at El Capitan.

RESTROOMS: Modern flush toilets, sinks, mirrors and coin-operated showers.

RESERVATIONS: Up to eight weeks in advance through MISTIX, 1-800-444-PARK. Group camps can be reserved up to six months in advance through MISTIX.

CHECK IN/ OUT: Noon.

FEES: $16/day in peak season (April 2-Oct. 30); $14/day off-peak. Same for *En Route camping. Hike & Bike camping* - $3/day per person. *Group camping* - $75/day at Ortega; $112.50/day at Cabrillo; $187.50/day at Drake.

DOGS: $1/day; not permitted on beach or trails.

MAX. STAY: Seven days (June-September); 15 days remainder of the year. Hike & Bike camping is limited to two nights; En Route camping to one night.

SECURITY: Park rangers and resident camp host

HOW TO GET THERE: From Santa Barbara, drive north on Highway 101; exit at El Capitan Beach.

REFUGIO STATE BEACH
#10 Refugio Beach, Goleta, CA 83117
(805) 968-1033

- Near-beach tent & RV camping
- Hike & Bike camping
- Group camping

Refugio State Beach is probably how most people imagine a California beach: A broad crescent of smooth, golden sand that's lined with palms and edged by an endless sky-blue sea. Unblemished hillsides of grass with dark green dots of evergreen oak rise up behind the park, not a sign of human habitation anywhere. The nearest cities of any significance – Buellton to the north and Santa Barbara to the southeast – are more than 20 miles away.

Follow the 1½-mile-long beach to the west around Refugio Point and you'll discover a beach where jags of rock suddenly emerge from the sand like some avant-garde sculpture. On the opposite end of Refugio, a bluff-top trail for bicyclists will lead you to El Capitan State Beach 2½ miles east.

The surf is fine for fishing, swimming and surfing. Lifeguards are on duty throughout the summer.

Refugio also has its own camp store, although it operates only during the summers and holiday weekends.

CAMPGROUND: There are 85 campsites squeezed between the sand on the south (Refugio is a south-facing beach) and railroad tracks on the north. Obviously, the farther you can get from the tracks, the better you are, although you're sure to know when a train is coming through regardless of where your campsite is. The tracks make a rather sharp turn by the park and the metal wheels screech as they scrape against the tracks.

Each site can accommodate either a tent or RV up to 30 feet long. They feature their own parking pads, fire rings with grill tops, tables and food lockers. Water spigots are nearby. There are no hookups or dump station. A creek runs through the center of the campground, which has the effect of creating two blocks of campsites. Each block is similar, with oaks, peppertrees and eucalyptus providing varying degrees of shade throughout the grass- and dirt-covered grounds.

Weathered rocks fringe the coast at Refugio State Beach

A third section of the campground, located east of the family campground, is reserved for groups of up to 80 campers and 25 vehicles. This is a very popular campground that's "always on reserve."

There's also a Hike & Bike section with room for up to 20 persons.

RESTROOMS: Modern, tiled facilities include flush toilets, mirrors, sinks, laundry tubs and private coin-operated showers.

FEES: $16/day in peak season (April 1-Oct. 30); $14/day off-peak. *Hike & Bike camping* - $3/day per person. *Group camping* - $120/day. **DOGS:** $1/day; not permitted on beach.

MAX. STAY: Seven days (June-September); 15 days remainder of the year. Hike & Bike camping is limited to two days.

RESERVATIONS: For family camping between March 25 and Dec. 1, you can make reservations up to eight weeks in advance through MISTIX, 1-800-999-PARK. It is on a first-come, first-served basis the rest of the year. Group camping may be reserved up to 120 days in advance year round through MISTIX.

CHECK IN/OUT: 2 p.m. in; noon out.

SECURITY: Park rangers and resident camp host.

HOW TO GET THERE: From Santa Barbara, drive north on Highway 101; exit at Refugio State Beach turnoff.

GAVIOTA STATE PARK
#10 Refugio Beach Road, Goleta, CA 93117
(805) 968-3294

• Near-beach tent & RV camping

This is a large park, 2,760 acres, that seems even larger because it's adjacent to the mammoth Los Padres National Forest, which looms to the rear. Essentially a canyon that opens out to the sea, Gaviota State Park features nine miles of trails up through hills of chaparral and coastal scrub. A quarter-mile walk along one of them leads to

The shallow, sandy shores at Gaviota lure swimmers and anglers

a hot spring where you might consider soaking yourself. A small creek also flows through the canyon and gives rise to stands of native sycamores, live oaks and willows.

The beach is wide and sandy and popular among swimmers and anglers. A lifeguard is on duty all through the summer. For those hoping to hook one of the area's halibut or perch, a pier juts into the sea for about 75 yards, providing a great spot from which to cast their lines. It also offers sightseers a superb view of the coastline and rolling interior. Just behind the beach, spanning the broad mouth of the canyon at maybe 75 to 100 feet above the ground, is a huge railroad trestle. You'll know when a train passes, but its elevation helps diffuse the sound.

CAMPGROUND: The campground has just undergone a complete remodel (scheduled to re-open for camping in the summer of 1995). Situated at the base of the canyon, it's basically an asphalt parking lot with islands of trees and bare dirt between rows of spaces. There are a total of 52 sites, each furnished with a table and fire ring with grill top. The spaces can fit RVs up to 30 feet, but only about 34 of them have enough ground to accommodate a tent. None of the spaces have hookups and the nearest dump station is at El Capitan State Beach.

The sand and surf is just a few hundred feet away.

RESTROOMS: Individual flush toilets, sinks, mirrors and coin-operated showers. All brand new.

RESERVATIONS: Gaviota has traditionally been a first-come, first-served campground. However, a survey was in process to determine if it should go on the reservation system (MISTIX). Call park for update.

CHECK IN/OUT: Noon.

FEES: $16/day in peak season (June 1-Sept. 30); $14/day off-peak.

DOGS: $1/day; not permitted on beach or trails.

MAX. STAY: Seven days (June-September); 15 days remainder of the year.

SECURITY: Park rangers and possible camp host.

HOW TO GET THERE: From Santa Barbara, drive north on Highway 101; exit at Gaviota State Park off-ramp.

JALAMA BEACH COUNTY PARK

c/o Santa Barbara County Parks Dept.
610 Mission Canyon Road, Santa Barbara, CA 93105
(805) 736-6316, 736-3504

- Near-beach tent & RV camping
- Group camping

Jalama Beach Park is a great getaway on a broad, beautiful sandy beach that's insulated from the rest of the world by miles of velvety smooth hills peppered with coastal scrub and evergreen oaks. The only way into the park is by way of a 15-mile road that lazily snakes through the hills and affords numerous panoramic views of the rambling countryside. It's a smooth, well-paved road although there are a few 10-mph curves to be negotiated. Count on a ride of 25-30 minutes.

The park itself looks brand new, although it was created more than 52 years ago. It's very open, with limited shrubs and neat islands of green doing their best to soften the extensive spread of asphalt. Campsites are situated along the beach as well as on the bluffs paralleling it.

The beach extends for about two miles in each direction. Activities include beach hiking, surfing, windsurfing and fishing. There are no lifeguards on duty here. Hiking inland is restricted because of the proximity of Vandenberg Air Force Base and surrounding private property. An on-site camp store is open all year during daylight

Seabirds gather along the tranquil beach

hours; you'll find it will fulfill most of your immediate requirements, including groceries, camping supplies and even hot, fast food.

Group camping is available on a limited basis between April 1 and September 15. After that, additional spaces become available and may be reserved (see below).

You'll find the park full virtually every day throughout the summer and holiday weekends. To prevent campers from making the 15-mile drive in vain, a big, lighted sign offers continuous reports on campground occupancy; it's a quarter-mile west of Highway 1 near the beginning of Jalama Road.

CAMPGROUND: There are 100 sites, including 15 with electrical hookups. Choose from beachfront sites or hilltop sites with superb views of the coastline. All are equipped with tables and fire pits. RVs of virtually any size can be accommodated, although not all sites can handle all sizes. Piped water is nearby. A dump station is also available, but none of the sites have sewer or water hookups.

RESTROOMS: These are first class, featuring private, tiled bathrooms with flush toilets, sinks and mirrors. Private coin-operated showers are located in a separate building.

RESERVATIONS: First-come, first-served basis throughout the year except for group reservations, which may be made up to one year in advance.

CHECK IN/OUT: 2 p.m. out; in anytime space is available. **Note:** Campers entering the park before 6 a.m. will be charged for the night before.

FEES: *Without hookups* - $13/day per vehicle ($10 for disabled); *with electrical hookups* - $16/day per vehicle ($13 for disabled). *Group sites* as follows: Area A (available Sept. 15-March 31) - $70/day for up to seven vehicles; Area B (available Sept. 15-March 31) - $130/day for up to 13 vehicles; and Area D (available all year) -$80/day for up to eight vehicles. **Note:** There is an additional $25 fee for each group reservation.

DOGS: $1/day; must be leashed or confined within a vehicle. Proof of rabies inoculation is required.

MAX. STAY: 14 days from April 1-Sept. 14; no limit the remainder of the year.

SECURITY: Four resident park rangers.

HOW TO GET THERE: From Santa Barbara, drive north on Highway 101; exit at Highway 1 (Lompoc/Vandenberg off-ramp) and follow it 14 miles to Jalama Road; turn left onto Jalama for another 15 miles to the park entrance.

RIVER PARK RV CAMPGROUND FACILITY
Highway 246 and Sweeney Road
(805) 736-6565

- Riverside RV camping
- Limited tent camping
- Hike & Bike camp
- Group camping
- En Route camping

River Park RV Campground is built along the banks of the Santa Ynez River, about eight miles from the coast, near the center of a valley bounded by the Santa Ynez Mountains to the south and the

Purísima Hills to the north. As the city of Lompoc's largest park, it encompasses 60 developed acres and 190 acres of open space.

Located on the outskirts of the city, the fields surrounding River Park are often ablaze with color. Mild year-round temperatures and dry summers are perfect for flowers such as sweet peas, larkspur, petunias, asters, marigolds and zinnias, all of which are grown here for their seeds. With 39,000 residents, however, Lompoc is no backwoods town; it's the county's third largest city, replete with the convenience of numerous stores, restaurants and other services.

The park features a dump station which is free to campers, $2 for all others. A picturesque day-use park with a lake and a smooth green carpet of grass is adjacent to the campground and features play equipment, an exercise path, volleyball courts and horseshoe pits.

Nearby points of interest include Vandenberg Air Force Base, one the nation's most important military and aerospace installations, just seven miles away, and Solvang, a pretty town with a distinctly Danish look to it – about 21 miles away.

CAMPGROUND: River Park is essentially an RV park consisting of a neat and tidy row of 34 spaces, each with full hookups, a parking pad, lawn area, table and grill. In addition, however, there's also a small grass-covered clearing with a few shrubs near the park entrance that's reserved for tenters. There are five tent-sites, each with its own table and fire ring.

RESTROOMS: Recently refurbished, the restroom facilities include flush toilets, sinks, mirrors and coin-operated showers.

RESERVATIONS: Except for groups, reservations are first come, first served throughout the year. Group camp reservations may be made by calling the Director of Parks & Recreation at (805) 736-6565. Summer weekends and holidays the camp is often filled.

FEES: (max. eight persons per site) *RV spaces* with full hookups - $15/day (same for *En Route* campers); *tentsites* - $10/day. *Hike & Bike* - $4/person per day.

DOGS: $1/day. Must be on leash.

MAX. STAY: 14 days (May 1-Sept. 30); 30 days remainder of year.

SECURITY: Resident park ranger and camp host.

HOW TO GET THERE: From Santa Barbara, drive north on Highway 1; exit on Route 246 and turn right for about a half-mile to the park entrance.

San Luis Obispo County

PISMO STATE PARK
555 Pier Avenue, Oceano, CA 93445
(805) 489-2684

- Near-beach tent & RV camping
- Hike & Bike camping

Shallow pools are great for exploring

This 1,000-acre park sits behind the dunes that parallel the northern tip of Pismo Dunes State Vehicular Recreation Area (see page 116). There are two campgrounds – Oceano and North Beach. Both accommodate either tents or RVs and are excellent, if not superior, alternatives to camping on the actual beach. Access to the beach is provided at both sites via sandy trails through the dunes and vary from easy to moderate. None is more than a few hundred yards long.

The weather here is moderate the year-round, temperatures averaging 60°. Expect frequent fog during summers, clear windy conditions in winter. The water is always cold, rarely rising above 58°.

CAMPGROUNDS:

Oceano: Located off of Pier Avenue in the southern end of Grover City, Oceano Campground has 40 tentsites and 42 RV sites with hookups for water and AC. All have their own parking pads. Campsites with hookups can accommodate RVs up to 36 feet; those without, up to 31. The grounds are generally grassy and moderately shaded by large eucalyptus and well-established pines. A freshwater lagoon flanks one side of the campground and provides a fun spot for easygoing canoeing and rafting. A very pleasant trail encircles it for those interested in a quiet amble.

North Beach: This campground is a mile north of the Oceano Campground along Highway 1. There are 103 sites capable of accommodating either tents or RVs up to 36 feet. The grounds are grassier than those at Oceano, but the trees are smaller and, thus, less shady. Each site includes its own parking pad, a table, fire ring with grill top, and food storage lockers. None has hookups, but there is an on-site dump station for use by campers at North Beach as well as Oceano.

RESTROOMS: Flush toilets, sinks, mirrors, AC outlets and showers are available at both Oceano and North Beach. The facilities at North Beach are newer and nicer.

RESERVATIONS: Reservations for Oceano Campground may be made throughout the year up to eight weeks in advance through MISTIX, 1-800-444-PARK. At North Beach Campground, reservations are accepted only for the period from May 26 through Sept. 5. North Beach is first come, first served throughout the rest of the year.

CHECK IN/OUT: 2 p.m. in; noon out.

FEES: *Without hookup* - $16/day in peak season (April 3-Sept. 5); $14/day off-peak. Sites *with electrical hookup* (at Oceano only) - $20/day in peak season; $18/day off-peak. *Hike & Bike* - $3/day per person.

DOGS: $1/day. Not permitted on trails. OK on beach.

MAX. STAY: Seven days (June-September); 15 days remainder of the year. *Hike & Bike* limit is two days.

SECURITY: Park rangers and resident camp hosts in both campgrounds.

HOW TO GET THERE: *(To Oceano Campground)* From Highway 101, take the Grand Avenue exit and turn left; turn left on Pacific Boulevard; turn right on Pier Avenue. *(To North Beach Campground)* From Highway 101, take the Grand Avenue exit and turn left; turn right on Pacific Boulevard and follow that for one mile to the campground entrance.

PISMO DUNES STATE VEHICULAR RECREATION AREA

Pier Avenue, Oceano, CA 93445
(805) 473-7220

- On-beach tent & RV camping

Hoping for a catch at Pismo

There are 2,000 acres of beach and sand dunes to be explored at Pismo State Vehicular Recreation Area, but what makes the preserve so special is you can do much of it by way of car or RV. It's the only place on the coast where the sand is firm enough to permit standard highway vehicles.

This is not to suggest you will never get stuck, however. High tides, heavy rains and blowing sand can trap vehicles and result in expensive towing service charges. Avoiding the beach during high tides and stormy weather and staying off the soft sand will minimize your risk of getting into trouble. Over a million people manage to do it every year. Rangers at each of the entrance stations make it one of their responsibilities to alert motorists of potential problems.

Dune buggies race across the beach

The beach is wide (approximately five miles long) and open to fishing, surfing, sailboarding and other aquatic activities. Beyond it rise 50- to 60-foot dunes, sections of which are open to off-road vehicles. This area is recognized as having the finest, most extensive coastal dunes remaining in the state.

Beyond the park, Grover City, Oceano and Arroyo Grande stand ready and willing to fullfil your every wish and command, from restaurants, grocery stores, filling stations and RV suppliers to rental outlets for dune buggies and other off-road vehicles.

Be advised that operators of all-terrain vehicles under 18 years of age must possess an appropriate safety certificate or be supervised by an adult who possesses a safety certificate. For complete information, contact the Foundation for Off Road Vehicle Safety, 1421 16th Street, Sacramento, CA 95814.

CAMPGROUND: Up to 1,000 vehicles are allowed on the beach at any one time. Upon reaching the camp, you simply drive south past marker post #2 and select whatever location seems best. You have a choice of beach or open-dune areas. All gear and supplies you need must be brought in. There is no water, tables, or fire rings. Remember, you need to haul out your trash.

Although off-roaders are permitted throughout the night and day, you'll generally find the noise level is minimal, muffled by the dunes and covered over by the constant surf.

RESTROOMS: Chemical toilets.

RESERVATIONS: Can be made up to eight weeks in advance through MISTIX, 1-800-444-PARK.

CHECK IN/OUT: Noon.

FEES: $6/day throughout the year.

DOGS: No extra fee; must be leashed at all times.

MAX. STAY: Seven days.

SECURITY: Park rangers are on patrol to 1 or 2 a.m. during the summer and they're always on call. Entrance stations are open to 1 a.m. in the summer; the rest of the time they're open to 6 p.m. except on Fridays (1 a.m.), Saturdays (midnight), and Sundays (10 p.m.).

HOW TO GET THERE: From Highway 101, take the Grand Avenue exit, turn left and follow it to the end of the road.

OCEANO COUNTY CAMPGROUND
Airpark Drive off Highway 1, Oceano, CA 93445
(805) 549-5219

• Near-beach tent and RV camping

Oceano Campground is a small rectangle of asphalt situated next to Oceano's airport. It's operated by San Luis Obispo County; don't confuse it with the much larger state-run campground of the same name, located about a half-mile north off Pier Avenue (see Pismo State Beach).

Although Oceano will accommodate tents, it probably shouldn't be your first choice. This is primarily an RV park. All spaces have hookups and the camping fees reflect that; if tenting, you'll be paying for the hookups whether you use them or not. Furthermore, there's very little ground space; most of each site is paved.

Immediately beyond the campground to the west lies Pismo State Beach. You can't actually see the water from the campground, but you can walk to it by heading north to Pier Avenue; figure on about a half-mile. A small creek runs alongside its northern edge. Across the street to the east is Oceano Park, a pleasant island of grass with picnic tables, grills and its own lake.

The campground includes its own little playground with slides, swings and other apparatus for very young children.

CAMPGROUND: There are 24 spaces that can accommodate RVs up to 40 feet. All have hookups for sewer, electricity and water. Just back into your space and you're ready to go.

RESTROOMS: Basic flush toilets and sinks; no mirrors. Coin-operated showers.

RESERVATIONS: First come, first served.

CHECK IN/OUT: Noon.

FEES: $20/day.

DOGS: $1.50/day. Must be leashed at all times.

MAX. STAY: 15 days within a 30-day period from April 1-Sept. 30; 30 days within a 60-day period the rest of the year.

SECURITY: Resident camp host.

HOW TO GET THERE: From Highway 101, exit at Grand Avenue and head west; turn left at Pacific Boulevard (Highway 1); turn right at Pershing; turn left onto Railroad Road; right on Airpark Drive to the campground.

MONTAÑA DE ORO STATE PARK
c/o Morro Bay State Park, Morro Bay, CA 93442
(805) 772-2560

- Near ocean tent and RV camping
- Environmental camping
- Horse camping
- En Route camping

Montaña de Oro means "Mountain of Gold." But don't go rushing in with a pan, a pick and other mining gear. The park's name is derived from the way the hills and bluffs light up in the spring, abloom with buttercups, California poppies and numerous other varieties of native flowers.

Montaña de Oro is one of the state's largest parks. Its 8,000 acres of precipitous peaks, valleys and seven-mile coastline draw more than 600,000 people annually. They hike, bike or ride horseback along its miles of trails and fire roads, and surf, beachcomb and explore tidepools along its crumbly shore. Nearly 40,000 of them opt to camp in one of its several campgrounds. Picnickers particularly enjoy Spooner's Cove, a broad crescent of golden sand equipped with tables and barbecue stoves; others enjoy making their own trails along a narrow finger of sand dunes three to four miles long that extends north of the main park.

CAMPGROUNDS:

The Family Campground, a quarter-mile inland of the coast, is the park's main campground and features 50 campsites for tents or RVs up to 24 feet. Ensconced within a pleasant clearing of grassy ground and shady pine trees, it provides tables, woodstoves, food lockers, potable wellwater and pit toilets. Parking pads are alongside each site.

The secluded setting at Spooner's Cove is great for picnics

Environmental Campgrounds: Those who would prefer to get deeper into the park, away from the day-users and traffic, may opt to stay in any one of four Environmental Camps within Montaña de Oro. Camps 1 and 2, named Bloody Nose Camp and Hazard Grove Camp respectively, are located in a sheltered grove of eucalyptus trees. Camps 3 and 4, named Badger Flat and Deer Flat, are on a ridge overlooking the ocean and subject to ocean winds, which can be particularly gusty in the spring and fall. Each campground has only one campsite, which can accommodate a maximum of eight persons. All have a picnic table and chemical toilet, but none has a fireplace or water. All require a walk of several hundred yards from the parking areas.

Horse Camps: Five horse camps, complete with corrals and parking for horse trailers, are also available. Two of them are group camps capable of accommodating up to 25 persons and 10 horses. The sites include picnic tables, pit toilets and water suitable for horses. Campers have to bring in their own drinking water. Access is by way of a mile-long dirt road leading down a moderate decline into a valley flanked by chaparral-covered walls on one side, leafy eucalyptus on the other.

RESERVATIONS: Up to eight weeks in advance through MISTIX, 1-800-444-PARK.

CHECK IN/OUT: 2 p.m. in; noon out.

FEES: *Family Campground* - $9/day peak season (April 3-Oct. 23); $7/day off-peak. *Environment Camps* - Same as family campground. *Horse Camps* - Family horse camps $16/day peak season for up to six horses; $14 off-peak. Group horse camps $50/day.

DOGS: $1/day. Must be leashed at all times. Prohibited from all trails and beaches. Dogs are not permitted in the environmental campgrounds.

MAX. STAY: Seven days (June-September); 15 days remainder of the year.

SECURITY: Park rangers and resident camp host.

HOW TO GET THERE: From San Luis Obispo, take Highway 101 to Los Osos Road; head west on Los Osos for 20 minutes. From Morro Bay, drive south on Rt. 41 for 10 miles; turn right on Los Osos and follow to the park entrance.

MORRO BAY STATE PARK
c/o Morro Bay State Park, Morro Bay, CA 93442
(805) 772-2560

- Near-coast tent & RV camping
- Hike & Bike camping
- Group camping
- En Route camping

One could hardly ask any more of a park. It is on the shore of Morro Bay. You can rent kayaks, canoes and rowboats, explore an isolated sand bar, hike trails, visit an on-site natural history museum, fish, golf on the adjacent 18-hole course or just enjoy the sweeping views of the bay, Morro Rock and the ocean.

There's a delightful café situated bayside in the park's marina. In fact, it's called the Bayside Café and serves lunch every day from 11 a.m. to 4 p.m., dinner Thursday through Monday from 4 to 9 p.m. Its menu offers everything from "Kid Stuff" starting at $3.95, to Bayside Burgers ($8.25) and pork loin medallions ($13.50).

Directly across from the café is the boat rental concession. Current rates vary from $6/hour for a canoe to $10/hour for a double kayak. Explore the bay or paddle your way across to the sand bar that stands between the bay and the Pacific.

The Morro Bay Museum of Natural History overlooks the marina and provides some of the best viewpoints in the park. The museum features interpretive displays about the area's complex ecosystem and its history. Mementos, books and posters are among items you can purchase here. It is open every day of the year from 10 a.m. to 5 p.m. (except Thanksgiving, Christmas and New Year's Day).

If golfing is your game, try the Morro Bay Golf Course, situated in the hills above the campground. The par 71 course will both challenge and delight with defiant greens and panoramic vistas. Fees are $20 on weekdays; $25 on weekends and $16 for twilight games after 1 p.m.

Spectacular views from atop the cliffs

Like most of the coastline along this part of California, you can count on the weather being mild throughout the year, though it is often foggy and overcast in the summer.

Morro Bay State Park is a mile or so from the town of Morro Bay, home to about 30,000 people.

CAMPGROUNDS: There are 135 individual campsites, including 20 with water and electrical hookups. They each have their own parking pad, table, rock fireplace/barbecue grill and food storage locker. Water spigots are nearby. Either tents or RVs up to 35 feet are easily accommodated. The grounds are well shaded with towering pines and eucalyptus trees. Their fallen leaves and needles carpet the campground.

On a hill rising above the campground in a grove of eucalyptus trees are two group sites: Chorro Campground, with space for up to 50 persons; and the adjacent Osos Campground, with space for 30 people. Tables, fire rings, grills and water spigots are provided.

RESTROOMS: The family campground features flush toilets, sinks, mirrors, AC outlets, laundry tubs and coin-operated showers. Group campground facilities are less generous, featuring a couple of flush toilets and exterior sinks; no showers.

RESERVATIONS: Up to eight weeks in advance through MISTIX, 1-800-444-PARK.

CHECK IN/OUT: 2 p.m. in; noon out.

FEES: *Family camping* (dry sites) - $16/day peak season (April 3-Sept. 5); $14/day off-peak. *Sites with water & electrical hookups -* $20/day peak season; $18/day off-peak. *Hike & Bike camping -* $3/day per person. *En Route camping -* $16/day peak season; $14/day off-peak. *Group camping -* $75/day for up to 50 persons at Chorro Campground; $45/day for up to 30 persons at Osos Campground.

DOGS: $1/day; permitted on trails with leash.

MAX. STAY: Seven days (June-September); 15 days remainder of the year. Hike & Bike camping - one day.

SECURITY: Resident park rangers and camp host.

HOW TO GET THERE: From Highway 101 at San Luis Obispo, exit on Highway 1 and drive 12 miles towards Morro Bay; exit on South Bay Boulevard and turn left; turn right on State Park Road (less than a half-mile); follow road to park entrance.

MORRO STRAND STATE BEACH
c/o Morro Bay State Park, Morro Bay, CA 93442
(805) 772-7434

• Beachside tent & RV camping

The strand lets you park right alongside a big, fat expanse of smooth, golden beach and low rolling sand dunes that stretch for three miles. There is a small community of cozy homes on the bluff above the park and downtown Morro Bay is just a mile or so south. This beach attracts fishing enthusiasts, windsurfers and kite fliers. The surf is reportedly pretty shallow and user friendly, although always cold. There are no lifeguards.

CAMPGROUND: The campground contains 104 sites capable of accommodating both tents and RVs up to 24 feet. It's essentially a parking lot with islands of shrubs trying hard to disguise this fact. But it still looks like a parking lot. If you're camping in a tent, be prepared for small patches of earth with room enough for a single tent, but just barely. Twenty-three of the campsites edge right up to the dunes. A hedge of shrubs forms a shield from the on-shore winds, which prevail most afternoons. Each site includes a a table and fire ring. Water is nearby, but there are no hookups or dump station.

RESTROOMS: Flush toilets, sinks, mirrors and AC outlets; no-cost outdoor rinse-off showers (cold water only).

RESERVATIONS: Camping dates from May 26 through September 5 can be reserved up to eight weeks in advance through MIS-TIX, 1-800-444-PARK. The rest of the year spaces are available on a first-come, first-served basis.

CHECK IN/OUT: Noon.

FEES: $16/day peak season (May 26-Sept. 5); $14/day off-peak.

DOGS: $1/day; permitted on beach with leash.

MAX. STAY: Seven days (June-September); 15 days remainder of the year.

SECURITY: Park rangers and resident camp host.

HOW TO GET THERE: From Morro Bay, drive north on Highway 1; turn left at Yerba Buena.

EL CHORRO REGIONAL PARK
c/o General Services, City Gov't Center, Room 460
San Luis Obispo, CA 93408
(805) 781-5200

• Inland tent & RV camping

Pastoral. Surrounded by rolling green hills as it is, there could hardly be a better word to describe El Chorro Regional Park. Historically, in fact, this 720-acre park was once used extensively by local ranchers for dairy production and cattle grazing. You can almost hear the mooing of cows. The park is clean and open.

The day-use area includes softball fields, horseshoe pits, a playground and several trails leading to scenic views and cool creekside oases.

Make sure to read the bulletin boards: They warn of the presence of mountain lions and poison oak.

The town of Morro Bay and its beaches is only 10 miles further west.

CAMPGROUND: There are 46 campsites on a high point above the day-use section of the park. They can accommodate either tents or RVs. A few of the sites are big enough to fit 35 to 40 footers. There are neither hookups nor a dump station.

Sites 1-24 seem to have been established longer than sites 25-46. The former have mature stands of eucalyptus, acacia, cypress and pine and, thus, offer appreciable shade. Sites 25-46 offer hardly any shade because the trees are still very young. However, that's bound to change within a few short years. Each site has a parking pad and grassy area, along with a table, grill and fire ring. Water spigots are placed intermittently.

RESTROOMS: Modern facilities include flush toilets, mirrors, sinks, hand-blowers and coin-operated showers (50¢/5 minutes).

RESERVATIONS: First come, first served.

CHECK IN/OUT: Noon.

FEES: $12/day.

DOGS: $1.50/day.

MAX. STAY: Seven days.

SECURITY: County park rangers.

HOW TO GET THERE: From San Luis Obispo, drive north on Highway 101; exit at the Pacific Coast Highway (1) and proceed west for six miles.

SAN SIMEON STATE PARK
750 Hearst Castle Road, San Simeon, CA 93452
(805) 927-2068

- Near-beach and hilltop tent & RV camping
- Hike & Bike camping

San Simeon State Park provides a great convenience to campers planning to tour the fabulous Hearst Castle, former home of the late newspaper publisher William Randolph Hearst. The park offers more than 200 campsites just four miles south of the popular attraction, which is open for tours every day of the year except for Thanksgiving Day, Christmas and New Year's Day.

However, you'll find the park is more than just a convenience. It's a pleasure as well, a relaxing, open area on the edge of a wide, sandy, driftwood-littered beach with a picturesque shoreline. Beachcombing is probably a better idea than swimming, as the water is rocky and signs warn of sleeper waves, rip currents and backwash. There are no lifeguards.

San Simeon Coastline

A pleasant, easygoing trail leads around the park for four miles through varying landscapes of coastal scrub, riverside woodlands, marsh and a forest of Monterey pines. Interpretive panels with information on wildlife and habitat tell you a little about what it is you're looking at and walking through. You'll also discover commanding views of the ocean and rolling, unspoiled hillsides that extend as far as the eye can see.

CAMPGROUNDS: There are actually two campgrounds at San Simeon – San Simeon Creek and Washburn. They're separated by a mile's drive, about 400 feet in elevation and by the quality of amenities.

San Simeon Creek is a developed campground situated near sea level, with paved roadways, parking pads, grassy lawns, established shrubs and a few Monterey pines. All 134 sites accommodate either tents or RVs up to 35 feet and include tables, fire rings with grills, and water. There are also horseshoe pits and a dump station, but no hookups. The beach is 100 yards away from the nearest campsite along an easy dirt trail. Its restroom facilities are of the state park system's newest genre, which provides individual restrooms featuring flush toilets, sinks and mirrors. There are also deep laundry tubs and individual coin-operated showers.

Washburn Campground is primitive by comparison. Located uphill of San Simeon Creek, the paved road turns to gravel and the landscape turns to endemic scrub and hard-packed earth. Some small pines have been planted, but, for now, they're all but invisible. The view is outstanding. One can see for miles in every direction. Each site does include a table and fire ring. Water spigots are also nearby. Restroom facilities consist of simple pit toilets.

Note: Campers at Washburn are prohibited from using the restroom facilities at San Simeon Creek.

RESERVATIONS: From March 15 through Sept. 30, reservations can be made up to eight weeks in advance through MISTIX, 1-800-999-PARK. Remainder of the year is first come, first served. If planning to tour Hearst Castle, you can also do so through MISTIX. This attraction draws nearly a million visitors each year; thus reservations are strongly recommended, especially through the summer and most weekends.

CHECK IN/OUT: Noon.

FEES: *San Simeon Creek* - $16/day peak season (May 27-Sept. 5); $14/day off-peak. *Hike & Bike* - $3/day per person. *Washburn* - $9/day peak; $7/day off-peak.

DOGS: $1/day; not permitted on trails.

MAX. STAY: 10 days (June-September); 30 days remainder of the year. Hike & Bike, 1-2 days.

SECURITY: Park rangers and resident camp host.

HOW TO GET THERE: From Santa Barbara, drive north on Highway 101 to San Luis Obispo; once in San Luis Obispo, take Highway 1 heading towards Morro Bay; follow Highway 1 north towards San Simeon; turn right at San Simeon Creek Road.

Monterey County

LOS PADRES NATIONAL FOREST
c/o Monterey Recreation District
406 S. Mildred Ave., King City, CA 93930
(408) 385-5434

- Near-coast tent and RV camping
- Hike & Bike camping
- Group camping

In Monterey County north of San Simeon on the way up to Big Sur, Los Padres National Forest hugs the sheer, spectacular coastline for many long, isolated miles. Within its wrinkled, rocky bulk there are several campgrounds, most of which are tucked into the mountains many winding miles from the coast. However, there are two that are but a quick, convenient turn off Highway 1: Plaskett Creek and Kirk Creek.

Plaskett Creek

Plaskett Creek sits at the base of the mountains off Highway 1 (about 35 miles south of Big Sur) in a flat, grassy enclave pleasantly punctuated by shady stands of mature pines and cypress trees. The impression is clean, green, spacious and welcoming. An asphalt path circles through the campground, built to accommodate both tents and RVs up to 30 feet. Each of the 45 sites has its own parking pad, table, fire ring and grill. Fresh water is nearby, but there are no hookups or dump station.

There are three *group campsites* at the southern end of the campground. Each can accommodate 50 persons for tent camping. Site 1 has parking space for seven vehicles; site 2 for 10 vehicles, site 3 for eight. Each site has tables, stoves, fire pits, and drinking water.

The entrance to Sand Dollar Beach is just across the highway from the campground. From its parking lot, a half-mile trail leads to a crescent-shaped beach, one of the widest expanses of sand along the Big Sur Coast. Jade Cove, a popular spot for beachcombers and rockhounds, is just two miles south. The nearest services are five miles north at the Pacific Valley store.

RESTROOMS: Modern flush toilets, sinks and mirrors. No showers or AC outlets.

RESERVATIONS: All except the group camps are first come, first served. Campers are advised to arrive by late Friday morning for spaces during the summer weekends, when the campground normally fills to capacity. Reservations for group camps may be made up to 360 days in advance by calling the National Forest Reservation Center from 9 a.m. to 9 p.m. (Eastern time) seven days a week at 800-280-2267.

CHECK IN/OUT: 2 p.m.

FEES: *Family campground* (max. 8 persons, 2 tents) -$15/day peak season (April 1-Sept. 30); $10/day non-peak. *Hike & Bike* - $3/day per person in peak season; $2/day non-peak. *Group camps* - $50/day.

DOGS: No extra charge. Must be leashed at all times and are permitted on trails.

MAX. STAY: 14 days.

SECURITY: Park rangers on patrol and resident camp host.

HOW TO GET THERE: From San Simeon, follow Highway 1 north for about 30 miles; watch for the Los Padres National Forest marker and turn right.

Kirk Creek

Kirk Creek is five miles north of the Plaskett Creek Campground. Its 33 campsites are spread along an open bluff about 100 feet above the ocean. Tents and RVs up to 40 feet are welcome.

An asphalt road meanders past individual campsites that have been cut into the tall, feathery, pale green pampas grass and dense coastal scrub that predominates. Each site has its own parking spur, table, fire pit and grill. Site #23 is reserved for Hike & Bike campers. There's a wild, unkempt look and feel about Kirk's Creek, probably because the vegetation is so high, thick and matted. By the same token, you'll find it ensures a high degree of privacy, your fellow campers all but hidden from sight.

Several steep trails lead to the beach below the bluff. It's sandy and popular among surfers. Hang gliders enjoy taking off from the Plaskett Ridge across the road (a free National Forest permit is required).

RESTROOMS: Modern flush toilets, sinks and mirrors. No electricity or showers.

RESERVATIONS: First-come, first-served basis all year long. The campground is frequently filled during the summer months, especially on weekends. Campers are advised to arrive by late Friday morning for spaces during the summer weekends.

CHECK IN/OUT: 2 p.m.

FEES: *Family campground* (max. 8 persons, 2 tents) -$15/day peak season (April 1-Sept. 30); $10/day off-peak. *Hike & Bike* - $3/day per person in peak season; $2/day non-peak. No group camping at Kirk Creek.

DOGS: No extra charge. Must be leashed at all times and are permitted on trails.

MAX. STAY: 14 days.

SECURITY: Park rangers on patrol and resident camp host.

HOW TO GET THERE: From San Simeon, follow Highway 1 north for about 35 miles; watch for the Los Padres National Forest marker and turn left.

LIME KILN STATE PARK
c/o Pfeiffer Big Sur State Park
Big Sur, CA 93920
(408) 667-2315

• Coastal canyon tent & RV camping in the redwoods

When this 707-acre parcel of Big Sur coast was put up for sale by the S. H. Cowell Foundation in 1994, the state jumped at the chance to acquire it. A Congressional Fact Sheet tells why:

Big Sur coastline

"Set between the Pacific Ocean and the Ventana Wilderness, part of the greater Los Padres National Forest, this remarkable property embodies the breathtaking beauty for which Big Sur is famous. Its ¾-mile coastline includes a rare sandy beach and sheer rocky cliffs exposed to the powerful Pacific surf. Directly above the property, Cone Peak rises 5,155 feet from the ocean in just 3.3 miles, making this the steepest coastal gradient in the continental United States. On exposed ridgetops, suspended over crashing waves, one can see the curve of the earth as the Pacific spreads to the south and west... In the deep, redwood-filled canyon, only a short hike from the coast, Limekiln Creek's fast-moving waters cascade over a spectacular 100-foot waterfall. For the adventurous explorer, a rare stand of old-growth redwood trees grows near the steep northern boundary of the property. Currently, annual visitation in Big Sur overwhelms accessible public open space. The Ventana Wilderness offers the area's most extensive recreational opportunities but suffers from a lack of public access through an almost unbroken wall of private landholdings bordering State Route 1. The Limekiln Canyon property could provide access to the wilderness area as well as highly accessible recreational opportunities within its own borders."

Up until August of 1994, in fact, Limekiln Canyon was site of a popular privately-operated campground from which campers could fish, hike and explore the rugged landscape. Trails meander throughout the area, including the lime kiln site from which this canyon derives its name. Still standing are three large ovens once used to bake the moisture from locally mined limestone. After drying, the white powder was placed in barrels and shipped to companies that used it to make cement.

Following an extensive renovation project, the state expected to reopen the campground in the spring of 1995.

CAMPGROUND: There are 41 campsites for tents or RVs up to 28 feet situated alongside both sides of Limekiln Creek beneath a mature forest of giant redwoods. Each site has its own parking pad, table and fire ring. None of the sites have hookups, but water is nearby. There is an existing dump station, but authorities were uncertain of its condition and useability. The campground is less than a quarter-mile from the beach, which provides good access for kayaking and other such activities. The water is always cold and rough, so swimming is not recommended. There are no lifeguards.

RESTROOMS: Flush toilets, sinks and coin-operated showers. These are the same restrooms that served the private campground brought up to current state standards.

RESERVATIONS: Contact park office at (408) 667-2315. Authorities were not sure if Limekiln would be a first-come, first-served campground, or be on the MISTIX reservation system.

CHECK IN/OUT: Tentative – 2 p.m. in; noon out.

FEES: To be determined.

DOGS: $1/day; permitted on beach, but not on trails.

MAX. STAY: Tentative – seven days (June-Sept.); 15 days remainder of the year.

SECURITY: Park rangers.

HOW TO GET THERE: From Carmel, drive south on Highway 1 for 56 miles. It's two miles south of Lucia at Rockland Landing.

JULIA PFEIFFER BURNS STATE PARK
c/o Pfeiffer Big Sur State Park, Big Sur, CA 93920
(408) 667-2315

• Coastal bluff tent camping

At 3,580-acres, Julia Pfeiffer Burns State Park is the second largest of three state parks located within 17 miles of each other on the Big Sur coast. In terms of visitors and campers, however, it's last. Visitor attendance figures from the State Department of Parks &

Recreation report it received just 85,049 visitors in the last 12-month period; only 1,049 of them were campers.

This is not to suggest the scenery is any less spectacular than that found at the other two parks. In fact, it's quite similar, from the precipitous peaks that rise up to 3,000 feet above the coastline, to the groves of giant redwoods growing in the steep canyons. In fact, Julia Pfeiffer Burns State Park offers something unique – a 1,680-acre underwater park. Here, experienced scuba divers can explore a surrealistic world of submerged canyons, caves, tunnels and natural bridges (permits required).

The rugged cliffs of the Big Sur coastline

The real reason Julia Pfeiffer Burns receives so few visitors is apparently because it hasn't been bulldozed, paved, plumbed and wired to the extent some other parks have. In other words, the park is relatively primitive. Travelers seem to know that just 11 miles further north, there are flush toilets and other user-friendly conveniences.

CAMPGROUND: One good example of JPB's rather limited facilities is the campground. There are two sites here, both requiring a quarter-mile hike from the nearest parking lot. Saddle Rock and South Garden are west of the Pacific Coast Highway in a forest of cypress trees with a panoramic view of the ocean and high, rugged coastline. Expect lots of wind, frequent fog and chilly temperatures even during summer. Each site accommodates a maximum of eight campers and is furnished with a storage cabinet and fire pit. Water is available from the restrooms at the parking lot.

RESTROOMS: Pit toilets near the campsites.

FEES: $16/day peak season (April 5-Oct. 25); $14/day off-peak.

DOGS: Prohibited.

MAX. STAY: Seven days.

CHECK IN/OUT: 2 p.m. in; noon out. Sites may be occupied early if vacant.

SECURITY: Resident park ranger.

HOW TO GET THERE: Julia Pfeiffer Burns State Park is off Pacific Coast Highway (1), 11 miles south of its better-known neighbor, Pfeiffer Big Sur State Park (see below), which is where campers must register. There, you will receive directions to the sites along with a parking permit that allows you to keep your vehicle overnight in the day-use parking at Julia Pfeiffer Burns.

PFEIFFER BIG SUR STATE PARK
Big Sur, California 93920
(408) 667-2315

- Mountainside tent & RV camping
- Bicycle camping (not for hikers)
- Group camping

At 810 acres, Pfeiffer Big Sur State Park doesn't sound very large. But it feels like it, starting with the ride along the precipitous Pacific Coast Highway (Highway 1). Whether you're coming from San Francisco 150 miles to the north, or Los Angeles 300 miles south, it's a relatively slow, windy route, much of it along a spectacular two-lane roadway that dips, curves and climbs along one of the most dramatic unions of earth and sea on this planet.

Then there are the wrinkled slopes and formidable peaks and valleys of the Santa Lucia Mountains into which the park is set, and the redwood forests that can rise over 200 feet, dwarfing anything smaller than the mountains in which they grow. Add to the park the vast 167,323-acre Ventana Wilderness that all but surrounds it and the word "big" seems inadequate.

The most amazing thing about all this is the accessibility and convenience available within this wilderness once you're here. There's a 61-room lodge right next door to a convenience store just inside the park entrance. And there are dozens of additional cabins, cottages, motel rooms, grocery stores

The Santa Lucia Mountains loom over tiny campers at Pfeiffer Big Sur

and restaurants hugging the highway just a mile or so north. It's particularly interesting to learn the area has had electricity only since the 50s, and it still doesn't extend for the entire length of the coast or far inland.

For those willing to rough it, though, there are plenty of opportunities, from swimming and fishing in the Big Sur River which flows through the park, to hiking along more than 240 miles of trails in the park and beyond.

Although Pfeiffer Big Sur does not actually touch the coast, a two-mile ride down a narrow winding road will lead you to Pfeiffer Beach, a dramatic stretch of sea, sand and cliffs.

CAMPGROUND: Most of the park's 218 campsites here are situated along the Big Sur River, beneath a variable forest of redwoods, pines, sycamores, oaks and more. Shade is the rule. Ground cover is typically limited to fallen leaves, needles and dirt. The sites can accommodate both tents and RVs up to 27 feet. Each is furnished with picnic table, fire ring, barbecue grill and locker. Water spigots are placed intermittently.

There are also two adjacent group camps, each of which can accommodate up to 35 tent campers. These sites require a walk of 150 yards.

The bike camp is reserved solely for bicyclists. Hikers are directed to Julia Pfeiffer Burns State Park (11 miles south on Highway 1).

RESTROOMS: Some of the restrooms are more modern than others, but all have flush toilets, sinks, mirrors and AC outlets. The newer units also include coin-operated showers.

RESERVATIONS: Family campsites may be reserved any time of year up to eight weeks in advance; group camps may be reserved from the end of May through September 30 through MISTIX, 1-800-444-PARK. Bike camp is first come, first served.

CHECK IN/OUT: Noon.

FEES: $16/day in peak season (Mar. 25-Oct. 30); $14 day non-peak. *Group camp* - $52/day. *Bike camp* - $3/day per person (max. two days).

DOGS: $1/day; prohibited from trails.

MAX. STAY: Seven days (June-September); 15 days remainder of the year.

SECURITY: Park rangers and resident camp host.

HOW TO GET THERE: Follow the Pacific Coast Highway (Highway 1) to Big Sur. Daily bus service from Monterey and Carmel to Pfeiffer Big Sur is available from the end of May through the beginning of October. Each bus is wheelchair-accessible and can carry two bicycles. Latest fares are $2.50 per person one way; $1 for seniors, disabled and youths. For exact schedules and pick up points, call Monterey-Salinas Transit at 408-899-2555.

ANDREW MOLERA STATE PARK
c/o Pfeiffer Big Sur State Park #1, Big Sur, CA 93920
(408) 667-2315

• Riverside/meadow tent camping

This park is overshadowed by the better-known Pfeiffer Big Sur State Park less than five miles south of here and, thus, it's often overlooked. The former annually attracts over 460,000 visitors –

325,000 campers among them – while the latter draws slightly fewer than 100,000 visitors and barely 19,000 campers. These figures are all the more interesting when you discover that Pfeiffer Big Sur is relatively small, only 810 acres compared to Molera's whopping 4,800 acres.

Like the smaller park, Andrew Molera is graced with high mountain ridges, flowered meadows and evergreen forests of towering redwoods, ponderosa pines, oaks and madrones. Only Molera has a lot more of each. Molera also shares the same river, the Big Sur, as it meanders its way down to the coast. What's more, Molera has its own on-site stables for those who want to explore by horseback. And it has its own beach, too – 2½ miles of it – while Pfeiffer Big Sur doesn't have an inch. So, why one gets so much more attention than the other is sometimes hard to figure.

The fact of the matter is that Andrew Molera is mostly undeveloped. There's a small gravel parking lot off to the side of the Pacific Coast Highway and, in all candor, it doesn't look like much. To see anything of interest, visitors actually have to get out of their vehicles and walk, but they needn't walk far. The trail to the ocean is flat and barely a mile. There are more challenging routes, of course, including the East Molera Trail that leads 1,600 feet up into the mountains overlooking the park.

Those who would rather let a horse do the walking may consider one of several two-hour rides scheduled throughout the day. Prices range from $40 to $50 per person (reservations: 1-800-303-8664).

From the shoreline, visitors can often spot California gray whales as they migrate south from December through February. This is also a sea otter refuge area and home to harbor seals and sea lions. Fishing is permitted here, but camping is not. At high tide, the ocean reaches all the way to the base of the bluffs that rise above the sand.

CAMPGROUND: The quarter-mile hike to the campground is an easy one on a wide gravel trail that leads from the parking lot along the banks of the Big Sur, a tame, shallow river – more like a stream – until the winter rains begin. That's when crews come out and remove the bridges before the river washes them away.

The campground itself is situated in an open, grassy clearing punctuated by sycamores and skirted by an assortment of shrubs such as coffee berry, bush lupine, poison hemlock, manzanita and coyote bush.

Upwards of 280 campers have been known to set stakes here and it appears there's always room for one more. Except for an occasional summertime weekend and holidays, though, the meadow is rarely crowded.

The campground is furnished with tables, fire rings and running water. Campers are permitted to collect up to 50 pounds of driftwood from the beach, but dead and downed twigs, branches and logs in other areas of the park are protected. The camp host also sells wood for fires, which are permitted only in the campground fire rings.

RESTROOMS: Chemical toilets.

RESERVATIONS: First come, first served.

CHECK IN/OUT: No set times.

FEES: $3/day per person.

DOGS: $1/day. Must be leashed. Permitted on trails.

MAX. STAY: 3 days.

SECURITY: Park rangers and resident camp host.

HOW TO GET THERE: From Pfeiffer Big Sur State Park, drive north on Highway 1 about 5 miles. Entrance is on the left side of the highway. Daily bus service from Monterey and Carmel to Andrew Molera State Park is available from the end of May through the beginning of October. Each bus is wheelchair-accessible and can carry two bicycles. Latest fares are $2.50 per person one way; $1 for seniors, disabled and youths. For exact schedules and pick up points, call Monterey-Salinas Transit, 408-899-2555.

Santa Cruz County

SUNSET STATE BEACH

201 Sunset Beach Road, Watsonville, CA 95076
(408) 724-1266

- Near-beach tent & RV camping
- Hike & Bike camping
- Group camping
- En Route camping

If you like Brussels sprouts, you'll be in heaven at Sunset State Beach, which is surrounded by acres and acres of them. But even if you don't, you're sure to like this park. It features a big, wide sandy beach some three miles long and grand mounds of sand reaching as high as 50 feet. A large chunk of this 324-acre park sits above the beach and beyond the dunes on a grassy bluff that's peppered with fully matured Monterey pines.

The park's only significant drawback is its propensity for fog, especially in the summer months. But hey, it's great for Brussels sprouts!

Kayak enthusiasts take to the high seas

The beach is popular with all age groups, especially in July and August when the water is at its warmest (low 60s) and lifeguards are on duty. However, signs warn of recurring rip currents, so caution is advised, as always.

A glider port for remote-controlled models is situated on a bluff above the beach and regularly draws vicarious pilots who enjoy testing their skill in the steady ocean breezes.

Although clam digging was a popular activity in the 50s and 60s, there was so much of it the clam population was decimated. Today, you'll have a difficult time finding clams of legal size.

There isn't really much of an opportunity for hiking here except for a couple of trails that lead down from the campgrounds and through the dunes to the beach. Most of the dune area, incidentally, has been fenced off to help the restoration of plant life, which is crucial to its survival.

CAMPGROUNDS: The campground is located on the bluff behind the dunes and above the beach. Despite its 50-ft. elevation, there are very few campsites with any chance of an ocean view. But a little effort and a short walk can solve that problem.

The campground is divided into three sections: Dunes Camp, Pine Hollow and South Camp. All are about the same size and share the same amenities: spaces with individual parking pads, tables, fire rings and storage lockers. The grounds are generally grassy, with generous shade from big pines. Campsites, a total of 90, can accommodate either tents or RVs up to 31 feet. Water is available, but there are no hookups nor dump station facilities.

The group camp is near the campfire center and is limited to 50 people and 10 vehicles (maximum 18 feet). The Hike & Bike campsite is just round the corner.

RESTROOMS: These feature the latest conveniences, including flush toilets, sinks, mirrors and AC outlets. The newer units also have coin-operated showers. Group camp facilities feature some chemical toilets.

RESERVATIONS: Reservations for family campsites are accepted up to eight weeks in advance from Mar. 18-Oct. 31 by calling MISTIX, 1-800-444-PARK. The remainder of the year, campsites are first come, first served. Group camp reservations are available all year long through MISTIX.

FEES: *Family campers* (max. 8 persons) and *En Route campers:* $16/day in peak season (April 1-Oct. 31); $14/day off-peak. *Group camp* is $75/day. *Hike & Bike*, $3/day per person.

DOGS: $1/day; not permitted on beach.

MAX. STAY: Seven days (June-September); 15 days remainder of the year. Hike & Bike limited to two days. En Route campers: one day.

SECURITY: Park rangers and resident camp host.

HOW TO GET THERE: The park is about 4½ miles from Highway 1. From Monterey, drive north on Highway 1; exit at Riverside Drive (in Watsonville) and turn left onto Beach Road; turn right at San Andrea Road and left at Sunset Beach Road.

MANRESA STATE BEACH
205 Manresa Beach Road, La Selva Beach, CA 95076
(408) 761-1795

• Near-beach tent camping

This park is built on a bluff perhaps 75 feet up from a long, wide, sandy beach not unlike Sunset State Beach less than four miles south. It is a relatively new campground. Small pine and cypress trees have been planted and will one day mature and fill out. Right now, though, campsites are situated amid the rather sparse and humble coastal scrub – patches of wild grass with low-growing shrubs like sage and coyote brush.

The beach is beautiful but cold, the water rarely warming up beyond 58°, so bring your wetsuits. It's particularly popular among surfers. Lifeguards are on duty throughout the summer.

Adjacent to the park is a stylish community of new homes and condominiums as well as fields where such crops as strawberries, celery, cauliflower, broccoli and Brussels sprouts are grown.

A KOA campground is just a mile away; its campstore serves as a convenient source of food and camping items should an unanticipated need arise. Nearby Watsonville offers a big selection of major grocery stores, restaurants and other services.

CAMPGROUNDS: There are 64 walk-in tentsites at Manresa. To reach them, campers drive down to a small lot, have a maximum of 20 minutes to unload their gear, then drive uphill 150-200 yards to the overnight parking area. The resident camp host lives at the edge of the lot with a clear view of the parking lot as well as the campground.

Access to the beach is by way of either a paved 55-ft. trail (convenient for wheelchairs) or a stairway near the day-use parking lot.

Each site includes a table, fire ring and storage locker. Water spigots are nearby.

RESTROOMS: These are of the latest state park design, featuring private toilet rooms and coin-operated showers.

RESERVATIONS: Up to eight weeks in advance through MISTIX, 1-800-444-PARK.

FEES: $16/day from Easter through Labor Day; $14/day all other times. **Note:** This park is typically closed to camping from October 31 through March 1, with most campers directed to nearby Sunset State Beach.

DOGS: $1/day; permitted on beach with maximum six-foot leash.

MAX. STAY: Seven days (June-September); 15 days remainder of the year.

SECURITY: Park rangers and resident camp host.

HOW TO GET THERE: Manresa is less than four miles from Sunset State Beach and about seven miles from Highway 1. From Highway 1, exit at Riverside Drive; turn left on Beach Road; turn right onto San Andreas Road; turn left at Sand Dollar Road for about four blocks to the park entrance.

SEACLIFF STATE BEACH
101 Madeline Drive
Aptos, CA 95003
(408) 688-3222 or 688-3241

- RV camping
- En Route camping

The campground at Seacliff State Beach is always filled, regardless of the season or weather. It can count on more than 44,000 campers per year.

One reason may be the beach, a broad, two-mile stretch of sand along one of the safest, gentlest coastlines in the area. The water temperature may never get much above 60°, but in the water they go nonetheless – kids, parents, grandparents, too.

Another reason may be the *Palo Alto*, a cement-hulled relic originally built to serve as a supply ship in World War I. Before it could, however, the war ended. The *Palo Alto* was subsequently brought to Seacliff Beach, purposely scuttled at its current location, and converted into an amusement complete with 54-foot heated swimming pool, dance floor and carnival-type concessions. That was in 1930, and even then it attracted visitors from miles around. After two years, though, the company operating the attraction went broke, and the *Palo Alto* ultimately disintegrated into the rather exotic fishing platform it is today.

Yet a third reason may be the fossils that are founded embedded in the dramatic three-million-year-old cliffs lining the beach. Attendants at the on-beach Visitor Center can tell you all about it.

Then again, the main reason it's always filled may be simply because there are so few spaces to fill – just 26.

CAMPGROUND: All 26 spaces are set at the edge of the sand on a paved lot in the shadow of the sheer, 50-foot cliffs paralleling the beach. Spaces are for self-contained vehicles only and feature complete hookups. Watch out for flying golf balls. People residing in the homes atop the bluff have been known to practice their drives from the backyards overlooking the ocean.

RESTROOMS: There are three restrooms, all of which have flush toilets, sinks and mirrors. Only one offers coin-operated showers.

FEES: $25/day peak season (April 1-Oct. 31); $23/day off-peak. *En Route campers* pay the same fees for spaces without hookups.

DOGS: $1/day; not permitted on beach.

MAX. STAY: Seven days regardless of the time of year.

RESERVATIONS: Up to eight weeks in advance through MISTIX, 1-800-444-PARK.

CHECK IN/ OUT: Noon.

SECURITY: Park rangers and resident camp host.

HOW TO GET THERE: From Monterey, drive north on Highway 1; exit at State Park Drive and turn left to the park entrance.

NEW BRIGHTON STATE BEACH

1500 Park Ave. Hwy 1, Capitola, CA 96010
(408) 475-4850

- Near-beach tent & RV camping
- Hike & Bike camping
- En Route camping

New Brighton State Beach is a small park, just 94 acres. Its beach, like Seacliff State Beach adjoining it on the south, is sandy and wide with user-friendly surf (no lifeguards). A 40-foot cliff rises behind it, atop which the park's 114-site campground is spread out. A few easy hiking trails lead through forested areas as well as to the beach.

Groceries, restaurants, gasoline stations and other services are readily available in Capitola, just beyond the park.

CAMPGROUND: The campground meanders in a series of oblong loops on a bluff thickly covered with towering, deep green pines and oaks. Fallen leaves and needles create a welcome cushion on the ground.

Campsites are suitable for either tents or RVs up to 34 feet and include tables and fire rings. Water spigots are nearby. There's also an on-site dump station, but no individual hookups for sewer, water or electricity.

A railroad flanks one end of the park, but it's far enough from most campsites to be of minimal concern.

RESTROOMS: Include flush toilets, mirrors, sinks, AC outlets and coin-operated showers.

RESERVATIONS: From April 1 through Sept. 30, reservations may be made up to eight weeks in advance through MISTIX, 1-800-444-PARK. The rest of the year is first come, first served.

CHECK IN/OUT: 2 p.m. in; noon out.

FEES: *Family and En Route camping* - $16/day in peak season (April 1-Oct. 31); $14/day off-peak. *Hike & Bike camping* - $3/day per person.

DOGS: $1/day; not allowed on beach.

MAX. STAY: Seven days (June-Sept.); 15 days remainder of the year. En Route and Hike & Bike camping limited to one day.

SECURITY: Park rangers and resident camp host.

HOW TO GET THERE: Coming from Monterey, drive north on Highway 1; exit at Park Blvd. (in Capitola) and turn left after four blocks.

HENRY COWELL REDWOODS STATE PARK
101 N. Big Trees Park Road, Felton, CA 95018
(408) 438-2396

- Inland forest tent & RV camping
- Bike camping

Henry Cowell is a densely-wooded park of redwoods, pines, oaks and madrones reaching high overhead, their interwoven limbs and boughs creating a tweed-like canopy of shade while a verdant substory of ferns, shrubs and grasses luxuriates below. More than 75,000 people take to its 113 campsites each year. There's even a small campground exclusively for bicyclists.

Located 500 feet above sea level and six miles from the beaches in Santa Cruz, the park features a nature center, gift shop and 17 miles of horse and hiking trails. Except for the easy loop trail through the redwood grove, where giants reach up to 285 feet and 10 to 12 feet in diameter, most trails require steep uphill climbs.

When winter rains raise the water level of the San Lorenzo River, the park also becomes a mecca to anglers eager to hook their limit of steelhead trout and salmon.

The rain makes for rather boggy camping, however, which is no doubt the reason the campground is usually closed from the end of October to mid-February. Check with park for exact dates.

CAMPGROUND: The sites accommodate either tents or RVs up to 35 feet and include individual parking pads, tables and fire rings. There are no hookups, but water spigots are placed intermittently throughout the grounds. There was a dump station until budget cuts forced officials to eliminate the service.

RESTROOMS: Modern flush toilets, sinks, mirrors and coin-operated showers.

RESERVATIONS: For camping dates between March 15 and Oct. 31, reservations can be made up to eight weeks in advance through MISTIX, 1-800-444-PARK. The campground is first come, first served the rest of the time.

CHECK IN/OUT: Noon

FEES: $16/day from March 15-Oct. 31; $14/day the rest of the season. *Bicycle camping* - $3/day per person. **Note:** The park is closed to camping from the end of October to mid-February.

DOGS: $1/day; not permitted on most trails.

MAX. STAY: Seven days. Bicyclists – 2-day limit.

SECURITY: Park rangers and resident camp host.

HOW TO GET THERE: From San Francisco, drive south on Highway 1; exit at Ocean Blvd. and turn left; Ocean becomes Graham Hill Road. The park is about five miles from Highway 1.

San Mateo County

BUTANO STATE PARK
1500 Cloverdale Road, Pescadero, CA 94060
(415) 879-0173

• Deep forest tent & RV camping

This is a very green place in the Santa Cruz Mountains. It is set in a canyon about 200 feet above sea level with ridges on either side climbing up to 1,700 feet. In addition to being very green, it's very shady, thick with redwoods, moss-trimmed Douglas firs, oaks and madrones. If you want to take pictures, use fast film or plan on long exposures.

The ground is cushioned with the rich, nutritive slough of plants, animals and insects that have been living, breeding and dying here for thousands of years. Out of it all springs a profusion of plant life, from gorgeous ferns to purple calypso orchids, one of Butano's star attractions. The dark, frequently damp environment also gives rise to bright orange chanterelles, the thick-fluted mushroom coveted by gourmets. Be warned: It also hosts stinging nettle and poison oak in abundance.

Through this copious compost crawl such peculiar creatures as the Banana slug, a bright yellow fellow up to six inches in length that helps grind down forest litter into spongy topsoil; the California newt, a large brown salamander with bright orange belly; and the Pacific giant salamander, which not only barks, but bites if threatened.

Towering redwoods at Butano

An estimated 20 miles of hiking trails and 15 miles of fire roads wind through the 3,800-acre park, leading from the coastal grassland at the park entrance to the chaparral-covered ridges enclosing the canyon.

Minimize the risk of tick bites by staying on the trails, and be forewarned about yellowjackets, pesty wasps that can detect open softdrinks and food items from great distances and will sting if provoked.

CAMPGROUND: There are 39 developed campsites. Twenty-one of them are drive-in sites capable of accommodating either tents or RVs up to 27 feet. These have their own parking pads as well as tables, fire rings and food lockers. There are no hookups, but water spigots are located throughout the campground.

The other 18 are walk-in sites requiring an easy 20-150-yard hike from the parking lot. Like the nearby drive-in sites a little further up the road, they include tables, storage lockers and fire rings. All are heavily shaded beneath giant redwood and fir trees.

RESTROOMS: Drive-in sites have access to modern facilities consisting of flush toilets, sinks, mirrors and AC outlets. However, there are no showers anywhere in the park. The walk-in sites are furnished with pit toilets.

FEES: $14/day in peak season (April 1-Oct. 31); $12/day off-peak. Fees are the same for both drive-in and walk-in campsites. *Hike & Bike* - $7 per site (maximum eight people). Unlike most other parks, Butano does not have an area exclusively reserved for Hike & Bike camping. It simply allows Hike & Bike campers to use any regular camping site if it's available; if filled, park rangers may allow camping in the picnic area.

DOGS: $1/day; not permitted on hiking trails.

MAX. STAY: 15 days year round; seven days for Hike & Bike camping.

RESERVATIONS: For campsites from Memorial Day through Labor Day, you can make reservations up to eight weeks in advance through MISTIX, 1-800-999-PARK. It's first come, first served the rest of the year.

CHECK IN/OUT: Noon.

SECURITY: Park rangers and resident camp host.

HOW TO GET THERE: From San Francisco, drive south on Highway 1; turn left at Gazos Creek Road (about five miles south of Pescadero). The park entrance is 3½ miles from Highway 1; the campground another 1½ miles further.

HALF MOON BAY STATE BEACH

95 Kelly Avenue, Half Moon Bay, CA 94019
(415) 726-8820

- On or near-beach tent and RV camping
- Group camping
- Hike & bike camping
- En Route camping

Francis, Venice, Dunes and Roosevelt – together, these four small beaches form Half Moon Bay State Beach, a strip of sand vaguely reminiscent of a half-moon-shaped crescent about 25 miles south of San Francisco. An ice-plant-covered bluff rises gently behind the beach, the parking lot just beyond that. A 2¼-mile trail paralleling the outer edge of the parking lot lets joggers, hikers and horseback riders run, walk or gallop the whole length of the park. South of Kelly Avenue horses can even take to the beach. Stables are located about 1½ miles north of the park.

The ocean here is cold the year round, rarely (if ever) breaking 60°F. There are also strong rip currents. What's more, there are no lifeguards on duty any time of year.

At the edge of the park is the charming village of Half Moon Bay, where all manner of requirements may be fulfilled, from antiques to video rentals, hardware to fast foods.

CAMPGROUNDS:
There are 55 sites capable of accommodating either tents or RVs up to 36 feet. Fourteen of the sites are exclusively for RVs; two are solely for tents; all the others are either/or.

Setting your stakes atop the bluff at Half Moon Bay

A few of the sites are located on a bluff overlooking the beach. These are surrounded by ice plants and require a short walk of 25 to 50 feet from the parking lot. The others are set on grassy islands situated between rows of asphalt drive-ways. Parking spaces beside each campsite are provided.

None of the sites have hookups, but water spigots are spaced throughout the campgrounds and there is a dump station. Each site also has a table and fire ring with grill top.

Group camping is allowed at the Sweetwood Group Camp, located north of the main campground off of Dunes Beach. This site can accommodate up to 50 people for tent camping only. Facilities include tables, fire rings, chemical toilets and a large grassy field suitable for a variety of activities. Parking is limited to 12 vehicles.

Hike and Bike camping is at the north end of the main camp-ground.

En Route camping is allowed in the Francis Beach day-use parking lot whenever the main camping ground is filled to capacity.

RESTROOMS: Except for the chemical toilets provided at the Sweetwood Group Camp, Half Moon Bay Park features flush toi-lets, sinks, stainless steel mirrors and AC outlets. There's also a large dressing area. However, the only showers are the cold, non-enclosed rinse-off type. Note that these facilities have seen a lot of hard use and they show it.

RESERVATIONS: First come, first served except for group camp-ing, which can be reserved up to eight weeks in advance through MISTIX, 1-800-444-PARK.

CHECK IN/OUT: Noon.

FEES: $14/day peak season (May 1-Oct. 31); $12/day off-peak. *En Route camp* is the same. *Hike & Bike* - $3/day per person. *Group camp* - $75/day.

DOGS: $1/day. Must be leashed at all times. Permitted on beach.

MAX. STAY: Seven days (May 1-Oct. 31); 14 days the rest of the year.

SECURITY: Park rangers and round-the-clock, on-site camp host.

HOW TO GET THERE: From San Francisco, drive south on Highway 1 to Half Moon Bay, exiting at Kelly Avenue; turn right on Kelly to the park entrance, about a half-mile away.

Northern California

San Francisco, Marin, Sonoma, Mendocino,
Humboldt and Del Norte Counties

An Overview

Northern California isn't famous for movie studios or high-voltage theme parks. In the northern part of the state, things are measured on a far grander scale than any man-made attractions. Here, *Fantasyland* is a forest of 2,000-year-old redwoods towering more than 300 feet overhead. *Adventureland* consists of miles of rivers swollen with coho salmon and steelhead trout. The bears, elk and other animals, though they don't sing and dance, are real as can be.

Much of the Northern California shoreline, running north from San Francisco almost 400 miles to the Oregon border, is fashioned on a grand scale, too. Consisting of jagged rock, precipitous cliffs and brutal steel-blue surf, it can be a veritable war zone where wave upon thunderous wave slams against defiant rock in a frantic effort to hammer it into sand. It's a far cry from the balmy, user-friendly surf and sandy, suntanned shores typical of Southern California.

In this country, much of which seems to have been built for giants, the human presence is dwarfed. The towns, often picturesque, with a distinct Victorian flavor, are small, few of them having populations of more than 500. The only skyscrapers are the ones growing leaves.

Population is relatively thin throughout. You'll notice a dramatic difference almost immediately upon leaving the San Francisco area. As soon as you're north of the Golden Gate Bridge, density drops from more than 16,000 people per square mile (in San Francisco), to 446 people per square mile in Marin County. By the time you reach Mendocino County, density is down to a lonesome 22 persons per square mile. Del Norte County (at the very top of the state) is even lonelier at 20.

Highway 1 (Pacific Coast Highway) is the lifeline along much of this coast. It twists and turns with the terrain, a single lane in each

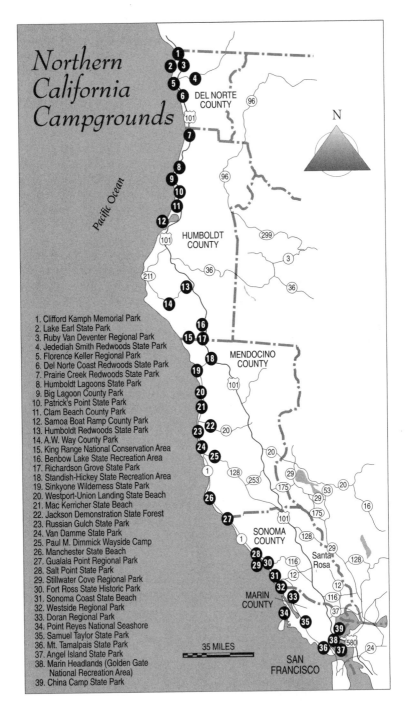

Northern California Campgrounds

N

Pacific Ocean

DEL NORTE COUNTY

HUMBOLDT COUNTY

MENDOCINO COUNTY

SONOMA COUNTY

Santa Rosa

MARIN COUNTY

SAN FRANCISCO

1. Clifford Kamph Memorial Park
2. Lake Earl State Park
3. Ruby Van Deventer Regional Park
4. Jedediah Smith Redwoods State Park
5. Florence Keller Regional Park
6. Del Norte Coast Redwoods State Park
7. Prairie Creek Redwoods State Park
8. Humboldt Lagoons State Park
9. Big Lagoon County Park
10. Patrick's Point State Park
11. Clam Beach County Park
12. Samoa Boat Ramp County Park
13. Humboldt Redwoods State Park
14. A.W. Way County Park
15. King Range National Conservation Area
16. Benbow Lake State Recreation Area
17. Richardson Grove State Park
18. Standish-Hickey State Recreation Area
19. Sinkyone Wilderness State Park
20. Westport-Union Landing State Beach
21. Mac Kerricher State Beach
22. Jackson Demonstration State Forest
23. Russian Gulch State Park
24. Van Damme State Park
25. Paul M. Dimmick Wayside Camp
26. Manchester State Beach
27. Gualala Point Regional Park
28. Salt Point State Park
29. Stillwater Cove Regional Park
30. Fort Ross State Historic Park
31. Sonoma Coast State Beach
32. Westside Regional Park
33. Doran Regional Park
34. Point Reyes National Seashore
35. Samuel Taylor State Park
36. Mt. Tamalpais State Park
37. Angel Island State Park
38. Marin Headlands (Golden Gate National Recreation Area)
39. China Camp State Park

35 MILES

direction, and speeds faster than 30 mph are impractical along much of the way. Halfway up from San Francisco, a large, crumbly range of mountains ultimately forces Highway 1 inland, where it merges into the faster, more efficient Highway 101.

Northern California is sweater country, with year-round highs in the 50s and 60s, the lows just 10° cooler. Have a raincoat ready, too, particularly between November and March. Actual rainfall amounts vary considerably according to where you are on the coast and the local elevation. At the region's southern end north of San Francisco, you can count on about 20 inches a year; at its northern end, rainfall will be three to four times as much. Along the Lost Coast region, where the King Range ascends to more than 4,000 feet, 100 or more inches is normal.

Even when it's not raining, you stand a good chance of cloud cover, mist and fog. This gives the coast a mystic quality but also obscures the sun almost half the time.

Getting There

You have only one practical option if flying in on a commercial airline: San Francisco International Airport. Flying into Crescent City, Eureka or any other airport north of San Francisco can double or triple your fare.

Rail service is available, although it can become a long drawn-out affair and include bus transfers. From San Francisco to Crescent City, for instance, would involve nearly 12 hours of travel, including almost nine hours on a bus. However, the fare is just $61 round trip. Contact Amtrak for schedules: 1-800-USA RAIL.

Attractions

The real magic of northern California is the great outdoors – its rivers, forests and dramatic shoreline. And there are almost 40 state, county, national parks, and national forests along or near the coast where you can bask in it. But the area is not without more human attractions as well. Many of them are not much more than roadside sideshows like the Living Chimney Tree, trees you can drive cars through and Confusion Hill, where the laws of physics seem to have gone awry and water appears to run uphill. Numerous roadside stands also offer shoppers the opportunity to buy redwood burls, carvings and other souvenirs. Have your checkbook or charge card ready!

Other attractions include the Avenue of the Giants, a scenic 33-mile stretch of highway that lets you explore acres of giant old-growth redwoods without leaving your car; the Skunk Train, a relic from the old logging days that now transports tourists instead of logs on scenic rides through redwood country; and the Pacific Lumber Company Museum, where you can lead yourself on a free tour of the world's largest redwood saw mill.

History buffs will also enjoy visiting a wide range of historical sites, including Fort Ross, established by Russian traders in the early 1800s. And, of course, connoisseurs of fine wine won't want to miss the wineries in Napa and Sonoma counties.

San Francisco County

ANGEL ISLAND STATE PARK

P.O. Box 318, Tiburon, CA 94920
(415) 435-1915

• Primitive tent camping

One of the really amazing things about the San Francisco Bay area is that there are still places like Angel Island. Picture a 758-acre hideaway in the midst of San Francisco Bay, virtually uninhabited and undeveloped, while all around sprawls the most densely populated region in the state. To reach the hideaway, simply hop a ferry or your own boat – if you have one. In less than an hour, you'll have escaped the sprawl and feel as though you've traveled back in time 100 years or more.

Timing this little trek is important, however. In spring, winter and fall, you may find yourself the only visitor on the island except for the state park staff. But to visit Angel Island during the summer months, especially on weekends, is to visit with thousands of

A view of Angel Island from the mainland

others trying to escape the sprawl with you. Ayala Cove, where visitors disembark, may very well be teeming with picnickers from the arrival of the first boat to the departure of the last. (The park is open from 8 a.m. to sunset.)

Often you can escape the crowds simply by hiking along the island's 12 miles of roads and trails (watch out for the guided tram tours). They lead to nearly every part of the island including Mt. Livermore, the island's highest point at nearly 800 feet. There, you'll have an unobstructed 360-degree panorama of the entire bay area. Wherever you go, you're sure to enjoy some of the most spectacular views anywhere.

About 10 miles of the roads are also open to bicycles, which you can rent from the Cove Café, the only concession on the island. Rates are $10/hour or $25/day. Of course, you can also bring your own bike on the ferry, space permitting.

The café also sells shirts, hats, film, ice, charcoal, beer, wine, coffee, sandwiches, pizza and other fast food. It operates daily throughout the summer, weekends only in spring and fall, and is closed in winter.

Although most of the island is covered in grass and non-native eucalyptus trees, signs of Angel Island's previous lives continue to endure, including a Civil War camp, immigration station (Ellis Island of the West), military embarkation center (World Wars I and II), Nike Missile base and prisoner of war camp. Remnants include old bunker gun emplacements, troop barracks and immigrant quarters. There's a visitors center and museum with exhibits and photographs of the island's history and environment.

The island has a few accessible beaches, too, although swimming is generally not advised. The water is always cold (56-58°) and subject to strong currents that can race along at 5 to 6 knots per hour.

CAMPGROUND: Angel Island has nine campsites in four areas. Each site can accommodate up to eight campers and includes a barbecue grill, food locker and water spigot. Park rangers caution campers not to bring too much gear. About one in 20 arrives on the island over-equipped, with no easy way to carry their gear to the campsite. Among items essential to campers is charcoal or a camp-stove since fires are not permitted anywhere on the island.

Campers should also verify ferry schedules. Make sure the ferry is operating on the days you plan to arrive and leave. Remember,

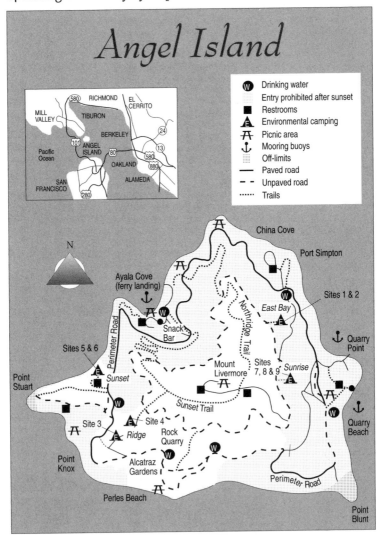

schedules change throughout the year. Sometimes service is provided only on weekends. Weather can affect schedules, too.

Sites 1 and 2 are located two miles from Ayala Cove (where the boats dock). Count on a relatively flat 45-minute walk. Site 1 is in a clearing of pine trees and coast live oak and has a view of East Bay; Site 2 is 50-75 yards beyond #1 and is surrounded by pines with no immediate view. Both are generally protected from the wind. A single pit toilet, located close to site 2, services both sites.

Sites 3 and 4 are less protected from the wind, but they're the most popular campsites because of the outstanding views of San Francisco and Golden Gate Bridge. Site 3 is a 1¼-mile walk from Ayala Cove. It's set in a clearing next to Battery Wallace, an old gun emplacement that kids love to explore. Eucalyptus and cypress trees surround the clearing, which is covered with a thin growth of grass. Site 4 is 100 yards uphill in another clearing surrounded by eucalyptus trees. A single pit toilet, located next to site 3 (100 yards from site 4), services both.

Sites 5 and 6 are less than one mile from Ayala Cove and should take no more than 20 to 25 minutes to reach. These two are a stone's throw from each other in a clearing surrounded by an eclectic mix of pines, oaks, madrones and eucalyptus trees. The water's edge is a short but steep hike down a dirt trail, which can be quite slippery after a rain. There's no real beach and swimming is not recommended, but you can get a good view of Tiburon, a community across the bay. Restrooms are five minutes up the access trail. Unlike those at the other campsites, these feature modern flush toilets, sinks, mirrors, even soap and paper towels. But there are no showers or AC outlets. Expect to share the facilities with trail walkers during the summer months.

Sites 7, 8 and 9 require the longest hike, about two miles from Ayala Cove. All three are located on a cleared step of land; one side of the clearing rises while the other side drops off. Because of the tall, thick eucalyptus trees that surround this area, there are no immediate views. A single pit toilet services all three sites.

FEES: $9/day in peak season (April 1-Oct. 31); $7/day off-peak.

DOGS: Not permitted.

MAX. STAY: Seven consecutive days.

RESERVATIONS: Up to eight weeks in advance through MISTIX, 1-800-444-PARK.

CHECK IN/OUT: Noon.

SECURITY: Resident park rangers.

HOW TO GET THERE: You can reach the island by private boat or one of several public ferries originating from San Francisco, Vallejo and Tiburon. Schedules vary with the season and are influenced by weather. Fares from San Francisco are $9 for adults; juniors (12-18) $8; and children (5-11) $4.50. For information on fares from other points and current schedules, call any of the following.

- Tiburon Ferry (from downtown Tiburon): (415) 435-2131
- San Francisco Ferry (Red & White Fleet, Pier 43-1/2): (415) 546-2896 or (800) 229-2784
- Vallejo Ferry (Blue & Gold Fleet): (707) 64-FERRY

Marin County

GOLDEN GATE NATIONAL RECREATION AREA (MARIN HEADLANDS)
(415) 331-1540

- Near-beach & inland tent sites
- Inland backpack camping
- Inland group camping

With more than 16,000 people per square mile, San Francisco ranks as the most densely populated county in California. But just over the Golden Gate Bridge in as lovely a part of the Bay Area as you will find is a near-pristeen 26,000 acres of rolling hills and undeveloped coastline.

This is the Marin Headlands, part of the Golden Gate National Recreation Area, a 74,000-acre preserve of natural and historical

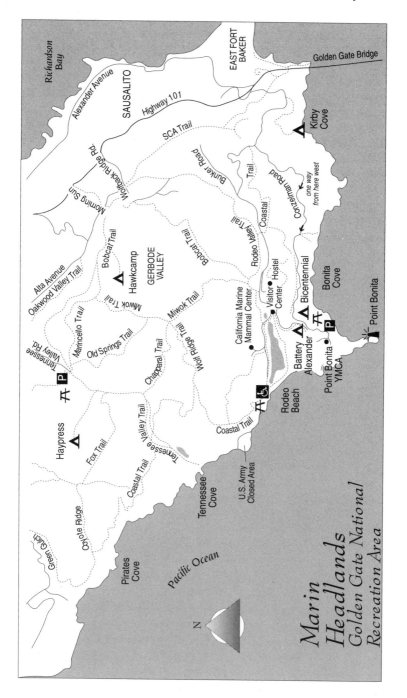

Marin
Headlands
Golden Gate National
Recreation Area

enclaves fringing the coast of San Mateo, San Francisco and Marin Counties. Established in 1972, the area's redwood forests, beaches, grassy hillsides, marshes, rocky shoreline and historic forts, lighthouses and gun batteries draw more than 18 million visitors a year, making it one of the most heavily visited national parks in the country.

That the Marin Headlands is not covered with condominiums and resort hotels is nothing short of a miracle. Except for some quirky turns of events and a few astute local leaders, in fact, there would be a city of more than 25,000 persons here today. Marincello, as it was to be called, was actually on the drawing boards in the 60s when money, interest rates, politics and other factors postponed and eventually dashed the developer's dreams.

Lucky for us, because today the beauty of the area can be enjoyed by all. Instead of a city, there are four *free* campgrounds and one group campsite. Maximum stay in these campgrounds is three nights annually per permit holder.

Kirby Cove Campground

Kirby Cove is the perfect place to view the Golden Gate Bridge

This is undoubtedly the most popular of the campgrounds. It is a mile off Highway 101 and you need a combination to unlock the barricade that prevents casual sightseers from driving down the narrow dirt access road leading to the campground. Park Rangers will reveal that combination, which is regularly changed, when you pick up your permit.

Nestled beneath a shady grove of giant cypress, pine and eucalyptus trees in a secluded valley, Kirby Cove is sure to surprise and delight you. Most surprising is where you will find yourself – at the mouth of San Francisco Bay *west* of the Golden Gate Bridge. Stroll the gravelly beach (its name before it became Kirby Cove) for an uncommon perspective of the city of San Francisco framed by the famous red-orange bridge. It's difficult to believe you're so close, yet so far from it all.

When the fog rolls in, though, as it frequently does, you'll start to believe. Sensors mounted on the bridge activate tuba-like foghorns as soon as the air gets thick enough. Then, every 10 seconds, you'll hear two long blasts followed seconds later by three short French Horn-pitched responses originating from the other side of the bay. Expect this to happen frequently and at any time. Don't expect to sleep through it!

Nevertheless, it's an experience you'll never "fogget." Kids will have a great time exploring the long-abandoned gun battery built into the bluff above the beach. It once helped guard the bay from potential intruders.

CAMPGROUND: There are only four campsites, each site accommodating a *minimum of two* and maximum of 10 persons. They're well shaded and spaced. Each has a picnic table, fire ring and barbecue pit. Parking is in a lot at one end of the campground. Dirt trails lead to the numbered campsites which may be several hundred feet away. Bring your own water; none is available at Kirby Cove.

RESTROOMS: Handicapped-accessible pit toilets (no showers).

RESERVATIONS: May be made up to 90 days in advance by calling (415) 331-1540 between 9:30 a.m. and noon, or by coming to the Marin Headlands Visitor Center between 9:30 a.m. and 4:30 p.m. All camping permits must be picked up in person at the Visitor Center. **Note:** Kirby Cove is closed during the rainy season, from approximately late October to April, because access is difficult when the road gets wet.

CHECK IN/OUT: Noon.

FEES: No charge.

DOGS: Prohibited (except guide dogs).

MAX. STAY: Three nights annually.

SECURITY: Resident camp host.

HOW TO GET THERE: From San Francisco, cross the Golden Gate Bridge. Exit at the Alexander Ave. off-ramp, staying to the left as it leads under Highway 101; follow signs to the Golden Gate National Recreation Area. None of the campgrounds are clearly designated, so ask park rangers for specific instructions when checking in to obtain your permit. Watch for the Kirby Cove access road on your left, shortly after you pass the first viewing site at Battery Spencer. After getting through the barricade, the cove is another eight tenths of a mile downhill.

Bicentennial Campground

This is a small campground situated in a flat clearing that's flanked by a wall of cypress on one side and a brushy slope on the other. A few staggered cypress trees also pop up around the campground just for fun. Hiking trails lead to the rugged Bonita Cove coastline.

Although primitive, Bicentennial is occupied virtually every weekend throughout the year and most weeknights during the summer months. In fact, the occupancy rate from late May to mid-September is reportedly about 100%.

CAMPGROUND: There are just three tent sites, each of which accommodates up to two people with one tent. Parking is in a roadside lot from which you must make a two-minute walk downhill along an easy gravel trail. There's a picnic table but no fire rings or grills. No fires are allowed.

RESTROOMS: One chemical toilet; water nearby.

RESERVATIONS: May be made up to 90 days in advance by calling (415) 331-1540 between 9:30 a.m. and noon, or by coming to the Marin Headlands Visitor Center between 9:30 a.m. and 4:30 p.m. All camping permits must be picked up in person at the Visitor Center.

CHECK IN/OUT: Noon.

FEES: No charge.

PETS: Prohibited (except guide dogs).

MAX. STAY: Three days annually.

SECURITY: Patrolled by park rangers.

HOW TO GET THERE: From San Francisco, cross the Golden Gate Bridge. Exit at the Alexander Ave. off-ramp, staying to the left as it leads under Highway 101; follow signs to the Golden Gate National Recreation Area. Bicentennial is across from the Battery Alexander, the group campground, but it's not marked, so ask the park rangers for specific instructions when checking in to obtain your permit.

Haypress Campground

Haypress is in an old dairy farming area under a shady grove of eucalyptus trees at the end of a dead-end ravine. It's a one-mile hike to Tennessee Beach, which is not recommended for swimming.

CAMPGROUND: There are five sites, each of which can accommodate up to four people with two tents. Each has a picnic table, but that's it. Fires are not allowed. There's no water either, so campers must haul in their own supply.

One site is specifically designed to accommodate wheelchairs. Group camping is allowed, but only from November 1 to March 31.

RESTROOMS: Chemical toilets

RESERVATIONS: This campground is used mostly on weekends; it's seldom crowded or even occupied during weekdays. Reservations are always recommended, however, and may be made up to 90 days in advance by calling (415) 331-1540 between 9:30 a.m. and noon, or by coming to the Marin Headlands Visitor Center between 9:30 a.m. and 4:30 p.m. All camping permits must be picked up in person at the Visitor Center.

CHECK IN/OUT: Noon.

FEES: No charge.

MAX. STAY: Three days annually.

PETS: Prohibited (except guide dogs).

SECURITY: Patrolled by park rangers.

HOW TO GET THERE: From San Francisco, cross the Golden Gate Bridge. Exit at the Stinson Beach-Highway 1 off-ramp and stay to the left as it takes you under Highway 101; turn left at Tennessee Valley Road (about a ½-mile from the highway) and follow that two miles to the Haypress parking lot. The campground is an easy ¾-mile walk from there, so you'll have to backpack in all supplies and equipment, including water.

Hawkcamp Campground

Hawkcamp was once slated to be the center of Marincello, a dream community of about 25,000 people. But the "dream" never materialized and today, instead of 25,000 residents, you'll find only 12.

The most primitive of the area's campgrounds, Hawkcamp is nestled in a small oasis of Monterey pines surrounded by barren, treeless hills.

CAMPGROUND: There are just three sites, each of which can accommodate up to four persons. They're furnished with picnic tables, but no grills or water. Fires are prohibited.

RESTROOMS: Chemical toilet

RESERVATIONS: Like Haypress Campground, Hawkcamp is used mostly on weekends. Reservations are always recommended, however, and may be made up to 90 days in advance by calling (415) 331-1540 between 9:30 a.m. and noon, or by coming to the Marin Headlands Visitor Center between 9:30 a.m. and 4:30 p.m. All camp permits must be picked up in person at the Visitor Center.

CHECK IN/OUT: Noon.

FEES: No charge.

MAX. STAY: Three days annually.

DOGS: Prohibited (except guide dogs).

SECURITY: Patrolled by park rangers.

HOW TO GET THERE: From San Francisco, cross the Golden Gate Bridge. Exit at the Alexander Avenue off-ramp, staying to the left as it leads under Highway 101; follow signs to the Golden Gate National Recreation Area and the Visitor Center. Hawkcamp requires a 3½-mile hike up the Bobcat Trail. All supplies and equipment, including water, must be backpacked in.

Battery Alexander Group Camp

Scout units, school kids on a fieldtrip and other groups will find camping in and around this historic military fortification fun as well as educational. The battery can accommodate 15 to 80 persons and is set on a promontory above San Francisco Bay.

Battery Alexander is one of numerous gun emplacements that were built along this coastal strip over the past 100 years to help protect San Francisco Bay from invasion. Today, they're all obsolete, even the once state-of-the-art Nike missile bases, the last of which closed in 1974.

CAMPGROUND: The campground is in a clearing alongside Bunker Road, across the way from Bicentennial Campground. Outside the thickly walled bunker, you'll find tentsites with fire pits, drinking water and picnic tables; inside the bunker, there are a limited number of bedsprings and electricity (bring your own sleeping gear).

RESTROOMS: Chemical toilets.

RESERVATIONS: May be made up to 90 days in advance by calling (415) 331-1540 between 9:30 a.m. and noon, or by coming to the Marin Headlands Visitor Center between 9:30 a.m. and 4:30 p.m. All camping permits must be picked up in person at the Visitor Center.

CHECK IN/OUT: Noon.

FEES: No charge. However, a $25 refundable key deposit is required for access into Battery Alexander.

DOGS: Prohibited (except guide dogs).

MAX. STAY: Three days annually.

SECURITY: Patrolled by park rangers.

HOW TO GET THERE: From San Francisco, cross the Golden Gate Bridge. Exit at the Alexander Avenue off-ramp, staying to the left as it leads under Highway 101; follow signs to the Golden Gate National Recreation Area. Ask for specific instructions at the Visitors Center.

CHINA CAMP STATE PARK
R.R. No. 1 Box 244, San Rafael, CA 94910
(415) 456-0766

- Off-the-bay tent camping
- Hike & Bike camping
- En Route camping

Old Chinese village at China Camp

Had you visited here back in the 1880s, you would have found a thriving Chinese fishing village on the edge of the bay. You would have seen nets draped along the pier, thousands of shrimp drying in the sun, and a modest cluster of shops and homes to service and shelter the nearly 500 fishermen and their families who emigrated here from Canton, China.

Today, you'll find a 1,640-acre park featuring extensive intertidal, salt marsh, meadow and oak habitats, panoramic views of the north San Francisco Bay, and over 10 miles of trails for hikers, bikers and horseback riders.

Except for low tide when the water is simply too shallow for fishing, you can also find spots where skillful anglers hook sturgeon, perch, bass and flounder. At the site of the historic old village, where a few shaky buildings still stand, visitors use the adjacent cove to boat, swim, windsurf and sunbathe. Protected as it is by a wall of high ridges to the west, China Camp is frequently sunny when the rest of the bay area is engulfed by fog. The park boasts more than 200 fog-free days a year as well as mild ocean-tempered temperatures.

China Camp is only five miles from Highway 101, three miles from downtown San Rafael, and just a 30-minute drive across Golden Gate Bridge from San Francisco.

CAMPGROUND: Backranch Meadows Campground is a quarter-mile from a marshy area that looks out to the north and east across San Pablo Bay. There are 30 campsites divided into upper and lower sections. Sites 1-15 are spaced along the bank of a small gurgling creek. Sites 16-30 are on a rise about 20 feet above. Both sections are an easy walk (30-100 yards) from the parking lot.

All campsites are tucked cozily beneath a forest of moss-covered oak and laurel and feature picnic tables, food lockers and fire rings. Although wood may not be gathered in the park, it can be purchased from the resident camp host. Water spigots are near each site.

RESTROOMS: Brand new tiled restrooms add a fine touch to the camping experience here. Private bathrooms include flush toilets, sinks, mirrors and AC outlets. Showers are coin operated.

RESERVATIONS: Up to eight weeks in advance through MISTIX, 1-800-444-PARK.

CHECK IN/OUT: Noon.

FEES: $14/day in peak season (May 1-Oct. 31); $12/day off-peak. *En Route* campers pay the same. *Bike & Hike* campers - $3/day per person.

DOGS: $1/day; not permitted on trails.

MAX. STAY: Seven days (June-September); 15 days remainder of the year.

SECURITY: Park rangers and resident camp host. The camp host locks the gate every night at around 8 or 9 p.m., and opens it promptly at 8 a.m. During that time, vehicles can neither leave nor enter the campground.

HOW TO GET THERE: From San Francisco, drive north on Highway 101 across the Golden Gate Bridge; exit at Central San Rafael; take a right at the first stop light (2nd Street). This ultimately turns into Pt. San Pedro and takes you straight to the park (about four or five miles from Highway 101). Once you enter the park, the campground is three miles in.

MT. TAMALPAIS STATE PARK
801 Panoramic Highway
Mill Valley, CA 94941
(415) 388-2070

- High country tent sites
- Oceanfront tent sites & cabins
- Group camping
- Horse camping
- En Route camping

Rising well above the rest of Marin County at 2,571 feet is the dark green prominence of Mt. Tamalpais (Tamal-pie-us), nucleus of a 6,300-acre park of deep canyons and high ridges, redwood groves and chaparral-covered slopes, airy grasslands and oak woodlands just 19 miles from San Francisco. More than 1.3 million visitors flock to the park every year to hike, bike and horseback ride its 50-plus miles of trails and fire roads. Nearly 32,000 of those visitors choose to camp within its five designated campgrounds.

Pantoll Campground

Pantoll features 16 family tentsites, each furnished with a table, stove and food locker. They're generous in size and widely spaced on roller coaster terrain beneath the ample shade of Douglas firs and oaks. Phones, drinking water, firewood and restrooms with flush toilets (but no showers) are located near the parking area, about 100 yards from the campground.

Raccoons are evidently a nuisance judging from bulletin board alert. Some of the "world's most poisonous mushrooms" grow among these hills as well.

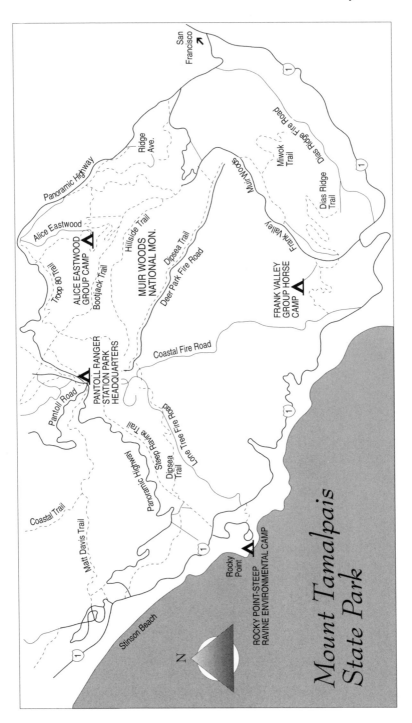

San Francisco

Panoramic Highway

Ridge Ave.

Dias Ridge Fire Road

Miwok Trail

Dias Ridge Trail

Muir Woods

Frank Valley

Alice Eastwood

Hillside Trail

Dipsea Trail

Troop 80 Trail

ALICE EASTWOOD GROUP CAMP

Bootjack Trail

MUIR WOODS NATIONAL MON.

Deer Park Fire Road

FRANK VALLEY GROUP HORSE CAMP

PANTOLL RANGER STATION PARK HEADQUARTERS

Coastal Fire Road

Pantoll Road

Steep Ravine Trail

Panoramic Highway

Dipsea Trail

Love Tree Fire Road

Coastal Trail

Matt Davis Trail

Rocky Point

ROCKY POINT-STEEP RAVINE ENVIRONMENTAL CAMP

Stinson Beach

N

Mount Tamalpais State Park

RESTROOMS: Modern toilets, sinks and mirrors; no showers.

FEES: $14/day in peak season (April 1-Oct. 31); $12/day off-peak. Same fees for *En Route* campers.

RESERVATIONS: Pantoll is a first-come, first-served campground all year long. No reservations are accepted. With only 16 sites, it can be tough to get into during the summer months.

CHECK IN/OUT: 2 p.m. in; noon out.

DOGS: $1/day; not permitted on trails or in undeveloped areas.

MAX. STAY: Seven days.

SECURITY: Rangers on patrol during the day. The park ranger's office is at the entrance to the campground. It is, reportedly, a very safe campground.

HOW TO GET THERE: From San Francisco, take Highway 101 north and exit at the Stinson Beach off-ramp (Highway 1). At Panoramic Highway, turn right and follow that to the Pantoll Campground.

Rocky Point/Steep Ravine Environmental Campground

Picture a tenacious shelf of rock jutting out from the edge of the mainland and into the ocean, refusing to crumble and wash away even after hundreds, more likely thousands, of years of continuous ocean beatings. An equally stubborn groundcover tightly hugs the

earth's surface, giving a green-gray tint to the rock. At its back, steep, rocky slopes loom, rising above a crumbling rocky shoreline, evidence that the ocean has made some progress over the centuries. But equally evident is the certainty the battle won't be over for a long, long time.

You can see how this camp got its name!

This is the campground alternately known as Rocky Point or Steep Ravine, about four miles downhill from the Pantoll Campground. You can tent here or take shelter in one of the 10 rustic cabins, each of which includes a small wood stove, picnic table, sleeping platforms and an outdoor barbecue. The six nearby tentsites include a table, fire pit and food locker. Water is nearby.

RESTROOMS: Pit toilets; no showers.

RESERVATIONS: Up to eight weeks in advance through MISTIX: 1-800-444-PARK. Only one vehicle and a maximum of five people are allowed per cabin or tentsite.

CHECK IN/OUT: 2 p.m. in; noon out.

FEES: *Tentsites* - $9/day in peak season (April 1-Oct. 31); $7/day off-peak. *Cabins* - $30/day all year.

DOGS: Not allowed.

MAX. STAY: Seven days.

SECURITY: A barricade blocks casual visitors from entering the mile-long access road from Highway 1. After you receive confirmation of your reservation from MISTIX, you will have to call the park for the combination, which is changed regularly.

HOW TO GET THERE: From the Pantoll Campground, follow the Panoramic Highway downhill three miles to Highway 1 and turn left. The Rocky Point-Steep Ravine access road will be on your right one mile down the road.

Alice Eastwood Group Camp

There are two adjoining camps designed for organized groups. One can take up to 50 people and 20 vehicles; the other, half as many. Both are located in a very shady canyon of coastal redwoods and are furnished with tables, water, sinks and grills. The larger of the two also has a camp fire center, including large fire pit with seating around it.

RESTROOMS: Pit toilets; no showers.

FEES: *Large camp* - $75/day; *small camp* -$37.50/day.

RESERVATIONS: Up to 180 days in advance through MISTIX: 1-800-444-PARK.

DOGS: $1/day; not allowed outside the developed camping area.

MAX. STAY: Seven days.

SECURITY: Park rangers patrol the area; there's also a gate that barricades the entrance. For the combination, you must call the park after making your reservations.

HOW TO GET THERE: From San Francisco, take Highway 101 north and exit at the Stinson Beach off-ramp (Highway 1). At Panoramic Highway, turn right. Take a left at Alice Eastwood Road and follow it to the group camp.

Frank Valley Group Horse Camp

This one is set in a usually dry, grassy valley dotted with oaks about 1½ miles west of Muir Woods. It accommodates up to 50 people and 12 horses. Tables, fire rings, water, two water troughs and 12 corrals are provided. Horses are restricted to fire roads and specially designated trails.

RESTROOMS: Pit toilets; no showers.

FEES: $16 per horse up to two horses; $2 additional per horse. A refundable $25 cleaning deposit is required for groups of more than eight horses.

RESERVATIONS: Call park at least two weeks in advance, (415) 388-2070.

DOGS: $1/day; not permitted outside the developed camping area.

MAX. STAY: Seven days.

HOW TO GET THERE: Take Highway 1 north towards Muir Beach; turn right onto Frank Valley/Muir Woods Road, which is a mile north of the Muir Beach turnoff. Follow steep, windy road to the campground.

SAMUEL P. TAYLOR STATE PARK
P.O. Box 251, Lagunitas, CA 94938
(415) 488-9897

- Inland tent and RV sites
- Hike & Bike camp
- Group camps
- Horse camp
- En Route camp

This 2,882-acre park of rolling hills is in the center of Marin County, less than an hour's drive from San Francisco and only seven miles from the Point Reyes National Seashore. Its proximity to San Francisco and surrounding communities make Samuel P. Taylor a heavily-used facility, drawing in excess of 157,000 visitors annually in recent years. More than half of those visitors are campers, which only seems natural since this is one of the first areas in the country to offer camping as a recreational outlet. Businessman Sam Taylor, namesake of the park, opened a resort hotel and campground here in 1874 and it soon became one of the area's most popular weekend getaway spots.

Pastimes at the park include wading and fishing in nearby lakes and streams, hiking along numerous trails and horseback riding. You'll also note lots of bicyclists of all ages rolling through the park. A three-mile bike trail makes it easy and safe to explore numerous scenic points.

There are several campgrounds, including one for families, two for groups, one for hikers and bikers, and another for campers on horseback.

CAMPGROUNDS: The main campground includes 60 campsites, 35 of which may be used as either RV or tent sites, the remaining 25 exclusively for tents. None have hookups. All are in a heavily forested grove of coastal redwood. The sites are ample in size and generously separated, each furnished with a table, fire ring, grill, food locker and parking space. Many, if not all, are also completely enclosed by their own wooden fence, much like a small yard.

RESTROOMS: Flush toilets, sinks and mirrors. Some also have coin-operated showers (50¢ for five minutes).

FEES: $14/day in peak season (April 1-Oct. 31); $12/day off-peak. Same rates for *En Route* camping.

DOGS: $1/day; not permitted on trails.

MAX. STAY: Seven days

RESERVATIONS: For camping dates between April 1 and Oct. 31, you can make reservations up to eight weeks in advance via MIS-TIX, 1-800-444-PARK. From November through March, the park shifts to a first-come, first-served basis, with no reservations accepted.

CHECK IN/OUT: 2 p.m. in; noon out.

SECURITY: Park rangers and resident camp host.

Group Camps

There are two group camps in the Madrone Group Area, about 300 yards west of the park entrance on Sir Francis Drake Boulevard. Each is situated beneath the cooling canopies of madrones, oaks and tanoaks – important in this usually warmer side of the park. There are tables and fire rings, flush toilets, but no showers. One campground can accommodate a maximum of 50 persons and 20 vehicles. The smaller group campground can accommodate up to 25 persons and 10 vehicles.

FEES: *Large campground* - $75 per night; *small campground* - $37.50

RESERVATIONS: For group camping reservations between April 1 and Oct. 31, call MISTIX up to eight weeks in advance, 1-800-444-PARK. Contact park directly from November through March.

Hike & Bike Camp

Available on first-come, first-served basis throughout the year. No reservations accepted. Cost: $3/night, two-night maximum stay. This camp is adjacent to the family campground and shares the same restrooms. Tentsites for up to 16 people include tables and fire rings.

Devil's Gulch Horse Camp

This camp is located in the bottom of a fairly steep canyon with a small stream and can accommodate RVs as well as tents. There are picnic tables, fire rings, water and flush toilets, but no showers or hookups.

One side of the canyon is heavily wooded with Douglas fir; the other side is covered with grass. The camp has a corral, hitching racks, watering troughs and a camping area for up to 25 people. More than 18 miles of trails provide access to most park areas and the adjoining Golden Gate National Recreation Area offers even more.

FEES: $16/day for up to two horses, $2 per additional horse up to a total of four horses. More than four horses results in another $16/day charge. Refundable cleaning deposit also required.

RESERVATIONS: Call park directly, (415) 488-9897.

MAXIMUM STAY: Seven days.

HOW TO GET THERE: From San Francisco, head north on Highway 101. Exit at Sir Francis Drake Highway and follow it west for 16 miles to the park entrance.

POINT REYES NATIONAL SEASHORE
Point Reyes Station, CA 94956
(415) 663-1092

- Primitive hilltop, valley and coastal tent camping

Probably... hopefully... you won't notice it, but the Point Reyes peninsula is moving, the whole thing – beaches, sand dunes, hills, valleys and all. The movement usually is very gradual, about two inches a year, but sometimes, as in the 1906 San Francisco earthquake, it leaped forward 20 feet in just 45 seconds. A wooden fence that was once connected still stands – now separated by more than 20 feet – as testimony to the big jolt that was centered in the town of Olema less than a mile from this park's Visitor Center.

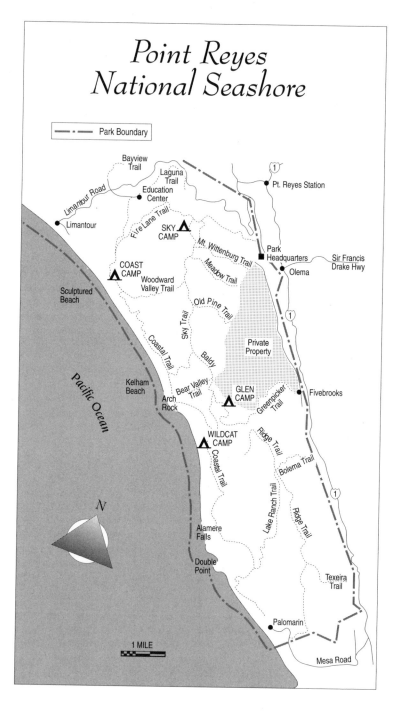

Point Reyes National Seashore

You can hike to that fence and most other areas of this 65,300-acre park along more than 140 miles of horse and hiking trails. About 35 miles of trails are open to bicyclists as well. They will lead you to the forested Inverness Ridge which peaks at about 1,400 feet, to rolling hills and freshwater lakes, to grass-brushed sand dunes, broad sandy beaches and brackish lagoons.

They also lead to four primitive hike-in campgrounds: Sky Camp, Coast Camp, Glen Camp and Wildcat Camp. Each campsite has a picnic table and food storage locker. Toilet facilities are limited to pit toilets, and the availability of drinking water is subject to well conditions. Water from streams and lakes is not potable.

Individual campsites can handle from four to eight campers. All except Glen Camp will accommodate groups of from 10 to 25. **Note:** wood fires and pets, are prohibited.

Although most of the peninsula is pure, splendid wilderness, you needn't be very far from civilized conveniences. There are three stables and a bike rental shop close by, plus numerous restaurants, cafés, markets, bakeries and other services in the towns of Drake's Beach, Inverness, Point Reyes Station, Olema and Marshall.

CAMPGROUNDS

Sky Camp is an easy 2.7-mile walk from the Bear Valley Visitor Center to its 1,025-ft. elevation on the western slope of Mt. Wittenberg. This is an inland campground with 12 sites on a grassy clearing dotted by occasional fir and cypress trees. Campers can opt to cut a mile off their hike by beginning the trek from the Sky Trailhead on Limantour Road.

Coast Camp is an easy two-mile hike down the beach from the Limantour Beach parking lot. It's a bit shorter if you take the Laguna Trail just past the Youth Hostel. You'll find 14 sites set on a bluff of about 200 yards from the beach. There are no trees, just bushy, low-growing coastal scrub. Half of the sites are partially shielded from the offshore winds in a small protected pocket.

Glen Camp requires a 4.6-mile walk along the mostly flat Bear Valley Trail starting at the Visitor Center. It's ensconced in a wooded valley. All 12 sites were recently renovated.

Wildcat Camp takes the most hiking to reach, about 6½ miles from the Visitor Center through a series of meadows and hills. The campground is situated in an open flat area near a small stream. The beach is a short walk away. Four group sites capable of handling 10 to 25 campers and three individual campsites (maximum of four campers each) are set on the bluff a short walk from the beach.

RESERVATIONS: Accepted up to two months in advance by calling the Visitor Center at (415) 663-1092, Mondays through Fridays between 9 a.m. and noon. Reservations are strongly recommended for weekends and holidays.

CHECK IN/OUT: Check in by 10 a.m. on weekends and holidays; 2 p.m. all other days. Campers with reservations who don't arrive by the check-in time **must** call and notify rangers of their delay or risk forfeiting their campsite to those on a first-come, first-served waiting list. If arriving after 5 p.m., campers must call on the day of arrival to make arrangements for picking up their permit.

FEES: None.

DOGS: Not permitted.

MAX. STAY: Four nights per visit; maximum 30 nights per year.

SECURITY: Park rangers on patrol.

HOW TO GET THERE: Campers may either hike or horseback ride to the campsites. Maximum number of horses or pack animals in any campground is eight at Sky, Coast and Wildcat, and four at Glen Camp.

Sonoma County

DORAN REGIONAL PARK
P.O. Box 372, Bodega Bay, CA 94923
(707) 875-3540

- Beachfront tent and RV camp
- Group tent camp

Doran Beach Regional Park is situated along a slim, 1½-mile-long finger of land that juts out from the mainland into the Pacific. It separates Bodega Harbor from Bodega Bay and is less than a quarter-mile wide in most places. A paved road runs through the middle of it, providing easy access to campgrounds and day-use areas on either side.

The shoreline is smooth and friendly, covered with a powdery white sand. Red clusters of ice plants thrive in the dry rolling sand beyond the beach well out of reach of the salty surf.

Along either side of the peninsula, you'll find it is normally gentle and safe for swimming, although the water is cold the year round. Even in the summer, 58°F is about as warm as it gets. But there's plenty to do from shore, including clam digging and fishing. Whales pass by on their annual migration up and down the coast from about January through April. Those venturing into the water can search for the elusive abalone (April-November except for July) or set traps for Dungeness crab from mid-November to June.

The weather is mild all year long, averaging highs of about 67° in summer, and just 10° cooler during winter. Summer is dry but prone to fog, with rain more or less replacing the fog during the fall and winter.

The park's five campgrounds provide 138 individual campsites. Four of them accommodate both tents and RVs; only the Miwok Campground is restricted to tent campers.

Facilities include a dump station and boat launch. The nearest stores, restaurants and other services are in the town of Bodega Bay two miles north.

Miwok

At Miwok, you'll find an asphalt parking lot in the middle of the campground with tentsites all around it. A few of the spaces are shaded by large cypress trees, but the majority are fully exposed, spaced out on the undulating sand just above the beach. Picnic tables and fire pits grace each site and water spigots are nearby. Restroom facilities are very modern and convenient and include flush toilets, mirrors, sinks, electrical outlets, and no-cost, private warm water showers.

Miwok is also the only group camp in the park. It can take groups of 25 to 50 persons.

The Four Others

The remaining campgrounds, Cove, Gull, Jetty and Shell, look as though they were designed for RV campers, although tenters are as welcome as any Winnebago. However, you'll find some sites better suited to tents than others. Each space has its own parking pad, table, and fire pit or barbecue grill. Water is near each site, but there are no hookups. As at the Miwok campground, there is a central restroom at each campground. Except for a couple of chemical toilets at the Shell Campground, restrooms include flush toilets, private hot showers (no charge), sinks, mirrors and AC outlets.

FEES: $14/day, maximum of eight persons, two RVs and one passenger vehicle per campsite.

RESERVATIONS: First-come, first-served basis only throughout the year except for group reservations, which can be made up to one year in advance.

CHECK IN/OUT: 2 p.m. out.

PETS: $1/day. Pets must be leashed at all times; permitted on beach.

MAXIMUM STAY: 10 consecutive days (but no more than 30 days in a calendar year).

SECURITY: Camp host on site 24 hours a day.

HOW TO GET THERE: From the town of Bodega Bay, drive south for several miles on Highway 1 until you reach the entrance to the Doran Regional Park on your right.

WESTSIDE REGIONAL PARK

P.O. Box 372, Bodega Bay, CA 94923
(707) 875-3540

• Bayside tent and RV sites

Westside Regional Park is situated across Bodega Harbor from Doran Regional Park, on a relatively flat peninsula that protrudes from the main coastline in the shape of a large handgun. It forms the north rim of Bodega Harbor.

CAMPGROUND: This park is basically a parking lot. There are 47 sites that can accommodate tents as well as most RVs. The campground has obviously been designed with RVs in mind. Picture five rows, each comprised of eight or nine diagonally-drawn pull-through spaces. Each has a gravelly picnic area furnished with a table and fire ring. Water spigots are placed intermittently throughout the campground. Hookups are nowhere to be seen, but there is an on-site dump station.

One edge of the park is built along the mudflats of Bodega Harbor and features a boat launch. The view is fine but the shoreline is muddy and no swimming is allowed. The opposite side is lined by Bay Flat Road, the only way on and off the peninsula. Aside from the tall cypress trees that border the edge of the road, there's scarcely a tree or shrub in the park. This is popular place among fishing enthusiasts.

RESTROOMS: Top-notch restrooms feature flush toilets, sinks, mirrors, AC outlets and free hot showers.

FEES: $14/day, maximum eight persons, two RVs and one passenger vehicle per site.

RESERVATIONS: First-come, first-served basis throughout the year.

CHECK IN/OUT: 2 p.m. out.

DOGS: $1/day. Must be leashed at all times.

MAX. STAY: 10 consecutive days (but no more than 30 days in a calendar year).

SECURITY: Camp host on site 24 hours a day.

HOW TO GET THERE: From the town of Bodega Bay, drive north on Highway 1 to Bay Flat Road; turn left on Bay Flat Road for a mile until you reach the park entrance on your left side.

SONOMA COAST STATE BEACH

3095 Highway 1, Bodega Bay, CA 94923
(707) 875-3483

- Edge-of-dunes tent & RV camp
- On-the-beach tent & RV camp
- Walk-in riverside tent camp
- Redwood forest tent camp
- Hike & Bike camp

Explore the rocky coast at Sonoma

Sonoma Coast State Beach is much bigger and much more complex than it may sound. Besides its wide, sandy beaches, it includes steep cliffs, forested canyons and 1,000 acres of sand dunes. There are 5,000 acres in all, including 10 miles of coastline. The towns of Bodega Bay and Jenner, on the southern and northern ends of the park respectively, offer restaurants, small grocery stores and numerous other services.

Nearly three million visitors are drawn to Sonoma Coast State Beach each year. They come to fish, watch whales, explore tide pools, comb beaches, picnic, hike and ride horseback. But one thing they aren't encouraged to do is swim. The water here is always cold (49-60°F), the rip currents strong, and the backwash and sleeper waves large and unpredictable. Much of the coast is rocky, too, all of which make for very dangerous swimming conditions. More than 81 people have been swept away from the beaches of Sonoma County since 1950.

More than 92,000 visitors choose to camp here each year. There are four campgrounds, including two walk-ins and two drive-ins.

Bodega Dunes Campground

This campground is right off Highway 1 just a mile north of the town of Bodega Bay. It's a spacious facility with lots of cypress trees for shade and shrubs for privacy. There are 98 generously proportioned sites staggered along both sides of an asphalt road that

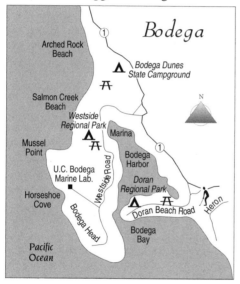

loops through the campground. Campsites can accommodate either tents or RVs up to 31 feet. There's also a section for hikers and bikers. Many of the spaces back up against the edge of the dunes, held in place by tufts of grass, ice plant and other low-growing ground cover. Three trails lead several hundred yards across the dunes to a long, broad stretch of beach.

Each campsite has its own parking pad, table and fire pit. There are occasional water spigots and a dump station, but no hookups.

RESTROOMS: Excellent facilities with flush toilets, sinks, mirrors, AC outlets and coin-operated showers.

FEES: $14/day in peak season (April 1-Nov. 30); $12/day off-peak. $3/day for *Hike & Bike* camping.

RESERVATIONS: Up to eight weeks in advance through MISTIX, 1-800-444-PARK.

CHECK IN/OUT: Noon.

DOGS: $1/day; not permitted on the trails or beach.

MAX. STAY: 10 days (June-Sept.); 30 days remainder of the year. Two days for Hike & Bike camping.

SECURITY: Park rangers and resident camp host.

HOW TO GET THERE: From the town of Bodega Bay, drive north about one mile; turn left at Bodega Dunes sign.

Wright's Beach Campground

High bushes offer protection on Wright's Beach

Like Bodega Dunes five miles to the south, Wright's Beach Campground is just off of Highway 1. Simply follow the turnoff down and around the bluff to a big, wide sandy expanse of shoreline. You'll find 31 campsites at the very edge of the beach, 10 of which have completely unobstructed views of the Pacific; the others are set back a ways and ensconced within walls of thick green shrubs.

The sites can accommodate both tents and RVs up to 27 feet in length. All feature their own rocky, gravelly pads with tables; most also have fire pits. There are water spigots, but no hookups or dump station.

RESTROOMS: Flush toilets, sinks, mirrors and AC outlets, but no showers.

RESERVATIONS: Up to eight weeks in advance through MISTIX, 1-800-444-PARK.

CHECK IN/OUT: Noon.

FEES: $19/day in peak season (April 1-Nov. 30); $17/day off-peak.

DOGS: $1/day; not permitted on beach.

MAX. STAY: 10 days (June-Sept.); 30 days remainder of the year.

SECURITY: Park rangers and resident camp host.

HOW TO GET THERE: From Bodega Bay, drive north about six miles; exit at the Wright's Beach turnoff.

Willow Creek Environmental Campground
(closed from Nov. 1-March 31)

Willow Creek is three miles south of Jenner. You'll actually have to leave your car in a parking lot and hike to reach it. Willow Creek is intended for those who want to get deeper into nature or, at least, farther away from civilization. The required hike, however, is neither long nor strenuous. Depending on the location of your particular campsite, you'll have to walk anywhere from 90 to 770 yards, most of it along a flat dirt trail. Expect a 10- to 15-minute walk at the most.

The campground sits alongside the Russian River, although only one (#10) of the 11 campsites is on the river's edge. Sites 1-4 are on the edge of a meadow backed up against a community of willow trees; site 5 is in an alder grove; sites 6-8 in a grove below the meadow; site 9 in a grassy area at the edge of a grove; and site 11 at the top of a meadow near the woods.

The willows stay leafy until well into October, after which the campground closes for the winter; the rising river and frequent rain simply makes it inaccessible.

During the summer, the flow of the Russian River slows and a sand bar forms at the mouth, essentially closing it off from the Pacific. This results in the formation of a rather substantial lake which, although cold, is popular with swimmers and kayakers. Once the river starts flowing again, steelhead trout and salmon draw lots of anglers.

Each site includes a table, and all but #5, where the danger of fire is exceptionally high, have a fire ring. There is no water, so campers have to bring their own supplies.

RESTROOMS: Pit toilets; no showers.

FEES: $9/day.

RESERVATIONS: Up to eight weeks in advance through MISTIX, 1-800-444-PARK.

CHECK IN/OUT: 2 p.m. in; noon out.

DOGS: Not permitted.

MAX. STAY: Seven days.

SECURITY: Park rangers

HOW TO GET THERE: From Bodega Bay, drive north on Highway 1; exit right on Willow Creek Road (just before you cross the Russian River). A half-mile from the highway, turn left onto a dirt road. You'll pass through two livestock gates – remember to close them after you – before reaching the parking lot.

Pomo Canyon Environmental Campground
(closed to camping Nov. 1-March 31)

This campground is four miles past the Willow Creek Campground in a canyon of redwood trees. It's backed up against a forest of fir owned by the Louisiana Pacific Lumber Company, which makes it seem even larger and more remote than it really is.

There are 21 campsites here, two of which are accessible to the handicapped. Each has its own table and fire ring. Fresh water is available. Other features include a large campfire center and hiking trails. Sites are short, easy walks from the campground parking lot.

RESTROOMS: Pit toilets; no showers.

FEES: $9/day.

RESERVATIONS: First come, first served.

CHECK IN/OUT: 2 p.m. in; noon out.

DOGS: Not permitted.

SECURITY: Park rangers.

HOW TO GET THERE: From Bodega Bay, drive north on Highway 1; exit right on Willow Creek Road (just before you cross the Russian River. Continue past the Willow Creek Campground turn for two or three miles until you see a sign on your right. Follow the dirt road until you come to the campground.

FORT ROSS STATE HISTORIC PARK
19005 Highway 1, Jenner, CA 95450
(707) 847-3286

• Near-beach tent & RV camping

This park's 3,315 acres roll smoothly and gracefully along the edge of the sea, a pastoral series of moderate hills and dales, covered with grass. The park is largely treeless until a dark green blanket of tanoaks and redwoods begins to cover the elevated slopes half a mile or so to the east.

Historic Fort Ross

The park is named after a Russian settlement (derived from *Rossiia*, the word for Russia) that was established here in 1812 by the Russian-American Company, a commercial hunting and trading business with strong ties to the Russian nobility, including the Czar. The primary purpose of the settlement, which included a fort, was to hunt sea otters and to raise food to support its outposts in Alaska. After the otter supply thinned and agricultural efforts proved disappointing, the settlement was disbanded in 1841.

The fort, most of which was reconstructed following a devastating fire that consumed a large part of the original structure in 1970, is the most popular attraction, drawing more than a 140,000 visitors a year.

The cove at Fort Ross

CAMPGROUND (open only from April to November): The Fort Ross Reef Campground is little known and attracts only 6,200 campers a year. Until last year, it didn't even have a sign to identify it. Located two miles south of Fort Ross and the main park entrance, it consists of 20 campsites which can accommodate both tents and RVs up to 17 feet. They're staggered within the redwoods, willows and shrubs growing along both sides of a dirt road. Each site has its own parking space and includes a table and fire pit, although absolutely no fires are permitted between August and October due to the high risk of fire. There's also piped-in water, but no hookups or dump station.

The dirt road leads down to a small rocky cove with a large kelp bed offshore and rollicking surf. It's popular among abalone hunters, but much too rough and cold for casual swimming.

RESTROOMS: Flush toilets and sinks. No showers.

FEES: $10/day.

RESERVATIONS: First come, first served.

CHECK IN/OUT: Noon

DOGS: Not permitted.

MAX. STAY: 14 days.

SECURITY: Park rangers.

HOW TO GET THERE: From Jenner, drive north on Highway 1 for 10 miles and watch for the Ft. Ross Reef Campground sign; turn left.

STILLWATER COVE REGIONAL PARK
22455 Highway 1, Jenner, CA 95450
(707) 847-3245

* Bluff-top tent & RV camping near the ocean
* Hike & Bike camping

"Stillwater Cove" is an appropriate tag for this little loop in the shoreline. Facing south, the cove is well protected from the onslaught of surf that attacks more open beaches. In fact, Stillwater Cove is one of the safer beaches along the Sonoma Coast. It's particularly popular among abalone divers who prize the coveted red mollusks clinging to the rocks offshore, sometimes just a few feet below the water.

Although the cove, with its safe and easy access to the ocean, is by far the park's strongest attraction, hikers also enjoy exploring the rest of the park. An easy mile-long trail leads through a canyon to a classic red schoolhouse, complete with belltower, that was built over a century ago. Within another year or two, the park expects to nearly double in size with the addition of 100 adjacent acres. Preparation of the new acreage is now in the planning stage.

For provisions, you'll find a limited selection of groceries, deli items and gasoline at the Ft. Ross Store two miles south. Gasoline, sodas and beer are also available from the Ocean Coast Store a mile to the north. For a more complete selection, including propane and other camping supplies, you'll have to drive to Stewart's Point General Store (12 miles north).

CAMPGROUND: The campground and day-use area sit about 250 yards from the cove, across Highway 1 and up a 60-foot bluff that you can negotiate by driving or walking up a multi-tiered staircase of well over 100 steps. More sunny than shady, the park covers over 100 gently rolling grass-covered acres. Mature pines and firs pop up haphazardly, gracing some of the campsites with reliable shade. However, most are in full sun.

There are 23 campsites which can accommodate both tents and RVs. The larger ones can host RVs as long as 32 feet or more. A few of the sites are pull-throughs. All have picnic tables, fire rings with grill tops and their own parking pads. The campground also has a dump station and water spigots, but there are no hookups.

There's also a Hike and Bike area featuring a table and fire ring.

RESTROOMS: Flush toilets, sinks, AC outlets, mirrors and private warm water showers (no charge at present). Deep dishwashing tubs with hot water are located behind the restrooms.

FEES: $14/day (max. eight persons per site). *Hike & Bike* camping is $3/day per person.

RESERVATIONS: First-come, first-served basis. Frequently crowded throughout abalone season, which runs from April through November (with the exception of July).

CHECK IN/OUT: 2 p.m.

DOGS: $1/day; permitted on beach and trails, but must be leashed at all times.

MAX. STAY: 10 consecutive days; 30 days/year. No established limit for Hike & Bike camping.

SECURITY: Park rangers and resident camp host.

HOW TO GET THERE: Stillwater Cove is 15 miles north of Jenner, 22 miles south of Gualala just off Highway 1. Watch for the Stillwater Cove Park sign.

WWW reserve america.com.
cal-parks.ca.gov.

SALT POINT STATE PARK
25050 Coast Highway 1, Jenner, CA 95450
(707) 847-3221

- Near-coast tent & RV camping
- Walk-in tent camping
- Hike & Bike camping

Salt Point State Park, 90 miles north of San Francisco and 20 miles north of Jenner, is on one of the most picturesque sections of coast in all of California. Here, a golden crust of crumbled sandstone fights a dramatic but futile battle against a relentless teal-blue sea. Hidden along its wrinkled and rugged six-mile length, however, are dozens of tiny coves with simple sandy crescent beaches.

But not all coves promise sand. Gerstle Cove, for instance, has virtually none but, as one of the first underwater reserves in the state, it does provide skin and scuba divers a unique opportunity to explore a rich, unspoiled community of marine life. The cove and all its denizens are completely protected by law. You can fish anywhere else in the park, but not here.

With almost 6,000 acres, Salt Point State Park offers a myriad of land-based activities. Hike, bike or ride horseback along the park's many miles of trails and fire roads. From sea level to its ridge 1,000 feet up, the landscape blends from coastal brush and grasslands into forests of pine, fir, madrone, tanoak, and redwood. At the park's highest point, you'll even find a pygmy forest where poor growing conditions have produced fully mature cypresses, pines and redwoods only a few feet in height.

Adjacent to the park is the 317-acre Kruse Rhododendron State Reserve, which includes an additional five miles of hiking trails through fir, redwood and tanoak forest and across bridges spanning seasonal streams and fern-filled canyons. In May, the forest bursts into bloom with patches of pink-blossomed rhododendron.

Several groups of Indians once lived, fished and hunted in the area. Traces of their villages are still evident and protected by both state and federal laws as important archelogical sites.

The charred, leafless skeletons of burnt trees are a result of recent wild fires, a constant danger during the area's dry summers. Ironically, you'll find much of the dead wood is eventually felled, cut up and sold to campers as, you guessed it, firewood.

CAMPGROUNDS: Of the park's 400,000 annual visitors, more than 61,000 are campers who have the choice of several campgrounds.

Closest to the coast is the *Gerstle Cove Campground*, on the west side of Highway 1 about 100 yards from the edge of the sea. Its 30 sites are set within a forest of fir, pine, tanoak and cypress and can accommodate tents and RVs up to 31 feet. Each site includes its own parking spur, table and fire pit with grill top.

The *Woodside Campground* is ensconced within a similar landscape, although at a slightly higher elevation just east of Highway 1. Its 80 campsites are strung along two loops and, as with the campground at Gerstle Cove, feature parking spurs, tables and fire pits. Tents and RVs up to 31 feet can be accommodated. The **Hike & Bike Campground** is near the entrance station. There are dump stations at both campgrounds as well as water spigots, but there are no hookups.

There are 20 additional *walk-in campsites*. From the parking lot, plan on an easy half-mile hike along a mostly level dirt trail. The landscape continues with tall stands of fir, pine and tanoak.

At one time, there were also five environmental campsites and a group camp, but fire destroyed them in November 1993. There are currently no plans to re-open the environmental sites, but park district officials are more optimistic regarding the group camp. Even so, it is doubtful that it will open before 1996.

RESTROOMS: The main campgrounds, Gerstle Cove and Woodside, and the Hike & Bike Campground each feature pump & flush toilets, sinks and mirrors. The area's limited water supply prohibits shower facilities anywhere in the park. "If we had showers," explained the camp host, "we'd never make it through the weekend."

FEES: *Woodside* and *Gerstle Cove Campgrounds* - $14/day in peak season (April 1-Nov. 30); $12/day off-peak. Woodside *walk-in sites* - $12/day in peak season; $10/day off-peak. *Hike & Bike camping* - $3/day per person.

RESERVATIONS: For campsites between March 1 and Nov. 30, reservations can be made up to eight weeks in advance through MISTIX, 1-800-444-PARK. The rest of the year is first-come, first-served.

CHECK IN/OUT: Noon check out.

DOGS: $1/day; not permitted on beaches, trails or walk-in camp-grounds.

MAX. STAY: 10 days; Hike & Bike 2-3 days.

SECURITY: Park rangers and resident camp host.

HOW TO GET THERE: From Jenner, drive north 20 miles on Highway 1; exit at Salt Point State Park turnoff.

GUALALA POINT REGIONAL PARK
P.O. Box 95, Gualala, CA 95445
(707) 785-2377

* Riverside tent & RV camping under redwoods
* Walk-in tent camping

Ferns, vines, shrubs and other substory plants luxuriate in the shade of this grove of towering redwoods situated along the banks of the crystaline Gualala River just east of Highway 1.

Approximately eight miles of interconnecting trails let you explore much of the park's nearly 200 acres; one of those trails follows the river to a long, sandy beach a mile to the west. A dramatic spot where the river empties into the ocean and steep cliffs rise abruptly to one side, the beach is typically littered with driftwood. The wood is yours for the taking, but the quantity is limited to an amount that you can carry by hand.

Divers frequent the beach in search of abalone from April to November. The beach opens straight out to the sea and has a steep dropoff; thus, it's prone to powerful sleeper waves that can easily knock over adults and carry them unsafe distances from shore. Casual swimming is not recommended. Besides, the water is always cold and there are no lifeguards.

If you really must swim, come during the summer months, when a sandbar builds up and effectively dams the river. This prevents the Gualala from emptying into the ocean and creates a sizeable lake suitable for swimming, kayaking and canoeing. Rental equipment is available in the nearby town of Gualala.

The same water can also give birth to huge squadrons of mosquitos during the warmer months. In fact, they're "some of the biggest mosquitos you've ever seen," reports one local resident.

Once the rainy season begins (October through April) and the river begins flowing again, steelhead trout arrive and so do the anglers. There are times, however, when the Gualala can overflow and, if that happens, the park closes.

Those interested in learning about the area's ecology and history can do so quite painlessly at the park's Visitor Center, open throughout the year Fridays through Mondays from 10 a.m. to 3 p.m. Here, you'll find interpretive displays and volunteers ready, willing and able to answer all your questions.

If you need supplies, the town of Gualala is just a mile away. Fuel, food, restaurants and other essentials are readily available.

CAMPGROUND: The park has a total of 26 campsites, seven of which are walk-in tentsites requiring an easy hike of 50 to 200 feet. All of the walk-in sites are next to or near the river within an area thick with redwoods and lush undergrowth. Each includes a picnic table and fire ring with grill top. Vehicles can be parked in the regular campground (space permitting) or near the park entrance.

The remaining 19 campsites have parking right next them. They include parking spurs as well as tables and fire rings and can accommodate either tents or RVs. The larger ones can host vehicles as long as 32 feet. A half-dozen of the sites back right up to the river, but all are within a stone's throw.

Water spigots are spaced throughout the park and a dump station is available. However, there are no hookups.

RESTROOMS: The city of Gualala's new sewer system has enabled the park to replace its previous pit toilets with a brand new facility featuring flush toilets, sinks, mirrors, AC outlets and coin-operated warm water showers.

FEES: $14/day (max. eight persons per site).

RESERVATIONS: First-come, first-served basis. Busiest time of year is July and August.

CHECK IN/OUT: 2 p.m.

DOGS: $1/day; permitted on beach and trails, but must be leashed at all times.

MAX. STAY: 10 consecutive days; 30 days/year.

SECURITY: Park rangers and resident camp host.

HOW TO GET THERE: Drive one mile south of the town of Gualala on Highway 1.

Mendocino County

MANCHESTER STATE BEACH
c/o Manchester District, P.O. Box 440
Mendocino, CA 95460
(707) 937-5804

- Sand dunes tent & RV camping
- Hike & Bike camping
- Group camping

A fallen forest of driftwood litters the wide sandy beach at Manchester State Park. And not only twigs, mind you. Picture whole logs – lots of them – strewn haphazardly along the shore for miles. Bleached grey by what must be many years of exposure to the sun, rain

Masses of driftwood make for interesting walks

and salt air, they resemble stone pillars from the tumbled ruins of some long gone seafront civilization. Discovering these *ruins* comes as quite a surprise because there's very little in the way of wood anywhere else. There are a few cypress and shrubs, but it's mostly dune grass and other low-profile growth working to keep the park's 1,400 acres of sandy mounds from blowing away.

Besides its dramatic driftwood, 50 pounds of which you're entitled to take, Manchester is also well known for the fishing opportunities it offers. It is one of the best surf-fishing beaches in Mendocino County. During the winter months, you can hook steelhead trout in the two creeks that flow the year round – Brush Creek near the center of the park and Alder Creek on the park's northern edge. Garcia River, just south of the park, is another choice fishing spot.

The hamlet of Manchester is located just a half-mile south of the park. Here, you can stock up on the basics. There's also a camp store at the KOA campground, right next to the park.

CAMPGROUND: There are 46 campsites spaced along an asphalt loop through the park at the edge of the sand dunes. The beach is a 15-minute walk through rolling mounds of soft sand. A few of the sites are shaded by lacey cypress trees, but most are in full sun surrounded by dune grass. Each campsite has its own parking spur, a picnic table and fire ring with grill. They can accommodate tents as well as RVs up to 32 feet. Water spigots are nearby, but there are neither hookups nor dump station.

For those wishing to delve deeper into the dunes, there are 10 environmental campsites that require a walk of about a mile to reach. A group campground can hold up to 40 campers with 12 vehicles up to 21 feet long. The Hike & Bike campground is located in a small clearing near the entrance to the park.

The closest phone is at the nearby KOA.

RESTROOMS: Pit toilets; no showers.

FEES: $9/day in peak season (April 1-Oct. 11); $7/day remainder of the year. *Hike & Bike camping* - $2/day per person. *Group camping* - $60/day (for up to 40 campers and 12 vehicles).

RESERVATIONS: First come, first served throughout the year except for the group campground, which can be reserved up to six months in advance through MISTIX, 1-800-444-PARK.

CHECK IN/OUT: 2 p.m. in; noon out.

DOGS: $1/day; permitted on beach and trails but must be leashed at all times.

MAX. STAY: 15 days. Hike & Bike camping three days.

SECURITY: Park rangers and resident camp host.

HOW TO GET THERE: From the town of Manchester, drive north on Highway 1 for a half-mile; turn left at Kinney Road and follow it a short distance to the park entrance.

VAN DAMME STATE PARK
c/o Mendocino District Headquarters
P.O. Box 440, Mendocino, CA 95460
(707) 937-5804

- Near-coast tent & RV camping
- Walk-in tent camping
- Hike & Bike camping
- Group camping
- En Route camping

Just three miles south of the charming, elegant cliffside town of Mendocino, this 2,163-acre park begins at a sheltered beach popular among abalone divers and extends inland through varying landscapes of sunny meadows, forested canyons thick with ferns, and a pygmy forest. Visitors can hike along its 10 miles of trails through moderate to steep terrain, bike on fire roads, fish for trout and salmon in Little River, or comb the beach. There's even a Visitor Center which offers a series of interpretive murals, videos as well as knowledgeable volunteers. It's open daily throughout the summer, with a reduced schedule during the rest of the year.

Of particular interest is the pygmy forest, which you can reach by either hiking or driving. The result of a unique combination of soils, climate and geology, the forest features decades-old trees less than an inch in diameter and only a few feet in height. Several species of plants are exclusive to this area.

CAMPGROUND: A split-level campground includes 74 family campsites capable of hosting either tents or RVs up to 30 feet. The lower level is situated at sea level in an area of redwoods a little more than a quarter-mile from the beach. Another quarter-mile or so up the road is the larger highland meadow campground. Here, at an elevation of 200 feet, the campsites sit beneath a thick canopy of redwoods, firs and tanoaks that surround a grassy open meadow. Campsites at both sections include their own parking spurs, food storage lockers and fire rings with grill tops. There is also piped water and a dump station, but no hookups.

For those who enjoy pack-in, pack-out camping in the depths of a dense, heavily shaded forest, Van Damme also offers 10 **hike-in campsites**. They're located an easy two miles up the lush Fern Canyon Trail on both sides of the Little River, a year-round stream flowing through tall redwoods. Each site consists of a cleared area with picnic table and fire ring. The only water is that provided by the stream, so campers are advised to bring their own drinking water or purify that taken from the stream. Heavy rainfall between November and February can flood the trails and make hiking impossible.

The **Group campground** is between the two levels. It can accommodate up to 50 campers and has parking for 15 vehicles. The **Hike & Bike campground** is nearby.

En Route camping is allowed during the busy season on the Van Damme Beach parking lot on the west side of Highway 1. Space is limited.

RESTROOMS: All but the walk-in campgrounds offer flush toilets, sinks and mirrors. Some also include coin-operated showers. Walk-in sites have pit toilets only.

FEES: *Family* and *En Route camping* - $14/day in peak season (April 1-Oct. 11); $12/day off-peak. *Walk-in camping* - $9/day in peak season; $7/day off-peak. *Hike & Bike camping* - $3/day per person. *Group camping* -$75/day.

RESERVATIONS: For camping between April 1 and Oct. 11, reservations can be made up to eight weeks in advance through MISTIX, 1-800-444-PARK. Group camping reservations for the same period may be made through MISTIX up to six months in advance.

CHECK IN/OUT: 2 p.m. in; noon out.

DOGS: $1/day; not permitted on trails or walk-in campsites, but okay on beach if leashed.

MAX. STAY: 15 days June-September; 30 days remainder of the year. Walk-in campsites seven days.

SECURITY: Park rangers and resident camp host.

HOW TO GET THERE: From Mendocino, drive south on Highway 5 for three miles; turn left at the park entrance.

PAUL M. DIMMICK CAMPGROUND
c/o Russian Gulch State Park
Highway 1, Mendocino, CA 95460
(707) 937-5804

• Riverside tent & RV camping

Located six miles east of Highway 1, this narrow 673-acre park follows 11 miles of Highway 128 on the north side of the Navarro River. As you drive through the park, you'll find yourself in a tunnel of redwoods, a thick second growth forest which parallels the entire length.

Anglers, canoers and kayakers particularly enjoy the park in the late winter and spring when the river runs deep and is full of steelhead and salmon.

During summers, temperatures here commonly hit 85 to 90° due to the park's inland location.

CAMPGROUND: The campground has 28 campsites beneath a shady grove of redwoods. They can accommodate both tents and RVs up to 30 feet. All have tables, food lockers and fire rings. Piped water is available from April to October. The campground is subject to flooding during heavy rain in the winter.

RESTROOMS: There are two cold water restrooms without showers.

FEES: $9/day in peak season (April 1-Oct. 11); $7/day off-peak.

RESERVATIONS: First come, first served.

CHECK IN/OUT: Noon.

DOGS: $1/day.

MAX. STAY: 15 days.

SECURITY: Park rangers and resident camp host.

HOW TO GET THERE: From Mendocino, drive south on Highway 1; turn left on 128 and head east for eight miles.

RUSSIAN GULCH STATE PARK
c/o Mendocino District Headquarters
P.O. Box 440, Mendocino, CA 95460
(707) 937-5804

- Near-beach tent & RV camping
- Horse camping
- Hike & Bike camping
- Group camping

This 1,300-acre park is nestled in a forested valley with a limited section of shoreline. From its rocky headlands, it affords you great views of the coastline and, if you're here between December and March, excellent opportunities to spot 40-ton grey whales on their migratory journeys to and from Mexico.

Its small sandy beach, sheltered from the open sea, provides scuba divers and kayakers easy access to the ocean and anglers a good base for surf fishing.

Turning inland, you'll be treated to numerous trails through a rolling forest of redwoods, firs and tanoaks. One of the trails leads to Russian Gulch Falls, which plunges for 36 feet before spilling into a creek that, during the winter months, teems with trout.

CAMPGROUND: The **family campground** is a small, heavily wooded facility with just 30 sites, each capable of accommodating tents or RVs up to 27 feet. All have their own parking pads, food storage lockers, tables and fire rings with grill tops. There is water, but no hookups or dump station.

Hike & Bike and group facilities are nearby. The group camp can handle up to 40 tent campers with parking space for 10 vehicles. No RVs or trailers are permitted.

A primitive **horse camp** with four tent campsites is near the northeast end of the park about three miles east of Highway 1 on County Road 409. You'll find a locked gate at the entrance. (When you register at the Russian Gulch entrance station, you get the combination.) It offers a water trough, picnic tables, fire rings and hitching posts. Like the other campgrounds, it is situated in a mixed forest of redwoods, firs and tanoaks. There's also a section of pygmy forest. While riding trails are limited in Russian Gulch, you'll find miles and miles of them in the adjacent Jackson State Forest – 52,000 acres of redwoods, fir, hemlock, pine, tanoak, alder and madrone.

RESTROOMS: Flush toilets, mirrors, sinks and, in one facility, hot coin-operated showers, are provided in the main campgrounds. The horse camp has pit toilets only.

FEES: *Family camping* - $14/day in peak season (April 1-Oct. 11); $12/day off-peak. *Group camping* - $60/day. *Hike & Bike camping* - $3/day per person. *Horse camping* - $12/day, maximum four campers and four horses.

RESERVATIONS: For camping in the family campground between April 1 and Oct 11, reservations can be made up to eight weeks in advance through MISTIX, 1-800-444-PARK. The Group camp can be reserved for the same period up to six months in advance. The park assumes a first-come, first-served basis the rest of the year. The Horse camp is usually first come, first served as well, but can be reserved by contacting Mendocino District Headquarters (see address and phone number above).

CHECK IN/OUT: Noon out.

DOGS: $1/day; not permitted on trails, but okay on beach if leashed.

MAX. STAY: 15 days (June-Sept.); 30 days remainder of the year. Hike & Bike: 2 day max.

SECURITY: Park rangers.

HOW TO GET THERE: From Mendocino, drive north on Highway 1 for two miles. Horse camp: From Russian Gulch, drive north on Highway 1 to County Road 409; take 409 east about three miles to the camp.

JACKSON DEMONSTRATION
STATE FOREST

P.O. Box 1185, 802 N. Main Street
Fort Bragg, CA 95437
(707) 964-5674

- Forested tent & RV camping
- Group camping
- Horse camping

Adjacent to Russian Gulch State Park is a rolling, mountainous 50,000-acre expanse of mixed forest. The terrain varies from flat on the old marine terraces near the coast, to very rugged on the east end. Elevation ranges from 300 to 2,100 feet and through it all are woven hundreds of miles of trails and logging roads, virtually all of them dirt and rock. Many are open to hiking, biking and horseback riding.

Bears and mountain lions are definitely part of this world, but they are rarely encountered. More likely to be seen are small animals like raccoons and insects, including ticks and mosquitos.

Seasonal hunting for deer, wild pigs and quail is permitted in certain areas of the forest (license required). But while there are an estimated 90 miles of streams that contain seasonal runs of coho salmon and steelhead trout, fishing is all but prohibited. The Department of Fish and Game traps the local catch and strips them of their eggs for hatchery use instead. You can see how it's done at the egg collection station, which is open to visitors.

Other points of interest include a Pygmy Forest Reserve and a tree identification trail, designed to help visitors recognize the major local tree species.

Foresters emphasize, however, that Jackson Demonstration State Forest is *not* a state park. Public recreation is only one of its concerns. Other equally, if not more important, concerns include the management of wildlife habitat and watershed, and the continuous growing and harvesting of trees for wood products.

CAMPGROUND: There are more than a dozen campgrounds within the forest, including several group horse camps. They're located in two main areas, *Camp One Area* and *Camp 20 Area*. Each has a resident camp host responsible for issuing campfire permits, maintaining the facilities, and providing information, brochures and directions to hiking trails and other areas of interest.

Some of the sites can accommodate RVs, others only tents. Most are accessible by car, although the winding, unpaved roads and their variable condition can make parts of the forest inaccessible to all but the most determined campers; four-wheel-drive vehicles may be required on some roads. Campgrounds are subject to closing at any time. Weather, time of year, ongoing logging operations and other forestry projects can be reason for closure.

Conditions are primitive throughout. There are no hookups of any kind, and the only available water is that flowing in the creeks and streams; it requires purification before drinking. Tables, fire rings and / or barbecue grills are provided at most of the campgrounds. Troughs and corrals are also provided at the horse camps. Some camps have nearby telephone service.

RESTROOMS: Pit toilets.

FEES: None.

RESERVATIONS: All campsites are first come, first served, except for group camps, arrangements for which must be made with the forest service a minimum of two weeks in advance. All campers must have a State Forest Campfire and Special Use Permit; these are obtainable *in-person* from the Jackson Demonstration State Forest Headquarters in Fort Bragg (address above) or from the camp hosts along Highway 20 and County Road 350 (follow the signs).

CHECK IN/OUT: Noon.

DOGS: No fee; must be leashed.

MAX. STAY: 14 days (a total of 30 days per year).

SECURITY: Forest rangers and two resident camp hosts

HOW TO GET THERE: Between Mendocino and Fort Bragg, there are several roads that lead into the Jackson Demonstration State Forest. The most accessible route is to take Highway 20 (located west of Willits and east of Highway 1 in Fort Bragg) east into the forest. Follow the signs to the camp hosts.

MACKERRICHER STATE PARK

c/o Mendocino District Headquarters
P.O. Box 440, Mendocino, CA 95460
(707) 937-5804

- Near-beach and near-dunes tent & RV camping
- Walk-in tent camping
- Hike & Bike camping

What most marks MacKerricher State Park is its 10 miles of beach and sand dunes. But that oversimplifies the character of its 1,600 acres, which annually attract 765,000 visitors, including 105,000 campers.

You should also know that MacKerricher provides one of the best viewpoints along the Mendocino coast, Laguna Point, for observing the California grey whale as it passes by the coast twice a year. Once the site of a Pomo Indian village, Laguna Point juts out from the coast like the beak of a giant hawk and elevates you well above the surf and sand. It also offers a handicapped-accessible boardwalk past the bluffs and intertidal areas to a seal-watching station where some of MacKerricher's resident harbor seals can be unobtrusively observed.

An attractive sandy beach awaits

Haul Road, a former logging road, provides hikers, bikers and joggers an extraordinary thoroughfare along which they can travel the entire length of the park. Although parts of the old road have been buried by sand or eroded, making the going tough at times, you'll be rewarded by spectacular views of the dunes and coastline up to the road's end at the mouth of Ten Mile River.

MacKerricher also has its own freshwater lake, Lake Cleone, where you can boat (non-motorized), sailboard and fish (it's stocked with rainbow trout every spring). It's also a great spot for hiking; a three mile trail completely surrounds it and affords ample opportunities for birdwatching and picnicking.

Horseback riding is permitted in designated trails as well as on the beach north of Ward Avenue. A concessionaire offering trail rides and boarding stables is just across Highway 1 from the park entrance.

For supplies, you can try either of two small grocery stores and a gas station located a quarter-mile north. With the town of Fort Bragg just three miles south, however, you will find a plentiful number of grocery stores, service stations, fast food restaurants and almost every other service and product readily available. From Fort Bragg, you can also catch a ride aboard the *Skunk*, originally a logging train established in 1885. Powered by either steam or diesel engines, the *Skunk* now carries passengers inland through 40 miles of scenic mountains and redwoods, concluding in the town of Willits.

CAMPGROUND: MacKerricher includes four family campgrounds with 142 sites, 11 walk-in tent sites and a Hike & Bike facility. The family campgrounds can accommodate both tents and RVs up to 35 feet. Each has its own parking spur, table, fire ring with grill top and storage locker. Water and a dump station are available, but there are no hookups. **West and East Pinewood Campgrounds** are nestled within a forest of coastal pine with appreciable shade. These campsites are among the furthest from the beach, some as far as a half-mile. If the walk seems excessive, consider driving the distance and parking in beachfront lots.

Cleone Campground is near the north shore of Lake Cleone and likewise shaded by stands of coastal pine.

Surfwood Campground sits along the south shore of Lake Cleone and is nearest to the main beach, a splendid, charcoal-colored sweep of sand that attracts surfers and anglers alike. Here, too, most sites are nestled within the shade of coastal pine.

The 11 **walk-in tentsites** are a 50-yard hike from the Surfwood Campground. Campers have to park in the nearby lot then pack-in and pack-out all supplies. The sites are set in a combination of forest and sand dunes and include tables and fire rings. Water is available. **Note:** the nearest restrooms are at the Surfwood Campground.

RESTROOMS: Brand new uni-sex restrooms feature the state's finest facilities, including private bathrooms with flush toilets, sinks, mirrors, AC outlets. Private coin-operated showers are also provided.

FEES: $14/day in peak season (April 1-Oct. 11); $12/day off-peak. *Hike & Bike camping* - $3/day per person.

RESERVATIONS: For camping between Apirl 1 and Oct. 11, reservations can be made up to eight weeks in advance through MISTIX, 1-800-444-PARK. The park assumes a first-come, first-served basis the rest of the year.

CHECK IN/OUT: Noon out.

SECURITY: Park rangers and resident camp host.

HOW TO GET THERE: From Fort Bragg, drive north on Highway 1 for three miles.

WESTPORT-UNION LANDING STATE BEACH
c/o Mendocino District Headquarters
P.O. Box 440, Mendocino, CA 95460
(707) 937-5804

- Coastal bluff tent & RV camps

Westport-Union Landing State Beach is a long and narrow treeless strip that runs along the west side of Highway 1 starting three miles north of the village of Westport. Views from the 30-40-foot bluff are outstanding, the sea stretching into the distance on one side, unspoiled green and gold hills rolling along the highway on the other.

A number of foot trails and stairways lead from the bluff to the broad, tawn-colored beach below. Although beautiful, the beach is subject to an extremely powerful backwash even with normal size surf. It has a steep dropoff which causes the water to pick up considerable momentum as it returns to the sea, creating enough force to sweep you off your feet and even tear off shoes and clothing.

Nevertheless, it is a superb setting for walking, beachcombing, and surf fishing (surf perch, cabezon, ling cod and greenling are the usual catches). From offshore, you may also enjoy abalone diving and spearfishing.

Golden hills give way to the beach

CAMPGROUND: There are seven camping areas with 130 campsites, the majority of which can accommodate either tents or RVs of virtually any length. Most sites have their own parking spurs, tables and fire rings with grills. Water is available, but there are neither hookups nor a dump station.

With Highway 1 paralleling the park, you should be prepared for the sound of traffic throughout the day and night, although the volume is usually pretty light once evening falls. And don't expect anything in the way of trees or shrubs for shade or privacy. Except for the scrub brush growing along the slope, there isn't a bush to be seen.

You'll find many of the campsites on the northern half of the park better suited to RVs, where they can often parallel park right next to the cliff's edge.

RESTROOMS: Nothing fancy, just pit toilets.

FEES: $9/day in peak season (April 1-Oct. 11); $7/day off-peak.

RESERVATIONS: First-come, first-served basis throughout the year.

CHECK IN/OUT: Noon out.

DOGS: $1/day; okay on beach and trails if leashed.

MAX. STAY: 15 days (June-September); 30 days remainder of the year.

SECURITY: Park rangers and resident camp host.

HOW TO GET THERE: From Fort Bragg, drive north on Highway 1 for 30 minutes. Watch for signs and turnoffs to the left.

SINKYONE WILDERNESS STATE PARK
P.O. Box 245, Whitehorn, CA 95489
(707) 986-7711

• Primitive near-coast tent camping

This area of California is often referred to as the *Lost Coast* because it is so unstable and its precipitous cliffs subject to frequent landslides. Collapsed piles of rock mark the park's 17 miles of coast as evidence. Less visible is the infamous San Andreas Fault, source of numerous earthquakes, which lies just offshore. A major highway can't exist here for very long and you'll notice that Highway 1 suddenly flees the coast and turns inland to merge with Highway 101.

Getting to the park requires some sacrifice. Whether entering from the north or south, you'll have to endure six to nine miles of rugged, unpaved road, portions of which narrow down to steep, single lanes at the cliff's edge. They're normally negotiable by passenger cars during the summer, but require four-wheel-drive in the winter months when the clay surface gets as slippery as butter. No doubt the park's difficult access accounts for its relatively small numbers of visitors (less than than 30,000 people a year).

For those who make the grade, however, the reward is an uncommon opportunity to partake of 7,000 acres of untamed wilderness. This extremely rugged land, composed of dense forests, prairies and peaks rising up to 1,900 feet, comes to a sudden and abrupt halt at the foot of the Pacific, its nearly vertical 200-foot bluffs separated from the water by nothing more than a thin strip of black sand beach and fan-shaped piles of talus.

If you're planning to stay for any length of time, bring everything you need. Plan for chilly, wet winters and cool, foggy summers. Temperatures range from the 40s to the 60s year round, although the frequent winds can make it seem even cooler. Spring and fall are generally clear, dry and sunny.

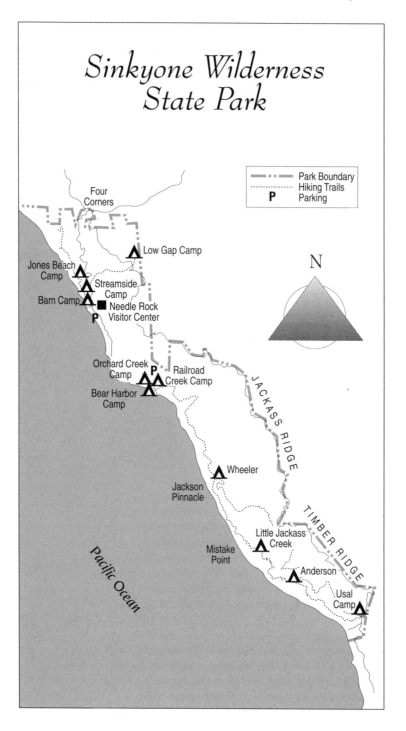

Sinkyone Wilderness State Park

Four Corners

Park Boundary
Hiking Trails
P Parking

N

Low Gap Camp

Jones Beach Camp

Streamside Camp

Barn Camp

Needle Rock Visitor Center

P

Orchard Creek Camp

P

Railroad Creek Camp

Bear Harbor Camp

JACKASS RIDGE

Wheeler

Jackson Pinnacle

TIMBER RIDGE

Little Jackass Creek

Mistake Point

Anderson

Usal Camp

Pacific Ocean

South End

Only one campground is open to vehicle camping – Usal Beach, at the extreme south end of the park. There are 15 drive-in sites, each including a picnic table and fire pit. Surface water from a couple of nearby creeks is usually available but must be treated before using. Otherwise, you should bring your own water supply.

The campground is in a valley that opens out to a broad sandy beach which draws lots of surf fishers. It's fun for beachcoming, too.

RESTROOMS: Pit toilets.

FEES: $9/night in peak season (May 1-Sept.30); $7/night off-peak.

RESERVATIONS: First come, first served.

CHECK IN/OUT: 2 p.m. in and out.

DOGS: $1/night; not permitted on trails, but okay on beach when leashed.

MAX. STAY: 15 days.

SECURITY: Park rangers.

HOW TO GET THERE: From Rockport, drive north three miles on Highway 1, take County Road 431 (Usal Road) north for six miles of rugged, unpaved driving. The road is passable for passenger cars in summer, but four-wheel-drive is recommended in winter.

North End

There are seven backcountry camps and three established trail camps providing nearly two dozen campsites in the northern half of the park. Most sites include tables, fire pits and pit toilets. Creeks provide water most of the year, but it should be treated before drinking. You can drive to within a few hundred yards of most campgrounds along Briceland Road, a thin stretch of dirt and gravel that enters the park from the north end and parallels the coast for approximately one-third the length of the park. Proceeding from north to south, they include:

Backcountry Camps

Jones Beach - Three sites just three-tenths of a mile from secluded Jones Beach Cove. Requires a 300-yard walk from Briceland Road.

Streamside - Three sites, one with an ocean view. About a quarter-mile walk from Lost Coast Trail.

Needle Rock - Two sites among firs and alders alongside a stream. Nice ocean views; black sand beach nearby. Parking is 75 yards away from Briceland Road. This is also location of the Sinkyone's Visitor Center, a converted turn-of-the-century ranch house. It offers interpretive displays, publications and registration for hike-in campsites. The camp host resides here.

The center has two bare-bones bedrooms – four wood walls and no furnishings except for a couple of elevated sleeping platforms – which can shelter up to four persons each. The fee is $14/day (per room, max. 4 persons) from May 1-Sept. 30; $12/day the rest of the year. These are first come, first served and used mainly during the wet season.

Orchard Creek - Three sites about 75 yards from Briceland Road in an old apple orchard.

Railroad Creek - Two sites a little further south of Orchard Creek, situated beneath a colony of eucalyptus trees.

Bear Harbor - Three sites just beyond Railroad Creek, in a meadow near Bear Harbor Cove, a popular spot among abalone divers, surf fishers, as well as beachcombers. Less than a half-mile walk from the end of Briceland Road.

Low Gap - This campground offers five inland sites alongside a stream about 200 yards from the north end of Usal Road.

RESTROOMS: Pit toilets.

FEES: $9/night in peak season (May 1-Sept. 30); $7/night off-peak.

DOGS: Not allowed.

MAX. STAY: 15 days

RESERVATIONS: First come, first served.

CHECK IN/OUT: 2 p.m. in and out.

SECURITY: Park rangers.

Trail Camps

The last three are trail camps requiring lengthy hikes (four to eight miles). These may or may not have fire rings or tables.

Wheeler - Four sites just over four miles from Bear Harbor. The vestiges of an old lumber mill town are evident. There's a black sand beach a quarter-mile away.

Little Jackass - 4½ miles from Wheeler are four more sites, two at the edge of a redwood grove, two closer to a beach with sea caves.

Anderson Gulch - The furthest south of all the campgrounds. Best approached from the Usal Trailhead (beginning at Usal Road, south end) – a five-mile hike. Set in a meadow with the ocean visible in the distance.

RESTROOMS: Pit toilets.

FEES: $3/night per person.

RESERVATIONS: First come, first served.

CHECK IN/OUT: 2 p.m. in and out.

DOGS: Not allowed.

MAX. STAY: 15 days.

SECURITY: Park rangers.

STANDISH-HICKEY STATE
RECREATION AREA
69350 U.S. Highway 101 #8
Leggett, CA 95585
(707) 925-6482

- Redwood forest tent & RV camping
- Hike & Bike camping

Standish-Hickey is gateway to the "tall trees country." Although coastal redwoods flourish in a narrow strip starting below Monterey, it's at this point where they really begin to tower. Within this park's 1,070 acres, however, much of the land was clear-cut or burned in 1945. As a result, almost all of the redwoods are second growth and mixed with other trees and shrubs, including Douglas fir, tanoak, and laurel. Of the few virgin redwood groves still surviving, one is located across Highway 101 from Hickey Campground.

The park is, nevertheless, a very shady, green place, with four main trails that range in difficulty from easy to strenuous. The Big Tree Loop Trail, 2.1 miles of moderate hiking, leads to the Captain Miles Standish Tree, a 225-foot giant that was already 800 years old when the Pilgrims landed on Plymouth Rock in 1620.

In the summer, visitors enjoy cooling off in the swimming holes of the South Fork Eel River, which bisects the park. In late fall and winter, when the rains begin, the swollen river summons both steelhead trout and salmon from the sea, with hundreds of anglers not far behind.

Standish-Hickey is often bypassed by travelers. It logs little more than 50,000 visitors per year, which means there are rarely crowds to contend with.

You can buy groceries and other basics across the highway from the park. For a wider selection, visit the town of Leggett, 1½ miles south.

CAMPGROUND: The park's three campgrounds – Hickey, Rock Creek and Redwood – include 162 sites for tents and RVs. Hickey and Rock Creek can host RVs up to 27 feet; Redwood is limited to 18 feet. All sites include their own parking spurs, fireplaces with grills, tables and food storage cupboards. There is water but no hookups or dump station.

All three campgrounds are situated along the banks of the river. Expect firs, madrones, redwoods and other trees to provide a reliable canopy of shade wherever you're camping.

Note: the campgrounds are open all year with the exception of Redwood, which is open only from May through September. Once the rains begin, the bridges accessing Redwood are actually removed to make way for the increased water flow.

RESTROOMS: Flush toilets, sinks, mirrors and coin-operated hot showers. Laundry tubs are nearby.

FEES: $14/day in peak season (May 1-Sept. 30 for *Hickey* and *Rock Creek*; May 1-Sept. 5 for Redwood); $12 in off-peak. *Hike & Bike camping* - $3/day per person.

RESERVATIONS: For camping at Hickey and Rock Creek between May 1 and Sept. 30, reservations can be made up to eight weeks in advance through MISTIX, 1-800-999-PARK. Same for Redwood between July 1 and Sept. 10.

CHECK IN/OUT: Noon.

DOGS: $1/day; not permitted on trails.

MAX. STAY: 15 days (June-Sept.); 30 days remainder of the year.

SECURITY: Park rangers and resident camp host.

HOW TO GET THERE: From Leggett, drive 1½ miles north on Highway 101.

Humboldt County

KING RANGE NATIONAL CONSERVATION AREA

Bureau of Land Management, Arcata Resource Center
1125 16th Street, Room 219, Arcata, CA 95521-5580
(707) 822-7648

- Coast and inland tent & RV camping

Immediately to the north of Sinkyone Wilderness State Park lies the 60,000-acre King Range National Conservation Area. Geographically, it's a continuation of the Sinkyone Wilderness, the *Lost Coast*, although the mountains get higher and the weather a bit wetter. Kings Peak, the area's highest point, tops out at 4,087 feet; rainfall typically measures 100 or more inches annually, twice that in extremely wet years.

The King Range extends for 35 miles beyond Sinkyone and up to six miles inland. Steep, winding, narrow dirt roads have been scribbled across the corrugated landscape along with miles of trails for hiking and horseback riding. Forests of Douglas fir, grasslands and chaparral support populations of black bear, black-tailed deer and herds of elk. They also attract a hearty brand of hiker, camper and angler.

As at Sinkyone, the range comes to an abrupt end at the edge of the sea, forming a giant wall of rock the likes of which are found at few other places on earth. At the foot of the wall, strips of black sand beach highlight the shoreline. Properly licensed off-road vehicles are permitted on the three miles of Black Sands Beach north of Shelter Cove.

You'll find the community of Shelter Cove offers a full range of services, including restaurants, two general stores, a daylight airstrip, boat launching ramp, several inns, a golf course and private RV parks and campgrounds. It's nestled on one of the few flat areas along the King Range.

CAMPGROUNDS: There are five *developed* campgrounds within the King Range. FEES vary from $5/day per campsite to no charge. There is no charge for dogs, which are permitted in campgrounds

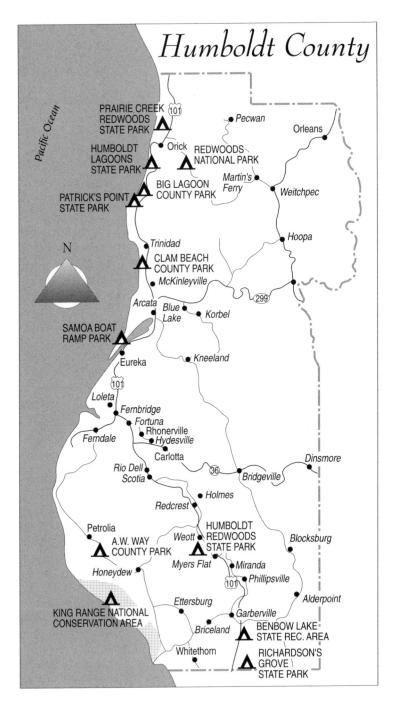

Humboldt County

Pacific Ocean

PRAIRIE CREEK
REDWOODS
STATE PARK

Pecwan

Orleans

Orick REDWOODS
NATIONAL PARK

HUMBOLDT
LAGOONS
STATE PARK

Martin's
Ferry

Weitchpec

BIG LAGOON
COUNTY PARK

PATRICK'S POINT
STATE PARK

N

Trinidad

Hoopa

CLAM BEACH
COUNTY PARK

McKinleyville

Arcata Blue
Lake Korbel

SAMOA BOAT
RAMP PARK

Kneeland

Eureka

101

Loleta

Fernbridge

Fortuna
Rhonerville
Hydesville

Ferndale

Carlotta

Rio Dell
Scotia

Dinsmore

36 Bridgeville

Holmes

Redcrest

Petrolia

A.W. WAY
COUNTY PARK

Weott HUMBOLDT
REDWOODS
STATE PARK

Blocksburg

Myers Flat Miranda

Honeydew

101 Phillipsville

Ettersburg

Alderpoint

Garberville

KING RANGE NATIONAL
CONSERVATION AREA

Briceland

BENBOW LAKE
STATE REC. AREA

Whitethorn

RICHARDSON'S
GROVE
STATE PARK

and on trails. However, they must be leashed at all times. MAXI-MUM STAY is 14 days. Water is normally available. RESTROOMS consist of pit toilets. There are no showers, hookups or dump stations. RESERVATIONS: All sites are first come, first served. Check in as sites become available; check out by noon. SECURITY consists of rangers on patrol.

In addition, backcountry camping is permitted virtually anywhere throughout the area. Camping on previously-used sites is encouraged to lessen the environmental impact. There's no charge for backcountry camping, but a campfire permit is required. These must be obtained in person at a California Department of Forestry office or Bureau of Land Management office anywhere in the state.

Wailaki Campground - 13 campsites at 1,000-foot elevation within a windy canyon about a mile inland. Accommodates both tents and RVs up to 25 feet. Affords easy access to Chemise Mountain Trail and self-guiding nature trail. No beach access. Wheelchair-accessible. FEES: $5/day per campsite. HOW TO GET THERE: From Highway 101 at Garberville, exit west on Shelter Cove Road for 17 miles; turn south on Chemise Mountain Road for 1½ miles.

Nadelos Campground - Located a half-mile north of Wailaki Campground. Includes nine inland tentsites (no RVs) at an elevation of 1,000 feet. Near Chemise Mountain Trail and a self-guiding nature trail. Wheelchair-accessible. FEES: $5/day per campsite. HOW TO GET THERE: From Highway 101 at Garberville, exit west on Shelter Cove Road for 17 miles; turn south on Chemise Mountain Road for 1½ miles.

Tolkan Campground - Nine inland sites at 1,840-feet above sea level. Accommodates both tents and RVs. However, the road to the campground is steep and should only be attempted with trailers and RVs no longer than 15 feet. Close proximity to Chemise Mountain Trail and self-guiding nature trail. Popular among deer hunters in fall. FEES: $5/day per campsite. HOW TO GET THERE: From Highway 101 at Garberville, exit west on Shelter Cove Road for 17 miles; turn north on Horse Mountain/King's Peak Road for 3½ miles.

Horse Mountain Campground - Nine sites at an elevation of 2,000 feet. Accommodates both tents and RVs up to 20-25 feet. Access to hiking and equestrian trails make it popular among hikers, horseback riders and deer hunters in fall. Summers are hot and dry. FEES: $5/day per campsite. HOW TO GET THERE: From High-

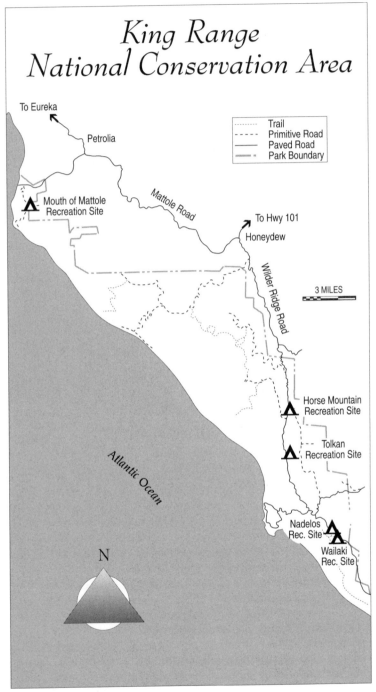

King Range
National Conservation Area

To Eureka

Petrolia

⋯⋯	Trail
---	Primitive Road
——	Paved Road
—··—	Park Boundary

Mattole Road

Mouth of Mattole
Recreation Site

To Hwy 101

Honeydew

Wilder Ridge Road

3 MILES

Horse Mountain
Recreation Site

Tolkan
Recreation Site

Atlantic Ocean

Nadelos
Rec. Site

Wailaki
Rec. Site

N

way 101 at Garberville, exit west on Shelter Cove Road for 17 miles; turn north on Horse Mountain/King's Peak Road for six miles.

Mouth of Mattole River - Five campsites for tents or small RVs (15-ft. max. recommended length) at the northern end of the King Range National Conservation Area where the Mattole River enters the sea. Campers may stake tents on the flat sandy beach or the campground. Be prepared for extremely windy conditions. Very popular for ocean- and freshwater fishing. You can also wade in the river. A four-mile hike along Lost Coast Beach Trail leads to the Punta Gorda lighthouse. FEES: None. HOW TO GET THERE: From Highway 101 at Garberville, exit west at either the Ferndale or South Fork/Honeydew turnoff; follow signs to Petrolia; exit at Lighthouse Road and follow five miles to campground.

RICHARDSON GROVE STATE PARK
c/o North Coast Redwoods, 1600 U.S. Highway 101
Garberville, CA 95542
(707) 247-3318 or (707) 946-2311

- Redwood forest tent & RV camping
- Riverside tent & RV camping
- Hike & Bike camping
- Group camping

These thousand acres have been a state park since 1922. Named after the 25th governor of California, Friend W. Richardson, the park is nestled in a small valley surrounded by mountains and hosts some of the oldest redwoods in existence; many of the trees in the main grove are estimated to be more than 1,000 years old. Rising more than 300 feet into the sky, their boughs and needles form a screen that subdues the sun and produces a perpetual twilight throughout the day, a blue-grey luminescence cherished by the colonies of ferns and tapestries of moss thriving at ground level.

Beyond the old growth groves of redwoods, where the sunlight becomes more intense, firs, oak, madrones, maples and laurels rise up to compete with each other, along with shrubby populations of manzanita, coyote brush, coffee berry and a variety of flowers.

Four loop trails, ranging from a gentle 1.6 miles to a strenuous four miles, allow visitors to explore the park's many facets. Interpretive programs and nature walks led by park staff are presented throughout the summer for all ages. Evening campfire programs, a tradition begun in the 1930s, feature songs, storytelling and informative talks.

A Visitor Center includes displays that explain and illustrate the history of the area; books, posters and other materials are on sale here. Next door, there's a concession-operated store with camping supplies, refreshments and gifts. Both the center and store are open daily from May through October.

Like much of the north coast, Richardson Grove is subject to significant rainfall, more than 68 inches a year, the bulk of it falling from November through March. Morning fog is common during summers as the cold currents of the Pacific wrestle with the heat of the inland valleys. Temperatures range from the upper 80s in July, August and September to lows in the 30s during the winter.

CAMPGROUND: Of the 122,000 visitors Richardson Grove receives each year, nearly half are campers. The park accommodates them with 170 family campsites in three campgrounds. **Huckleberry** and **Madrone Campgrounds** are situated in dense redwood groves west of Highway 101. Separated by Durphy Creek, each consists of approximately 36 campsites. They all have their own parking pads and can handle either tents or RVs up to 30 feet.

The third campground, **Oakflat**, is east of the highway along the east bank of the South Fork Eel River, which closely parallels Highway 101. Oakflat Campground sits among large oak, maple, fir and madrone trees and open grassy meadows. Sites have their own parking pads and can accommodate tents or RVs up to 24 feet.

With the approach of fall, the bridge that straddles the Eel River is removed in preparation for the rainy season and Oakflat is closed to camping until the following summer. In 1964, the river rose 46 feet, flooding the park and submerging Highway 101.

About a half-mile north of the Oakflat Campground is the **Group** camp, which can accommodate up to 40 persons and 10 vehicles (maximum 18 feet in length).

All campsites include fire ring, picnic table and food locker.

RESTROOMS: All restrooms include flush toilets, sinks and mirrors; half also have hot coin-operated showers.

FEES: $14/day in peak season (May 1-Sept. 30); $12/day off-peak.

RESERVATIONS: For campsites in Huckleberry and Madrone campgrounds between May 1 and Sept. 30, you can make reservations up to eight weeks in advance through MISTIX, 1-800-444-PARK. Advance reservations for campsites at Oakflat Campground can also be made through MISTIX for the July 1-Sept. 9 period.

CHECK IN/OUT: Noon out.

DOGS: $1/day; not permitted on trails.

MAX. STAY: 15 days (June-Sept.); 30 days remainder of the year except at Oakflat, which is open only during the summer.

SECURITY: Park rangers and resident camp host (spring through fall).

HOW TO GET THERE: From Garberville, drive south for eight miles on Highway 101; turn right at Richardson Grove exit.

BENBOW LAKE STATE RECREATION AREA

c/o North Coast Redwoods
1600 U.S. Highway 101, #8, Garberville, CA 95542
(707) 923-3238

- Riverside tent & RV camping
- Hike & Bike camping

This being Humboldt County – part of Northern California's redwood country – you might come expecting this to be another awesome grove of giant redwoods, thick with shade and lush layers of undergrowth. But not here. Instead, you'll find lacey stands of oaks and alders, grass typically dried to a golden hue and a lot of summer sunshine.

Some 25 miles inland from the coast, it's not uncommon for temperatures to hit 90 to 100 degrees in this valley. Fortunately, the South Fork Eel River affords visitors ample opportunities for cooling off and draws almost 70,000 people a year to the park. Probably the park's greatest attraction is Benbow Lake, created every summer by damming the Eel River. The lake provides 26 fluid acres for swimming, kayaking and other water sports. The Benbow Lake Yacht Club even offers guided canoe "hikes" (707-923-5242). But that's not all. It also serves as the setting for the popular **Summer Arts Festival, Jazz on the Lake, Shakespeare at Benbow Lake**, and **Reggae on the River** programs (call 707-923-2613 for additional information).

During the winter months, the river is allowed to flow freely again and offers excellent fishing for trout and salmon. With nearly 60 inches of annual rainfall, however, most of it coming in the winter, the Eel River can become quite torrential, spilling over its banks and flooding much of the park's 1,200 acres.

CAMPGROUND: Nestled on the banks of the river, the campground is one of the first areas to flood when the waters rise. And that no doubt explains why the campground is closed Nov. 1 through March 31. From April to the end of October, however, more than 18,000 campers choose this spot. There are 75 sites capable of accommodating tents or RVs up to 30 feet. Each has its own parking spur, table, fire ring with grill and storage locker. There's also a dump station and water, but no hookups.

RESTROOMS: One of the three restrooms includes private coin-operated showers; the others have free cold outdoor showers. All feature flush toilets, sinks and mirrors.

FEES: $14/day in peak season (May 1-Sept. 30); $12/day off-peak. $3/day per person for *Hike & Bike camping.*

RESERVATIONS: From May 1 through Sept. 30, campsites may be reserved up to eight weeks in advance through MISTIX, 1-800-444-PARK. The campground shifts to a first come, first-served basis the rest of the time it's open.

CHECK IN/OUT: Noon out.

DOGS: $1/day; not permitted on trails.

MAX. STAY: 15 days throughout the year. Hike & Bike camping, two days.

SECURITY: Park rangers and resident camp host.

HOW TO GET THERE: From Garberville, drive south for two miles; exit at Benbow Drive and follow signs to the campground exit.

A. W. WAY COUNTY PARK
c/o Humboldt County Parks
1106 2nd Street, Eureka, CA
(707) 445-7651

- Riverside tent & RV camping

This 20-acre pocket park sits in the middle of nowhere alongside the Mattole River in a grassy meadow punctuated with occasional firs, pines and poplars. It's 12-15 miles inland and can get pretty warm in summers when people take to the river. In the winter, the river fills with steelhead, and that's when the anglers take to it.

The nearest services are in the towns of Petrolia or Honeydew, eight miles drive in either direction from the park on Mattole Road. Both have a grocery store, gasoline station and propane.

CAMPGROUND: The mostly grassy campground consists of 30 sites capable of taking either tents or moderate-sized RVs. Each site includes its own parking spur, table, and fire ring. Water is available, but there are neither hookups nor dump station.

RESTROOMS: Two plumbed restrooms with sinks; one has an AC outlet, the other has a cold outdoor shower with privacy shield.

FEES: $10/day per vehicle. *Hike & Bike campers* - $3/day per person.

DOGS: $1/day.

MAX. STAY: 16 days per 28-day period.

RESERVATIONS: First come, first served.

CHECK IN/OUT: 1 p.m.

SECURITY: Occasional park staff and resident caretaker.

HOW TO GET THERE: From Garberville, drive 22 miles north on Highway 101; exit at South Fork/Honeydew and follow for 31 slow, winding miles through hills and valleys to the park entrance.

HUMBOLDT REDWOODS STATE PARK
P.O. Box 188, Weott, CA 955771
(707) 946-2409

- Redwood forest tent & RV camping
- Walk-in tent camping
- Hike & Bike camping
- Backpack camping
- Horse camping
- Group camping

This park attracts almost three-quarters of a million visitors a year. Nevertheless, as the third largest state park with more than 51,000 acres, it's considered a sleeping giant still waiting to be discovered.

Located 25 miles from the coast, the park hugs Highway 101 45 miles south of Eureka. It includes 17,000 acres of old growth redwood forest, almost 10% of all old growth redwood forests remaining in the world. More than 100 miles of hiking, riding and mountain bike trails snake along the mostly mountainous landscape, which varies in elevation from about 150 feet to 3,379 feet at Grasshopper Peak. The Eel River and numerous creeks run through the park like veins and arteries, promising trophy-sized steelhead and salmon to anglers during the winter months. In the summer, its swimming holes offer refreshing opportunities to swim, raft and cool off in the 80-90° temperatures.

Summer is the busiest time of year, with frequent organized hikes and campfire programs. The Visitor Center is open daily throughout the summer, too, offering exhibits, publications and audio-visual programs about the area. (The center is open intermittently throughout the rest of the year.)

One of the most effortless ways of exploring and enjoying the park is via the Avenue of the Giants, a 32-mile portion of old Highway

101 that winds through an unreal forest of giant old growth redwoods along the entire length of the park's eastern end. It's a few miles and takes a little longer to drive than the new Highway 101 which it closely parallels, but it also adds tremendous dimension to your journey. There are numerous motels, restaurants, fuel stations and other services along the way, so don't worry about breaking down. The avenue is also the only route to the Visitor Center and the park's main campgrounds.

Wildlife is abundant and includes black bears and mountain lions. In 1994, in fact, there were a half-dozen sitings of mountain lions. In spring and summer, but mosquitos pose a far more realistic concern.

Basic services are available along a string of small towns on the Avenue of the Giants.

CAMPGROUNDS: The park offers a variety of camping opportunities including three family campgrounds; two walk-in tent camps; five trail camps, two group campgrounds, a Hike & Bike camp, and a horse camp for groups or families.

Family Campgrounds

Hidden Springs, Burlington and **Albee Creek** can accommodate both tents and RVs up to 33 feet with a total of 249 campsites. Hidden Springs is set beneath a mixed forest of second growth redwoods, tanoaks and madrones; Burlington beneath second growth redwoods; and Albee Creek under a second growth redwood forest at the edge of an old, abandoned apple orchard that still bears fruit (and draws a lot of wildlife to it, including a recurring bear). All sites offer their own parking spurs, tables and fire rings with grill tops. Water spigots are placed throughout the campgrounds, but there are no hookups. The park's only dump station was recently decommissioned.

RESTROOMS: Flush toilets, sinks, mirrors, AC outlets and coin-operated showers. Albee Creek's showers are solar-heated and free of charge.

FEES: $14/day in peak season (May 1-Sept. 30); $12/day off-peak.

RESERVATIONS: Burlington - for camping between May 1-Sept. 30, reservations may be made up to eight weeks in advance through MISTIX, 1-800-444-PARK; Hidden Springs and Albee Creek reservations may be made for the May 27-Sept. 4 period.

CHECK IN/OUT: Noon.

DOGS: $1/day; not permitted on trails.

MAX. STAY: Burlington - 15 days (June-Sept.); 30 days remainder of the year; same for Hidden Springs and Albee Creek except these campgrounds are closed to camping Oct. 1-May 26.

SECURITY: Park rangers and seasonal staff; summertime resident camp host at Albee Creek only.

HOW TO GET THERE:

Hidden Springs - 154 campsites on the Avenue of the Giants, a half-mile from the town of Myers Flat. From Garberville, drive north on Highway 101 for 10 miles; exit onto the Avenue of the Giants and follow that to the Hidden Springs Campground.

Burlington - 56 campsites next door to park headquarters and the Visitor Center. From Hidden Springs Campground, drive five miles north on the Avenue of the Giants.

Albee Creek - 39 campsites. From Burlington Campground, drive north on the Avenue of the Giants; turn left (west) on Mattole Road for five miles to the campground.

Walk-In Tent Camping

Hamilton Barn and Baxter environmental campgrounds are located across Mattole Road from each other just beyond the Albee Creek Campground.

Hamilton Barn offers three sites beneath a mixed forest of tanoak, madrones, Douglas firs and second growth redwoods. Campsites are 100-150 yards apart. **Note:** this campground closes after Labor Day.

Baxter Camp is a little more forested, further back from the road and closer to the creek than Hamilton. It includes two campsites about 200 yards apart from each other. It's open all year long.

Each campsite features a picnic table, food locker, and fire pit. Water must be treated before use. Campers must walk approximately 100 yards to the campsites.

RESTROOMS: Pit toilets.

FEES: $9/day in peak season (May 1-Sept. 30); $7/day off-peak.

RESERVATIONS: For camping between Memorial Day weekend and Labor Day weekends, reservations may be made up to eight weeks in advance through MISTIX, 1-800-444-PARK. Thereafter, it works on a first-come, first-served basis. You may also register in person at either Albee Creek or Burlington Campgrounds.

CHECK IN/OUT: Noon.

DOGS: Not permitted.

MAX. STAY: Seven consecutive days

SECURITY: Park rangers.

HOW TO GET THERE: From the Avenue of the Giants, turn west on Mattole Road about 5½ miles (about a half-mile past the Albee Campground).

Trail Camping

These five campgrounds are located along the park's many miles of trails and are available on a first-come, first-served basis. Trail distances range from two to eight miles, which will vary according to where you start and what loops you follow. Except for Johnson Camp, the camps are open to bicyclists as well as hikers.

Johnson Camp is set within a forest of second growth redwoods and marked by two rustic but useable cabins left over from an old railroad tie-making camp. They offer nothing more than four wooden walls, a wooden floor and a roof.

Hanson Ridge Camp is a sunny place set amid the tanoaks. There are good views of the Bull Creek watershed and surrounding area.

Whiskey Flat Camp is situated beneath a shady grove of old growth redwoods.

Bull Creek Camp sits alongside the creek of the same name in a relatively open area of tanoaks and madrones. This is probably the warmest of all the campgrounds, with temperatures climbing into the 90s.

Grasshopper Camp is just beneath Grasshopper Peak, highest point in the park at 3,379 feet. To reach the camp, you must hike from an elevation of 250 feet to over 3,300 feet. It's a sunny area of Douglas firs and grass. Expect lots of hikers to pass by the campground on their way to the peak.

RESTROOMS: Pit toilets. Water should be treated before using.

FEES: $3/day per person.

RESERVATIONS: First come, first served. Registration required at either Albee Creek or Burlington Campgrounds.

CHECK IN/OUT: Noon.

DOGS: Not permitted.

MAX. STAY: Seven days.

SECURITY: Park rangers.

HOW TO GET THERE: Get trail map from park headquarters.

Williams Grove Group Camps

There are two sections to this campground: **Camp A**, located alongside the Avenue of the Giants with capacity for 60 campers and parking for 20 vehicles; and **Camp B**, set alongside the south fork of the Eel River with a capacity for 40 campers and parking for 15 vehicles. They're adjacent to each other in a combination of old and second growth redwoods and may be booked separately or together. They include tables, barbecues and require a short walk from the parking area.

RESTROOMS: New facilities include flush toilets, sinks and mirrors. There's no electricity, but lighting is provided by propane lights. No showers.

FEES: $90/day for *Camp A*; $60/day for *Camp B*; $150/day for both.

RESERVATIONS: For camping between May 27 and Sept. 4, reservations may be made up to six months in advance through MISTIX, 1-800-444-PARK.

CHECK IN/OUT: Noon.

DOGS: $1/day; not permitted on trails.

MAX. STAY: 15 days.

SECURITY: Park rangers.

HOW TO GET THERE: From Myers Flat, drive north on Avenue of the Giants one mile; turn left at Williams Grove.

Hike & Bike Camping

A short walk or ride off the Avenue of the Giants, Marin Garden Club Grove offers hikers and bicyclists respite from the road beneath a shady grove of second growth redwoods with alders and willows nearer the river. There are tables, fire rings and water.

RESTROOMS: Flush toilets and sinks. Campers may use shower facilities at Burlington, 1½ miles south.

FEES: $3/day per person.

RESERVATIONS: First come, first-served. Register at the other campgrounds.

CHECK IN/OUT: Noon.

DOGS: Not permitted.

MAX. STAY: Two days.

SECURITY: Park rangers.

HOW TO GET THERE: From Burlington Campground, hike or bike 1½ miles north on the Avenue of the Giants.

Horse Camping

The Cuneo Creek Horse Camp can accommodate both groups and individual families. There are some 75 miles of fire roads open to horseback riding within the park.

The group camp can handle 50 to 100 people with horses. It features group picnic tables, barbecues, corrals, water troughs, hitching posts and drinking water.

There also are five individual sites for families. Each has a table, fire ring, and limited corral capacity.

RESTROOMS: Newly constructed facilities include flush toilets, sinks, mirrors and coin-operated showers.

FEES: *Group camp* - $90/day. *Individual* sites - $16/day in peak season (Memorial Day weekend through Labor Day) for a family and up to two horses ($1 additional each additional horse); fee drops to $14/day in off-peak.

RESERVATIONS: For camping between Memorial Day and Labor Day, the group horse camp may be reserved up to six months in advance through MISTIX, 1-800-444-PARK. All other times, reservations are made directly through park headquarters: (707) 946-2409.

Individual sites are available on a first-come, first-served basis throughout the year. Campers self-register at the campground.

CHECK IN/OUT: Noon.

DOGS: $1/day; not permitted on riding trails.

MAX. STAY: 15 days.

SECURITY: Park rangers.

HOW TO GET THERE: From Avenue of the Giants, take Mattole Road west 6½ miles.

SAMOA BOAT RAMP COUNTY PARK

c/o Humboldt County Parks
1106 2nd Street, Eureka, CA 95501
(707) 464-7230

- Tent & RV camping
- Hike & Bike camping

This is basically a parking lot – wall-to-wall asphalt – maintained by the county, while all of the beach area around it is administered by the City of Eureka or other agencies. One of its main attractions is not part of the park at all – the Samoa Peninsula Off-Road Vehicle Recreation Area, located just a quarter-mile away. As the biggest dune area in the vicinity (125 acres), it attracts lots of *dune bugs* who enjoy racing through the sand in every manner of all-terrain vehicle you can imagine.

Until fairly recently, Samoa Boat Ramp County Park was also a popular fishing destination. However, fishing hasn't been all that good lately, resulting in a noticeable drop-off in popularity. You can also launch boats into Humboldt Bay, second largest deepwater port in California and home of the third largest colony of harbor seals on the Pacific Coast.

With Eureka, the cultural, political and economic hub of Humboldt County just across the bay, you'll find goods and services to fill your every requirement. For basic items though, you may find what you need right on the peninsula in the nearby communities of Fairhaven and Samoa. Just two miles away from the park, in fact, is the well known Samoa Cookhouse, the only cookhouse in the West still serving breakfast, lunch and dinner lumber-camp style (big tables and lots of food).

CAMPGROUND: There are 20 campsites, more accurately referred to as parking spaces best suited to RVs. Concrete picnic tables, fire rings with grill tops and water hookups grace most sites, which are capable of accommodating virtually any size vehicle. For the insistent tenter, however, there are some spaces with a sandy area upon which to set your stakes. Of course, you can also make camp on the asphalt.

RESTROOMS: Flush toilets, sinks, mirrors and AC outlets; no showers.

FEES: $8/day; $3/day for *Hike & Bike* campers.

RESERVATIONS: First come, first served (rarely filled).

CHECK IN/OUT: 1 p.m. out.

DOGS: $1/day; permitted on trails and beaches if leashed.

MAX. STAY: 16 days max. in any 28-day period.

SECURITY: Resident camp host and park personnel.

HOW TO GET THERE: From Eureka, drive north on Highway 101; exit left on Highway 255, passing over three bridges to a narrow peninsula across from Humboldt Bay. From 255, veer to the left onto New Navy Base Road and follow it to the park entrance. It will be on the left side of the road (facing Humboldt Bay), almost at the end of the peninsula.

CLAM BEACH COUNTY PARK
c/o Humboldt County Parks
1106 2nd Street, Eureka, CA
(707) 445-7651

• On-beach tent & RV camping

Clam Beach is a giant stretch of sandy shoreline where you can dig for razor clams, comb the beach, ride horseback or just picnic and enjoy the ample space and wide-angled ocean vista. It's also site of the Clam Beach Run, which attracts thousands of runners each year.

Clam Beach is situated alongside Highway 101 seven miles north of Arcata, a town of just over 15,000 people and home to Humboldt State University. Seven miles to the north lies Trinidad, a quaint little fishing village of 432 people. Closest of all is McKinleyville, where horses still have the right of way despite it being the fastest growing community in Humboldt County, with an estimated 11,000 residents. Local industry includes thriving bulb and tree farms, dairies, begonia gardens (often open to the public) and a nationally acclaimed manufacturer of goat cheese (Cypress Grove Chevre).

One of the best times to visit this area is in the spring, when the Azalea Reserve is abloom with native shrubs.

CAMPGROUND: There's a parking lot at both north and south ends of the park; within the three-quarters of a mile that divides them spread the scoops and swells of shallow sand dunes. Tent campers will find 20 campsites in this rolling landscape. All have concrete picnic tables and fire rings with grill tops. Beyond the dunes is a very broad expanse of smooth sand where you can also camp, although without benefit of either table or fire rings.

Signs warn of "DANGEROUS UNDERTOW" in the surf and caution against swimming or wading. Street-licensed four-wheel-drive vehicles are permitted on the sand; off-road vehicles are prohibited.

RVs of nearly any length can use either of the two parking lots, although they will find neither hookups nor dump station. Water spigots are nearby, however.

RESTROOMS: Chemical toilets; no showers.

FEES: $8/day.

RESERVATIONS: First come, first served.

CHECK IN/OUT: 1 p.m. out.

DOGS: $1/day; okay on beach. Must be leashed at all times.

MAX. STAY: 16 days maximum in any 28-day period.

SECURITY: County sheriff's department.

HOW TO GET THERE: From Arcata, drive north on Highway 101 for seven miles; exit at Clam Beach.

PATRICK'S POINT STATE PARK

4150 Patrick's Point Drive, Trinidad, CA 95570
(707) 677-3570

- Cliff-top tent & RV camping (near the ocean)
- Hike & Bike camping
- Group camping

"At Patrick's Point, you are on the front lines of a dramatic battle," explains a sign at one of the park's overlooks.

Standing at the edge of this 632-acre promontory you have an excellent view of the battle between the land and sea. From the top of its sheer, 100-foot cliffs come dramatic views of frothing surf, stubborn stacks of offshore rock and, in the spring and fall, 40-ton whales.

Expect to be fogged in morning and night throughout the year, particularly in the summer when it may hang in the air for days at a time. Spring and fall typically present the clearest days of the year; winter the wettest. Temperatures are moderate the year round, winter lows averaging 38°, summertime highs about 62°.

Camping in the woods

Patrick's Point trails also offer ample opportunity for exploration. Rim Trail extends for two miles along the edge of the cliff overlooking the ocean; at several points, steep quarter-mile paths lead down from the trail to the shoreline where you can examine tidepools or comb beaches. Semi-precious agates polished smooth by the surf and sand are a common discovery at Agate Beach, a long crescent of sand at the north end of the park.

Near the park entrance, local members of the Yurok Indian tribe have constructed an authentic Yurok village, which is open to the public daily during park hours. The Yuroks once lived in permanent villages north and south of the park and frequented the area now known as Patrick's Point in summer to harvest fish, mussels, sea lions and other game. Anglers still come here to catch ling cod, greenlings, sea trout and rock cod. Bears and raccoons are among the many animals you may encounter here. Rangers urge campers to wrap food carefully and store it in their vehicles, well out of sight and smell of these animals.

CAMPGROUND: Three family campgrounds – Agate, Abalone and Penn – offer a total of 124 campsites. Each has its own parking spur, table, stove and storage locker and can host either tents or RVs up to 31 feet. There are no hookups or dump station, but water faucets are nearby. Some campsites in the Agate and Abalone Campgrounds are close to the park's cliff. Penn Campground, adjacent to Abalone Campground, is set back from the cliff, about a half-mile from the beach.

Like Penn Campground, the Beach Creek Group Camp is a half-mile inland of the beach. It can accommodate up to 150 campers and 30 vehicles, and includes a covered cook shelter and campfire center.

Although situated in the heart of redwood country, you'll more than likely find yourself camped beneath spruce, hemlock, pine, fir or red alder, the predominant trees at Patrick's Point. Closer to ground level, you'll find a variety of thick shrubs and ground-covers, including deer fern, azalea, and rhododendron.

RESTROOMS: Flush toilets, sinks, mirrors and, in some cases, coin-operated showers.

FEES: $14/day in peak season (May 1-Sept. 30); $12/day off-peak. *Hike & Bike camping* - $3/day per person. *Group camp - $150/day.*

RESERVATIONS: For campsites from May 27-Sept. 5, you can make reservations up to eight weeks in advance through MISTIX, 1-800-444-PARK. Group camp reservations may be made any time of year up to six months in advance through MISTIX.

CHECK IN/OUT: Noon.

DOGS: $1/day; not permitted on trails or beaches.

MAX. STAY: 15 days from June-Sept.; 30 days remainder of the year.

SECURITY: Park rangers and resident camp host.

HOW TO GET THERE: Drive five miles north of Trinidad; turn left at Patrick's Creek and follow one-half mile to the park entrance.

BIG LAGOON COUNTY PARK

c/o Humboldt County Parks
1106 2nd Street, Eureka, CA
(707) 445-7651

- Lagoon-side tent & RV camping
- Hike & Bike camping

There's a reason they call this facility *Big Lagoon*. The large freshwater lake that shimmers before you makes it eminently clear. Separated from the ocean by a 600-700-foot-wide spit of land that disappears on occasion in the wetter months of winter, the 1,400-acre lagoon provides a popular recreational outlet to windsurfers, sailors and motor boat enthusiasts alike. It's open to fishing all year round too, trout being the prize catch.

Nearest services are in the little town of Trinidad, eight miles south on Highway 101.

CAMPGROUND: Twenty-five campsites which can accommodate both tents and RVs are situated in a densely shaded grove of Sitka spruce and fir on the inland side of the lagoon. Only a few of the campsites have any view of the lagoon, which is 30 to 40 yards from the nearest site. Each site includes a parking spur, table and fire ring with grill top. Water spigots are placed throughout the campground, but there are no hookups or dump station.

There's no set maximum to the length of RV here, although the loop through the campground is rather tight and narrow, making maneuverability a potential problem for larger units.

A broad, sandy beach is 100 to 150 yards from the campground. Swimming is not recommended due to strong undertow, but it's a nice place for a walk.

RESTROOMS: Newly built restrooms feature flush toilets, mirrors, sinks and AC outlets; however, there are no showers.

FEES: $10/day per vehicle. *Hike & Bike campers* - $3/day per person.

RESERVATIONS: First come, first served; reportedly packed every day throughout July and August. Best chances are to arrive early, before 10 a.m., and wait for openings as others leave.

CHECK IN/OUT: 1 p.m.

DOGS: $1/day; permitted on trails and beach if leashed.

MAX. STAY: 16 days per 28-day period.

SECURITY: Occasional park staff and resident camp host.

HOW TO GET THERE: From Eureka, drive north on Highway 101 40 miles (two miles past Patrick's Point State Park). Turn left at Big Lagoon Park Road and follow signs to the entrance, an estimated two miles from 101.

HUMBOLDT LAGOONS STATE PARK
Orick, CA 95555
(707) 488-2041

- Boat-in tent camping
- Environmental tent camping

Midpoint between Eureka on the south and Crescent City on the north, Humboldt Lagoons State Park consists of seven miles of mercurial beach and marshland that can shift, dissolve away and then rebuild at the whim of the weather and ocean tides. The park is named after three sizeable lagoons that comprise the bulk of its area. Largest of the three is Big Lagoon, 3½ miles long and more than 1,400 acres in size.

North of that is Dry Lagoon, which is not much more than a marsh today. Early farmers had drained the lagoon in a futile effort to grow currants. When that didn't pan out, the farmers left and the land reverted to its present state.

Stone Lagoon is one mile long and encompasses an estimated 520 acres. Like Big Lagoon, Stone Lagoon is separated from the ocean by a 600-700-foot-wide barrier of sand known as a spit. During the winter, the spits are liable to wash away, allowing the lagoons to spill into the sea. Lagoon levels can drop six to eight feet in a few hours. As conditions change, the surf and tide repair the beach, the lagoons refill and the cycle begins all over again.

This fluid landscape, which once drew goldminers by the score, continues to serve as a haven to more than 200 species of birds as well as the black bear. Food and trash storage precautions are required.

The closed-in beach offers fine strolling and surf fishing, but swimming is not recommended; it's simply too cold and rough.

The Visitor Center tries to maintain a daily schedule during the summer season; however, because it's staffed by volunteers, hours of operation are subject to change. It's generally closed from October through May.

Nearest services are in Orick, three miles north.

There are two campgrounds in Humboldt Lagoons State Park – Stone Lagoon and Dry Lagoon. In each case, you'll have to pack in everything you need, from water to firewood, then pack out all trash when leaving.

Stone Lagoon Campground

This is a boat-in site on the western shore of Stone Lagoon in a forest of alder, spruce and redwood. If you're interested in camping here, you must have your own boat, which can be launched from a small gravelly boat ramp next to the Visitor Center. It's on the eastern edge of Stone Lagoon alongside Highway 101. You can park in the Visitor Center's parking lot. The trip to the other side of the lagoon is about a quarter mile. You'll find six tent sites with food storage lockers, tables and fire rings.

RESTROOMS: Pit toilets.

FEES: $7/day.

RESERVATIONS: First come, first served. Self-register and pay fees at the *iron ranger* next to the bulletin board near the Visitor Center (just off Highway 101). The campground is rarely filled.

CHECK IN/OUT: Noon.

DOGS: Not permitted.

MAX. STAY: 15 days (June-Sept.); 30 days remainder of the year.

SECURITY: Occasional park ranger on patrol.

HOW TO GET THERE: From Eureka, drive north 43 miles on Highway 101. Park at the Visitor Center.

Dry Lagoon Campground

Another popular getaway in the summer months. It consists of six campsites in a brushy area punctuated with spruce. A couple of them have views of the ocean and all include a table and fire ring. Campers may either walk in or drive to the campground, set about ¾ of a mile west of Highway 101. Those driving in will need the combination to unlock the gate. The combination will be given to you after registering at either the Stone Lagoon Visitor Center, Prairie Creek Redwoods State Park or Patrick's Point State Park.

RESTROOMS: Chemical toilets.

FEES: $7 / day.

RESERVATIONS: First come, first served. Campers must register and pay fees at either Patrick's Point State Park, Prairie Creek Redwoods State Park or the Stone Lagoon Visitor Center.

CHECK IN/OUT: Noon.

DOGS: Not permitted.

MAX. STAY: 15 days (June-Sept.); 30 days remainder of the year.

SECURITY: Occasional park ranger on patrol.

HOW TO GET THERE: From Eureka, drive north 42 miles on Highway 101. Exit at the Dry Lagoon turnoff and follow the road to the gated campground entrance (veer to the left as the road forks).

REDWOODS NATIONAL PARK
1111 Second Street, Crescent City, CA 95531
(707) 464-6101

- Primitive walk-in tent camping
- Horse camping

This is a *park of parks* in a manner of speaking, for within its 110,000 acres exist three magnificent state parks – Prairie Creek Redwoods, Del Norte Coast Redwoods and Jedediah Smith Redwoods – the combined area of which forms over a quarter of Redwood National Park's total acreage. But while state and federal authorities work in close cooperation for the mutual benefit of the whole redwood coast, each maintains its individual identity, operating under its own regulations and personnel (refer to the individual state parks for details).

To the birds, bears, mountain lions, elk, and most people that live on or pass through this land, of course, the administrative facts of the redwood coast are immaterial. What matters most is the preservation and enjoyment of the some of the planet's most beautiful forests, beaches and cliffs which stretch for 40 miles between Orick and Crescent City.

Within this vast expanse, you can see the world's tallest trees, hike along 125 miles of trails, ride horseback and discover secluded beaches. From the precipitous Coastal Drive, outstanding panoramas reveal themselves at numerous points along eight miles of twists and turns. Trailers and motorhomes are not advised on the north part of the drive (detour on Alder Camp Road).

The Redwood Information Center is an absolute must, especially for first time visitors. A mile south of Orick just off Highway 101, it's an impressive treasure chest of information, including lots of literature, maps, interpretive displays and a knowledgeable staff.

CAMPGROUNDS: All camping within Redwoods National Park (excluding the state parks) is at primitive walk-in sites or horse camps equipped with basics such as tables and fire rings with grills. Troughs and corrals are also provided at horse camps. Water may or may not be available. Restroom facilities consist solely of pit toilets. Bears and mountain lions inhabit the area, but there have been no reported incidents.

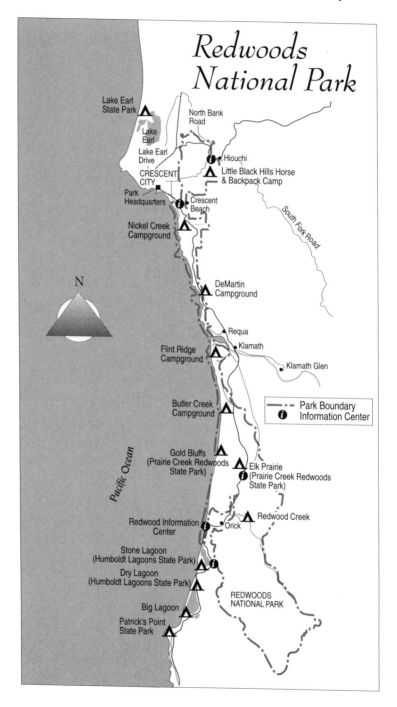

Redwoods
National Park

Lake Earl
State Park

North Bank
Road

Lake
Earl

Lake Earl
Drive

Hiouchi

CRESCENT
CITY

Little Black Hills Horse
& Backpack Camp

Park
Headquarters

Crescent
Beach

South Fork Road

Nickel Creek
Campground

N

DeMartin
Campground

Requa

Klamath

Flint Ridge
Campground

Klamath Glen

Butler Creek
Campground

Park Boundary
Information Center

Pacific Ocean

Gold Bluffs
(Prairie Creek Redwoods
State Park)

Elk Prairie
(Prairie Creek Redwoods
State Park)

Redwood Creek

Redwood Information
Center

Orick

Stone Lagoon
(Humboldt Lagoons State Park)

Dry Lagoon
(Humboldt Lagoons State Park)

REDWOODS
NATIONAL PARK

Big Lagoon

Patrick's Point
State Park

Little Bald Hills Horse and Backpack Camp sits 1,000 feet above sea level in a forest of firs, hemlocks and madrones. Once the site of an old ranch, the campground has potable water and a horse bar. Six miles beyond the campground there is access to extensive horse trails within national forest lands. For information on forest service lands, call the Gasquet Ranger Station at (707) 457-3131. HOW TO GET THERE: From Crescent City, take Elk Valley Road (199) to Howland Hill Road, six miles of gravel that's closed to motorhomes and trailers. The trailhead begins off Howland Hill Road at South Fork Road; hike or ride 3½ miles through redwoods and open prairies to the campsite.

Redwood Creek Backpack and Horse Camp is a small backcountry facility in an old growth redwood forest. Campers must obtain a backcountry permit in person at the Redwood Information Center (707-488-3461) prior to camping. There's water, a horse trough and a horse bar. Several trail loops will lead you on rides from three hours to three days in length.

On the longer trails, a couple of true backcountry camps, **Elam Camp** and **44 Camp**, offer respite from the trail. Elam has two sites with corral, tie down lines, non-potable water, bear-proof food lockers and a pit toilet. 44 Camp has four sites beneath a heavy forest canopy. You will find tie down lines, grills, picnic tables, a restroom, and bear-proof food lockers here. Water is available summers only. HOW TO GET THERE: From Orick, drive north on Highway 101; exit at Dryden and park in the Orick Rodeo grounds. Hike or ride a mile to Redwood Creek.

Butler Creek Campground is situated on a bluff above a rocky beach. There's a trail to the beach as well as water and an excellent view. HOW TO GET THERE: From Orick, drive north on Highway 101; exit at Davison Road, a dirt road on which trailers are prohibited. Follow Davison past Gold Bluffs Beach to Fern Canyon; park and follow the rolling Coastal Trail three miles to Butler Creek Campground.

Flint Ridge Campground features 10 sites on a hillside 100 feet above the ocean at the edge of a grassy meadow surrounded by a redwood and spruce forest. Good views of the coast and surrounding terrain. Potable water is available. No beach access. HOW TO GET THERE: From Orick, drive north on Highway 101 to Drury Scenic Parkway (old Highway 101); follow the parkway to the Coastal Drive and take that north to where it crests south of the mouth of the Klamath River. Park on the west side of the road and hike a quarter-mile to Flint Ridge Campground. **Note:** Trailers are not recommended on parts of Coastal Drive.

DeMartin Campground has 10 campsites on a small open grassy area at the edge of a forest of redwoods. Some have ocean views. Potable water is available. This is an active bear habitat and campers have to take special precautions. Food (and trash) must be stored in bear-proof lockers (provided) or hung from a tree 200 feet from the campsite at least 15 feet from the ground and 10 feet out on a limb from the trunk. All trash should be packed out when leaving. A rocky, sandy beach is accessible by trail. HOW TO GET THERE: There are two options. Drive north from Orick on Highway 101 and park on the east side of Highway 101 at mile marker 14.42 at the north end of Wilson Creek Bridge. From here, it's a half-mile hike to the campground. You may also park at the Redwood Hostel south of Wilson Creek off Highway 101 and hike three *steep* miles to the campground.

Nickel Creek has five campsites about 25 feet above the beach in a shrubby canyon bisected by a year-round creek. The rock and sand beach is 15 minutes away. Potable water is available. HOW TO GET THERE: Drive south from Crescent City on Highway 101 for three miles; exit at Endert's Beach Road (paved) and drive south. Park at the end of Endert's Beach Road and hike a half-mile to the campground.

FEES: None.

RESERVATIONS: First come, first served.

CHECK IN/OUT: No specific in or out times.

DOGS: No pets allowed.

MAX. STAY: 14 days.

SECURITY: Park rangers on patrol.

PRAIRIE CREEK REDWOODS STATE PARK
Orick, CA 95555
(707) 488-2171

- Redwood forest tent & RV camping
- On-beach tent camping
- Hike & Bike camping

If you find yourself in the midst of a herd of elk here, you shouldn't be surprised. This is home to the antlered giants that graze throughout portions of the park's 12,500 acres. You can often see them right next to Highway 101 in a prairie aptly named Elk Prairie.

As is generally the case along this part of the California Coast, you'll find incredible forests of redwoods as well as spruce and numerous other trees. Explore them along 75 miles of meandering trails. Don't miss Fern Canyon, a 50-foot wall of rock covered with a living tapestry of ferns. Gold Bluffs Beach offers a long, wide, sandy coast flanked by mounds of sand and golden bluffs that rise 100 to 150 feet straight up.

Insight into the history, natural and otherwise, of this area is offered at the Elk Prairie Visitor Center within the park. There's also an interpretive trail for the blind. If you're there in August, you may be interested in entering the annual Banana Slug Derby (check for actual date). The Banana Slug is bright yellow, several inches in length, and an important member of the redwood forest ecosystem. It helps break down plant debris on the forest floor. You can bring your own or borrow one of the park's. Park fees are waived the day of the derby.

About 50 miles north of Eureka, Prairie Creek is one of most popular state parks, drawing nearly a half-million visitors a year. Orick, just six miles south, provides the nearest basic services. Klamath is 12 miles to the north.

Of the Prairie Creek's numerous visitors, almost 70,000 of them are campers who avail themselves of the park's two main campgrounds.

Gold Bluffs Campground

Gold Bluffs Campground is situated along Gold Bluffs Beach. There are 25 sites here. Some of them allow you to park right next to your campsite. Others require a short walk into the dunes within full view of the Pacific, its outraged surf desperate to scramble up the beach. A number of the sites are protected from the wind and blowing sand by windscreens comprised of heavy duty log walls. All campsites have tables, fire rings with grill tops and bear-proof food storage lockers. Water is available, but there are no hookups or dump station.

Basic log walls offer campers protection

This is bear country, by the way, and the animals are active day and night. Proper food storage is required by state law. Mountain lions inhabit the area as well, along with occasional herds of elk. Plant life is sparse, dune grass being the most prevalent growth.

Make sure you have all your supplies. It's a long, bumpy ride back to Orick if you need anything.

RESTROOMS: A bit rustic, but they do include flush toilets, sinks and mirrors. The showers are outdoors but are enclosed by wood plank walls. When conditions are right, solar heat provides warm water, and there's no charge.

FEES: $14/day in peak season (May 1-Sept. 30); $12/day off-peak.

RESERVATIONS: First come, first served. This campground is very popular, so be prepared with alternate plans. "Every day is like a weekend in the summer."

CHECK IN/OUT: Noon out.

DOGS: $1/day; not permitted on trails, but okay on beach if leashed.

MAX. STAY: 15 days (June-Sept.); 30 days remainder of the year.

SECURITY: Park rangers.

HOW TO GET THERE: From Orick, drive 4½ miles north on Highway 101; exit left on Davison Road, a dirt road that feels as though you're driving across a washboard at times (trailers are prohibited). Portions of the road pass through tunnels of spruce and alder so dense that you're asked to turn your headlights on. Follow the road six miles to the campground. Fern Canyon is a couple of miles further.

Elk Prairie Campground

Elk Prairie Campground is inland of Gold Bluffs Beach and comprised of 75 sites in a shady forest of redwoods, alders and spruce. Each site can accommodate tents or RVs up to 27 feet and includes its own parking spur, table, fire ring with grill top and food storage lockers to discourage bears and raccoons. Water spigots are spaced throughout the campground and there is a dump station, but no hookups. The Visitor Center, located near the entrance to the campground, offers interpretive displays, publications for sale and knowledgeable staff. Nearest supplies are in Orick, six miles south.

Access to Gold Bluffs Beach is possible by way of several trails. The 4.2-mile James Irvine Trail is the most popular.

RESTROOMS: Modern facilities with flush toilets, sinks, mirrors and hot showers, soon to become coin operated.

FEES: $14/day in peak season (May 1-Sept. 30); $12/day off-peak.

RESERVATIONS: For camping between May 27 and Sept. 5, you can make reservations up to eight weeks in advance through MISTIX, 1-800-444-PARK.

CHECK IN/OUT: Noon out.

DOGS: $1/day; prohibited on trails.

MAX. STAY: 15 days (June-Sept.); 30 days remainder of the year.

SECURITY: Park rangers and resident camp host.

HOW TO GET THERE: Elk Prairie is three miles north of Davison Road, where you turn off to reach Gold Bluffs Beach. From Orick, drive north on Highway 101; exit at Drury Scenic Parkway. Watch for signs and turn left at the park entrance.

Del Norte County

DEL NORTE COAST REDWOODS STATE PARK

1375 Elk Valley Road
Crescent City, CA 95531
(707) 464-9533

- Dense redwood forest tent & RV camping
- Hike & Bike camping

This 6,375-acre park, two-thirds of it a dense forest of old growth redwoods, rises to an elevation of 670 feet before it comes to an abrupt end at the foot of the Pacific. Rugged trails will lead you down to the eight miles of wild coast below, which offers tiny hidden coves as well as roaring seas and beaches. A number of other trails take you to dramatic ocean views, colorful spreads of wildflowers, along streams and past remnants of the old railroad and lumbering operations, which once chugged, whistled and buzzed throughout the area.

In May and June, many native flowers, including western azalea and rhododendron, dab the forest with sprays of color.

The nearest services are located in Crescent City, seven miles north.

CAMPGROUND: The Mill Creek Campground is a little over two miles from Highway 101 in a lush ravine consisting of second growth redwoods, Sitka spruce, alder and maple. There are 145 campsites that accommodate either tents or RVs up to 31 feet. Each site has its own parking spur, picnic table and fire ring with grill top. There is piped-in water and a dump station, but no hookups.

RESTROOMS: Flush toilets, sinks, mirrors and coin-operated showers.

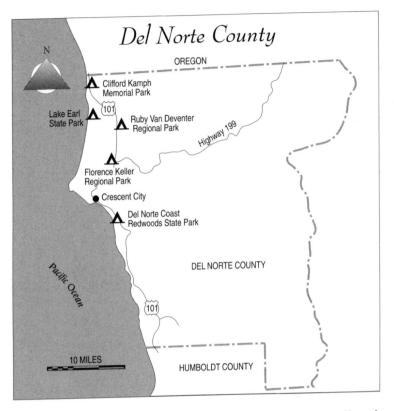

FEES: $14/day in peak season (May 1-Sept. 30); $12/day off-peak. *Hike & Bike* camping: $3/day per person.

DOGS: $1/day; not permitted on trails.

MAX. STAY: 15 days (June-Sept.); 30 days remainder of the year.

RESERVATIONS: For camping between May 21 and Sept. 5, you can make reservations up to eight weeks in advance through MIS-TIX, 1-800-444-PARK.

CHECK IN/OUT: Noon out.

SECURITY: Park rangers and resident camp host.

HOW TO GET THERE: From Crescent City, drive south on Highway 101 for seven miles; watch for turn-off on your left and follow for a little over two miles.

JEDEDIAH SMITH
REDWOODS STATE PARK

1440 Highway 199
Crescent City, CA
(707) 458-3310

- Redwood forest tent & RV camping
- Hike & Bike camping

Jedediah Smith Redwoods State Park is nine miles east of Crescent City and the coast. It has more than 9,500 acres, 7,000 of which are covered with redwoods. There are more than 30 miles of hiking trails and roads, some of which are available for horseback riding and bicycling. The Smith River, one of the cleanest rivers in the country, runs through the park and offers fishing, canoeing, kayaking, swimming and other water sports.

Near the center of the campground is the park's Visitor Center, where interpretive displays, park rangers and volunteers can answer many of your questions regarding the area's wildlife, history and geology. You may also purchase books, posters, photographs, tee-shirts and other souvenirs here.

Jedediah Smith was a well-known trapper and explorer who led the first party of white men overland into the California territory.

CAMPGROUND: There are 106 heavily shaded campsites suitable for either tents or RVs up to 36 feet. Each site has its own parking pad, picnic table and fire ring. There is drinking water and a dump station, but no hookups of any kind. Hike & Bike camping is also permitted.

RESTROOMS: Flush toilets, sinks, mirrors and coin-operated showers.

RESERVATIONS: For camping between May 21 and Sept. 5, reservations may be made up to eight weeks in advance through MIS-TIX, 1-800-444-PARK. The park reverts to a first-come, first-served basis the rest of the year.

CHECK IN/OUT: Noon.

FEES: $14/day in peak season (May 1-Sept. 30); $12 off-peak. $3/day per person for *Hike & Bike camping*.

DOGS: $1/day; not permitted on trails.

MAX. STAY: 15 days (June-Sept.); 30 days remainder of the year.

SECURITY: Park rangers and resident camp host.

HOW TO GET THERE: From Crescent City, drive north on Highway 101; exit on 199 and drive east to the park entrance.

RUBY VAN DEVENTER COUNTY PARK

c/o Del Norte County Parks and Recreation Department
840 Ninth Street, Crescent City, CA 95531
(707) 464-7230

• Redwood forest tent & RV camping

This park is seven miles from the coast on the north bank of the Smith River, a choice fishing ground for steelhead trout and salmon. The salmon generally begin showing in September or early October and continue through mid-December, when the steelhead take over, staying until March or the first part of April. The best fishing is said to be around Thanksgiving for salmon; the first week of February for trout.

Jedediah Smith Redwoods State Park, 10,000 acres of predominantly old growth redwoods and one of California's most popular state parks, is a nearby neighbor just three miles away.

CAMPGROUND: Nestled in a shady forest of redwoods, Ruby Van Deventer Campground is comprised of 11 sites which can accommodate both tents and RVs; the largest sites take RVs up to 22 feet. Each includes its own parking spur, table, fire ring and grill. Water is available but no hookups or dump station.

RESTROOMS: Flush toilets, sinks; no mirrors, showers or AC outlets.

FEES: $10/day (maximum eight persons per campsite).

RESERVATIONS: As far in advance as desired by calling Del Norte County, (707) 464-7230.

CHECK IN/OUT: Noon.

DOGS: No additional charge; must be leashed at all times.

MAX. STAY: 3 days (not rigidly enforced).

SECURITY: Resident camp host.

HOW TO GET THERE: Driving north on Highway 101, exit at Route 197 and follow for about 2½ miles to the park entrance.

FLORENCE KELLER COUNTY PARK

c/o Del Norte County Parks and Recreation Department
840 Ninth Street, Crescent City, CA 95531
(707) 464-7230

• Redwood forest tent & RV camping

This is redwood country and Florence Keller Campground is part of it. It's located five miles inland from the coast.

CAMPGROUND: All 32 campsites are set beneath an umbrageous canopy of redwoods. Ferns and other substory plants help fill in the space far below the towering crowns of the trees. Tents and RVs up to 27 feet regularly seek respite from the rest of the world here. (Note that size of the sites varies and not all can accommodate 27-ft. vehicles.) Sites include parking pads, tables, fire rings and grills. Water is also available, but there are no hookups or dump station.

RESTROOMS: Modern modes of convenience include flush toilets and sinks; however, there are no mirrors, showers or AC outlets.

FEES: $10/day (maximum eight persons per campsite).

RESERVATIONS: As far in advance as desired by calling Del Norte County, (707) 464-7230.

CHECK IN/OUT: Noon.

DOGS: No additional charge; permitted on trails but must be leashed at all times.

MAX. STAY: 3 days (not rigidly enforced).

SECURITY: Resident camp host.

HOW TO GET THERE: Driving north on Highway 101, exit to the left at Elk Valley Crossing; turn left at Cunningham and follow a quarter-mile to the entrance (on your left).

LAKE EARL STATE PARK
1375 Elk Valley Road
Crescent City, CA 95531
(707) 464-9533

- Near-coast walk-in tent camping
- Horse camping
- Group camping
- Hike & Bike camping

This is a laid-back, little-known facility. Statistics show it attracts fewer than 30,000 visitors a year; and only 500 of them are campers. For all it has to offer, though, that won't always be the case. Discovery certainly awaits. But, for now, it's peaceful, soothing and almost always crowdless.

About 15 miles south of the Oregon border, Lake Earl State Park extends over 5,000 acres of wetlands, wooded hillsides, grassy meadows, sand dunes and beaches. There are some 20 miles of trails here for hiking, bicycling and horseback riding. Sandy and relatively flat, they meander throughout the park's marshes, lakes, ponds, dunes and forested ridges.

For anglers, there's cutthroat trout in Lake Earl along with bass and crappie in Dead Lake. Salmon and steelhead teem in the nearby Smith River. And, of course, there's always surf perch just waiting to be lured in from the sea just a half-mile from Lake Earl's campgrounds.

The beach is often rough and always cold, the shore alternating from sand to gravel, depending on conditions. But it's as fine as any for a casual stroll and beach combing. Agates are plentiful.

Throughout the park, you may very well spot deer, coyote and raccoons on land, as well as sea lions, harbor seals and grey whales offshore. Hundreds of species of birds such as the rare Canadian Aleutian goose and the peregrine falcon flock to the adjacent state wildlife preserve.

Despite the pervasiveness of nature, however, you needn't be without the comforts of civilization. Crescent City and all that it offers is but 10 miles to the south. There's also a small store a few miles away in Fort Dick.

CAMPGROUNDS: The park includes two basic campground facilities. One is a **walk-in camp** which includes six sites, each featuring a food locker, picnic table and fire ring. Sites are just five minutes walk from the parking lot. Separated by distance as well as a variety of trees and shrubs, they're totally apart from each other and offer maximum privacy. The beach is a half-mile walk from here. There's also a road for those too tired for the ramble. One thing the park does not have is water, so bring your own. From time to time, the park ranger stacks firewood that's free for the taking to campers. Bring your own if you want to be absolutely sure.

The second facility is a **ride-in horse camp.** It includes 16 corrals and water trough (with hand pump delivering non-potable water) along with standard picnic tables and fire rings. When not used by horse campers, this camp is open to families, groups and backpackers. It's about a mile from the parking lot.

RESTROOMS: Pit toilets; no showers.

FEES: $7/day in peak season (June-Sept); $6/day remainder of the year. *Horse camping* - $12/day for up to eight persons and two horses; $2/day extra for each additional horse. *Group* camping: Contact park. **Note:** All fees must be paid at either the Mill Creek Campground in Del Norte Redwoods State Park south of Crescent City, or Jedediah Smith Redwoods State Park to the east. Upon paying, you'll receive a receipt and the combination that lets you unlock the gate into the parking area.

RESERVATIONS: First come, first served. Dick Goss, the camp ranger since inception of the park, says the park rarely fills up.

CHECK IN/OUT: No established times; usually no problem as long as campers vacate sites by sundown.

DOGS: No extra fee at present; permitted on beaches and trails but must be leashed at all times.

MAX. STAY: 15 days.

SECURITY: Park ranger.

HOW TO GET THERE: From Crescent City (seven miles north of the Mill Creek Campground in Del Norte Redwoods State Park), drive north on Highway 101; to its junction with Northcrest Drive. Follow Northcrest (which turns into Lake Earl Drive) six miles to Lower Lake Road; turn left at Lower Lake Road and proceed 2½ miles to Kellogg Road. Turn left at Kellogg and follow to the gated and locked camp road on your right.

From Jedediah Smith Redwoods State Park, turn left on US 199 as you exit the park; turn right on North Bank Road just before the bridge and follow for seven miles to the junction of Highway 101; turn left and go across the bridge. Turn right on Lake Earl Drive and proceed one mile to the Fort Dick store; turn right on Moorehead and follow to its junction with Lowe Lake Road. Turn right on Lower Lake, then left on Kellogg Road to the gated and locked camp road on your right.

Horse Camp: Same as the above except don't turn left at Kellogg Road; instead, continue north on Lower Lake Road for three miles to Pala Road; turn left and follow the parking lot at the end.

CLIFFORD KAMPH MEMORIAL COUNTY PARK

c/o Del Norte County Prks and Recreation Department
840 Ninth Street, Crescent City, CA 95531
(707) 464-7230

- On-the-beach tent camping

Clifford Kamph Memorial Park is just four miles from the Oregon border. It was created in the 40s in honor of a serviceman killed in World War II. The park affords fine views of the coastline on one side, and the beginning of the rolling, dark green Siskiyou Mountain Range on the other.

CAMPGROUND: This is a slender campground set on a grassy bluff 25 feet above the beach. As you drive in, the campsites are to your left, the camp host and restrooms to your right. The ocean stretches on forever directly in front of you. One of the eight campsites is actually below the bluff and on the beach, reachable by way of a 40-50-step stairway. Each site has a table, fire ring and barbecue grill. Water is available. The surf is cold and the park is popular among anglers.

RESTROOMS: Flush toilets, mirrors and AC outlets. No showers.

FEES: $5/day (maximum eight persons per campsite).

RESERVATIONS: May be made as far in advance as desired by calling Del Norte County, (707) 464-7230.

CHECK IN/OUT: Noon.

DOGS: No additional charge; must be kept on leash. Permitted on beach.

MAX. STAY: 3 days (not rigidly enforced).

SECURITY: Resident camp host.

HOW TO GET THERE: Driving north on Highway 101, exit to the left at Clifford Kamph Memorial Park.

Directory

DEL NORTE COUNTY

RV Rentals
Daryl's RV Village, Grants Pass   (503) 476-0897

Visitor Information   (800) 343-8300
Crescent City-Del Norte County   or (707) 464-3174
Chamber of Commerce
1001 Front Street
Crescent City, CA 95531

HUMBOLDT COUNTY

Camping Gear Rental   (707) 822-4673
Adventure's Edge Arcata   (707) 445-3035
Adventure's Edge Eureka   (707) 445-1711
Northern Mountain Supply, Eureka

Visitor Information   in state (800) 338-7352
Eureka/Humboldt County   out of state (800) 346-3482
Convention and Visitors Bureau
1034 Second Street
Eureka CA 95501

Shelter Cove Information Bureau   (707) 986-7069
412, Machi Road
Shelter Cove, CA 95589

LOS ANGELES COUNTY

Camping Gear Rental   (310) 821-9400
Sport Chalet, Marina Del Rey   (310) 316-6634
Sport Chalet, Torrance

RV Rentals   (310) 518-6182
Altman's Motorhome Sales and Rental, Carson   (310) 518-4487
California RV Rentals   (818) 960-1499
Cruise America Motorhome Rentals and Sales (800) 367-3687
El Monte RV Center, El Monte

Holiday Motorhomes Rental	(310) 202-0041
Luxury RV, Harbor City	(310) 618-8844
Moturis, Inc., Hawthorne	(310) 676-0999

Visitor Information

Beverly Hills Visitors Bureau	(310) 271-8174
239 S. Beverly Drive	or (800) 345-2210
Beverly Hills, CA 90212	

Catalina Island Chamber of Commerce	(310) 510-1520
and Visitors Bureau	
One Green Pier, P.O. Box 217	
Avalon, CA 90704	

Hollywood Visitor Information Center	(213) 689-8822
Janess House, 6541 Hollywood Blvd.	
Hollywood, CA 90028	

L.A. Convention and Visitors Bureau	(213) 624-7300
633 W. Fifth Street, Suite 6000	or (800) 689-8822
Los Angeles, CA 90071	

MARIN COUNTY

Camping Gear Rental

Star Rental Center, San Rafael	(415) 454-1225
Any Mountain Ltd., Corte Madera	(415) 927-0170
Marin Outdoors, San Rafael	(415) 453-3400
Marmot Mountain Works, Kentfield	(415) 454-8543
Narains, Berkeley	(510) 527-2509
Novato Sports Headquarters, Novato	(415) 897-5388

RV Rentals

Cruise America, Santa Rosa	(707) 526-1562
El Monte RV Center, Oakland	(800) 332-7878
Recreation Rentals, Petaluma	(800) 649-1221
Vacation RV Rental, El Sobrante	(510) 223-0328

Visitor Information

Marin County Chamber of Commerce	(415) 472-7470
and Visitors Bureau	
30 N. San Pedro Road, Suite 150	
San Rafael, CA 94903	

MENDOCINO COUNTY

Camping Gear Rental
G.I. Joe's Army & Navy Surplus, Ukiah   (707) 468-8834

Visitor Information
Ft. Bragg-Mendocino Coast Chamber   (707) 961-6300
of Commerce   or (800) 726-2780
332 N. Main Street
P.O. Box 1141
Ft. Bragg, CA 95437

MONTEREY COUNTY

RV Rentals
Family RV Motor Home, San José   (408) 365-1991

Visitor Information
Monterey County Tourism Center   (408) 385-1484
San Lorenzo Park, 1160 Broadway Street
King City, CA 93930

Monterey Peninsula Visitors and   (408) 649-1770
Convention Bureau
380 Alvarado Street, P.O. Box 1770
Monterey, CA 93942

ORANGE COUNTY

Camping Gear Rental
Adventure 16 Outdoor & Travel Outfitters   (714) 650-3301
Grant Boys, Costa Mesa   (714) 645-3400
                                                     or (714) 540-6333
HAX Rental Charters, Garden Grove   (714) 638-3640

RV Rentals
Altman's Winebago Sales & Rentals, Carson   (310) 518-6182
Bob's Motorhome Rentals, Anaheim   (714) 827-2810
Cruise America   (714) 241-0953
El Monte RV Center, Santa Anna   (714) 367-2201
Executive RV Center, Fullerton   (714) 680-0295
Luxury Motor Home Rentals, Harbor City   (310) 618-8844
Western RV Bookings (private RVs)   (909) 681-1919

Visitor Information

Anaheim Area Visitor and Convention Bureau   (714) 999-8999
800 W. Katella Avenue
Anaheim, CA 92802

Huntington Beach Conference & Visitors Bureau   (714) 969-3492
2100 Main Street   or (800) SAY-
Huntington Beach, CA 92648   OCEAN

South Coast Metro Alliance   (714) 435-2109
611 Anton Boulevard, Suite 760
Costa Mesa, CA 92626

SAN DIEGO COUNTY

Camping Gear Rental

Adventure 16 Outdoor & Travel Outfitters   (619) 283-2374

RV Rentals

AA Travel Time RV Inc.   (619) 234-2192
Adventure Motor Homes Rentals, El Cajon   (619) 579-8727
Blue Chip Motor Home Rentals, La Mesa   (619) 464-5252
Cruise America Motorhome Rentals, El Cajon   (619) 588-5261
Holiday On Wheels RV Rentals   (619) 234-9444
Leisuretime RV Rentals   (619) 527-2484
No Mileage Charge Motorhomes of Mission Valley (619) 278-6164
US Rentals, Chule Vista   (619) 422-1105

Visitor Information

Coronado Visitor Information Bureau   (619) 437-8788
1111 Orange Ave, Suite A   or (800) 622-8300
Coronado, CA 92118

San Diego Int'l Visitor Information Center   (619) 236-1212
11 Horton Plaza
San Diego, CA 92101

SAN FRANCISCO COUNTY

Camping Gear Rental

Dave Sullivan's Sport Shop, San Francisco   (415) 751-7070

RV Rentals

Cruise America Motorhome Rentals, Oakland	(510) 639-7125
El Monte RV Center, Oakland	(800) 332-7878
Happy Campers, San Francisco	(415) 777-4205
Go Vacations Calif., Inc., Hayward	(510) 888-9809
Moturis Inc., San Leandro	(510) 562-7566
Travel-Time RV Center	(800) 453-4386

Visitor Information

San Francisco Visitor Information Center   (415) 391-2000
Hallidie Plaza, Lower Level
900 Market Street, P.O. Box 429097
San Francisco, CA 94103

SAN LUIS OBISPO COUNTY

RV Rentals

Arnies Rental, Grover Beach	(805) 473-1610
B&J RV Storage, Arroyo Grande	(805) 481-4855
Earl's RV Rentals, Lompoc	(805) 736-5175
Pismo Dunes Sports & ATV Rentals, Oceano	(805) 489-4288
Scotties RV Rentals	(805) 461-1240

Visitor Information

Pismo Beach Convention & Visitors Bureau   (805) 773-4382
581 Dolliver Street   or (800) 443-7778
Pismo Beach, CA 93449

San Luis Obispo County Visitors Bureau   (805) 541-8000
1041 Chorro Street, Suite E   or (800) 634-1414
San Luis Obispo, CA 93401

SAN MATEO COUNTY

RV Rentals

El Monte RV Center, Dublin	(800) 845-7267
Go Vacations	(800) 845-9888
Travel-Time RV Center	(800) 453-4386
Vacation RV Rental at Dave's Camperland, El Sobrante	(510) 223-0328

Visitor Information
San Mateo County Convention & Visitors Bureau   (415) 348-7600
111 Anza Boulevard, Suite 410   or (800) 288-4748
Burlingame, CA 94010

SANTA BARBARA COUNTY

RV Rentals
Earl's RV Rentals, Lompoc   (805) 736-5175
T&L RV Rental Inc., Ventura   (800) 373-6825

Visitor Information
Santa Barbara Conference and Visitors Bureau   (805) 966-9222
510 State Street   or (800) 927-4688
Santa Barbara, CA 93101

SANTA CRUZ COUNTY

RV Rentals
Cruise America, Santa Clara   (408) 226-8512
Family RV, San José   (408) 365-1991

Visitor Information
Pajaro Valley Chamber of Commerce   (408) 724-3900
444 Main Street
Watsonville, CA 95076

SONOMA COUNTY

Camping Gear Rental
The Rental Place, Sebastopol   (707) 823-7686
Sonoma Outfitters   (707) 528-1920

RV Rentals
Country Roads RV & Marine   (707) 578-0881
Cruise America, Healdsburg   (707) 431-1951
Cruise America, Santa Rosa   (707) 526-1562
Recreation Rentals, Petaluma   (707) 765-1221
                                   or (800) 649-1221

Visitor Information

Sonoma County Convention& Visitors Bureau   (707) 586-8100
5000 Roberts Lake Road
Rohnert Park, CA 94928

VENTURA COUNTY

RV Rentals

Metro RV, Burbank   (800) 400-7544
                                              or (805) 645-0000
RV Owners Rental Network   (805) 522-0727
T&L RV Rental   (805) 653-0714

Visitor Information

Ventura Visitors and Convention Bureau   (805) 648-2075
89-C S. California Street
Ventura, CA 93001

DEPT OF FISH & GAME   (916) 653-7664
1416 Ninth Street,   24-hr recorded msg (916) 227-2244
Box 944209
Sacramento, CA 94244-2090

DEPT OF PARKS & RECREATION   (916) 653-6995
Box 942896
Sacramento, CA 94296-0001

MISTIX   (800) 444-PARK

NATIONAL PARKS   (415) 556-0560
Western Region Information Office
National Parks Service
Fort Mason, Bldg. 201
San Francisco, CA 94123

NATIONAL FORESTS   (415) 705-2874
USDA Forest Service
630 Sansome Street
San Francisco, CA 94111